A LEARNED SOCIETY
IN A PERIOD OF TRANSITION

SUNY series in Medieval
Middle East History

Jere Bacharach, Editor

A LEARNED SOCIETY
IN A PERIOD OF TRANSITION

The Sunni 'Ulama'
of Eleventh-Century Baghdad

DAPHNA EPHRAT

State University of New York Press

Published by
State University of New York Press, Albany

For information, address State University of New York Press,
State University Plaza, Albany, N.Y. 12246

Production by Diane Ganeles
Marketing by Patrick Durocher

Library of Congress Cataloging-in-Publication Data

Ephrat, Daphna.
    A learned society in a period of transition : the Sunni 'ulama' of the eleventh
century Baghdad / Daphna Ephrat.
        p.   cm. — (SUNY series in medieval Middle East history)
    Includes bibliographical references (p.   ) and index.
    ISBN 0-7914-4645-X (alk. paper) — ISBN 0-7914-4646-8 (pbk. : alk. paper)
    1. Ulama—Iraq—Baghad—History.   2. Religious institutions and associations
Iraq Bagdad—History.   3. Islam—Study and teaching—Iraq—Bagdad History.
I. Title.   II. Series

BP63.B34 E64 2000
297.6'1'095674709021—dc21

                                                                    99-054127

10 9 8 7 6 5 4 3 2 1

CONTENTS

The Framework of Inquiry
Institutionalization and Social Change
The 'Ulama' and the Problem of Self-Presentation
A Note on the Sources

The Coming of the Turks
The Appearance of the Madrasa

The Baghdadi 'Ulama' and Worldwide Scholarly
Networks
From Journeys to Schools

ACKNOWLEDGMENTS

This book began as a dissertation at Harvard University and represents the efforts and energies of many people over many years. I would like to take the opportunity here to thank at least some of the people and institutions that acted as midwife in its birth.

The Middle Eastern Department of Tel Aviv University deserves first mention as the spawning ground of my interest in the fascinating topic of Islamic and Middle Eastern history. A special thanks is extended to Ehud Toledano and Israel Gershoni for introducing me to the dynamic interrelationships of social and cultural history.

But it is to Harvard's community of teachers and scholars that I owe my greatest debts for giving me the opportunity to study in its most stimulating atmosphere. For financial support, I must thank the Graduate School of Arts and Sciences. For intellectual support, guidance, and encouragement, I thank my teacher Roy P. Mottahedeh, a trusted and kind mentor, under whose direction this book took shape. Without his inspiration and support, this book, as well as a great part of my academic education, would not have been possible. For leading me to a comparative approach to medieval Islamic history and helping me to hone my research tools, I am indebted to Thomas Bisson and his seminars of medieval European history.

Nehemia Levtzion of the Hebrew University of Jerusalem, my second adviser in the Ph.D. dissertation, goes my gratitude for sharing with me his vast knowledge of the historical legacy of the Muslim world, and for reading through several successive drafts of this work. I am also indebted to him for the opportunity to co-author in a series on Islamic history (published by the Open University of

Israel), which helped me to an understanding of events within the broad context of that field.

To the Center for Judaic Studies of University of Pennsylvania I owe great debt for giving me the opportunity to participate as a post-doctoral fellow in the most stimulating project on learning and literacy. In addition to financial and intellectual support, the center provided me with a unique forum for interaction and dialogue with scholars of the international community.

Various versions of this book also benefited from valuable comments by a number of other scholars, in particular Richard W. Bulliet, and the readers of the press whose names are unknown to me. To my colleagues and friends, Daniella Talmon-Heller and Meir Litvak, a special word of thanks for their support and friendship, as well as their generosity with their works and ideas. I am also much appreciative of the efforts of my editor Danna Har-Gil and technical editor Peggy Weinreich. While the contributions of all those who have helped me in the various stages of this project have been critical, I bear sole responsibility for any deficiencies.

Portions of this book were presented at the Center for Judaic Studies' weekly seminars and the annual colloquium in the spring of 1996 in Philadelphia; a Van Leer international workshop on the public sphere in Islamic societies in the fall of 1997 in Jerusalem; and an Israel Science Foundation research workshop on elites in the worlds of classical and medieval Islam in the winter of 1998 in Tel Aviv. I am grateful for the participants of each for their helpful comments.

Last but certainly not least, my family: my husband Oved, my children Noa, Daniel, and Omri, who suffered from their mother's late nights spent bent over books and computer; and my entire family for their support and belief in my goals.

A NOTE
ON THE TRANSLITERATION,
PERIODIZATION, AND DATES

In transliterating Arabic words, I have followed the rules of transliteration of the Encyclopaedia of Islam, with some slight variations. Thus, for the Arabic letter *qaf*, I have used the letter *q*, not *k*, and for *jim*, *j*, not *dj*. The letter *ayn* is represented by (ʿ), and the *hamza* by a simple apostrophe (ʾ). All Arabic words, other than those that appear frequently, are italicized. When an Arabic word is first introduced, it is defined, and the plural form is given in round brackets. For the sake of convenience, and to help the nonspecialist reader, diacritical markings for the Arabic letters *ha*ʾ, *sad*, *dad*, *ta*ʾ, and *za*ʾ, as well as those for long vowels, have not been inserted. For some Arabic words, plurals are formed simply by adding the English plural *s*—thus, madrasas, not *madaris*, and *ribats*, not *rubut*. Certain words and place names commonly used in the West are given their familiar Western spelling—Koran, not Qur'an; and Cairo, not al-Qahira.

Definition of the medieval period in the history of the Islamic lands of the Middle East is a matter of controversy. The very word *medieval* presents a number of problems. For some the period goes from the very beginning of Islam, in the seventh century A.D., up to about 1500, while for others it seems to begin much later. Chronological designations like "classical," "transitional," and "high medieval" periods are just as difficult to define, and also remain unresolved problems in the periodization of Islamic history as a whole. In this book the term "transitional period" is useful to the extent that it serves to draw attention to changes in the prime characteristics of the classical ʿAbbasid world—in particular the capital of the ʿAbbasids— from the coming of the Turks at the beginning of the eleventh century to the great Mongol invasions of the mid-thirteenth century. However, because most broad chronological designations are in any case anachronistic or artificial, or both, I have generally preferred to refer to specific centuries or dates, rather than to periods.

When a century or a date appears for the first time, it is given according to both the Islamic (A.H.) and Western (A.D.) calendars. Thereafter, I have generally used only the Western calendar. For dates of death and dates in the tables and graphs, I have used both systems of dating.

ABBREVIATIONS

AESC	*Annales: Économies, Sociétés, Civilisations*
AJSL	*American Journal of Semitic Languages*
BSOAS	*Bulletin of the School of Oriental and African Studies*
EI 1st edition	*Encyclopaedia of Islam*, 1st edition (Leiden, 1913–38)
EI 2nd edition	*Encyclopaedia of Islam*, 2nd edition (Leiden, 1954–)
GAL	*Geschichte der Arabischen Literatur*
IC	*Islamic Culture*
IJMES	*International Journal of Middle Eastern Studies*
IQ	*Islamic Quarterly*
JAOS	*Journal of the American Oriental Society*
JARCE	*Journal of the American Research Center in Egypt*
JRAS	*Journal of the Royal Asiatic Society*
MW	*Muslim World*
REI	*Revue des études islamiques*
SEI	*Shorter Encyclopedia of Islam*
SI	*Studia Islamica*
WZKM	*Wiener Zeitschrift für die Kunde des Morgenlandes*

ILLUSTRATIONS

6.1 The composition of the group of religious and civil officials
     according to school affiliation and geographical origins
     (409/1018– 549/1154)

Genealogical Charts

A.1   Banu Ya'la
A.2   The Tamimis
A.3   Banu Musa al-Hashimi
A.4   The Samads
A.5   The Damaghanis
A.6   The Zainabis
A.7   Banu Sabbagh
A.8   The Shashis
A.9   The Bishrans
A.10 Banu Dust an-Nishapuri

Maps

1. Baghdad between 400 and 700 A.H. (Buyid, Seljuk, and Mognol
    Periods). Source: G. Le Strange, *Baghdad During the Abbasid
    Period*, 3rd edition (London, 1972), facing page 231 [first pub-
    lished in 1900].
2. Later East Baghdad, ibid., facing page 263.

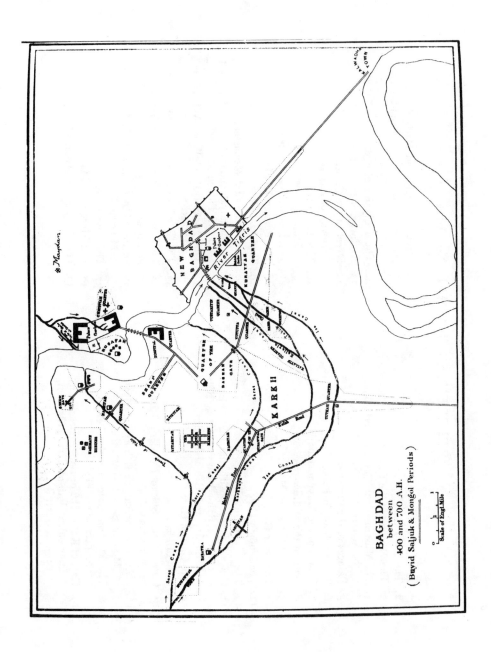

BAGHDAD
between
400 and 700 A.H.
(Buyid Saljuk & Mongol Periods)

Scale of Engl.Mile

REFERENCES TO MAP No. VIII.

1. The Ḥasanî Palace.
2. The Tâj Palace.
3. The Mosque of the Caliph.
4. The Mustanṣirîyah College overlooking the Wharf of the Needle-makers.
5. Palaces of the Princess.
6. The Rayḥânîyîn Palace.
7. Palace of the Maydân Khâliṣ.
8. Gate of the Willow-tree.
9. Gate of the Date Market.
10. The Badr Gate."
11. The Nubian Gate.
12. The Public Gate.
13. Outer Precincts, with the three Gates called Bâb-ad-Duwwâmât, Bâb 'Ullayân, and Bâb-al-Ḥaram.
14. The Garden Gate.
15. Gate of Degrees.
16. Gate of the Sultan (Modern Bâb-al-Mu'aẓẓam).
17. Gate of Khurâsân or Bâb-aẓ-Ẓafarîyah (Modern Bâb-al-Wusṭânî).
18. The Ḥalbah Gate and the Belvedere (Modern Bâb-aṭ-Ṭalism).
19. Gate of Kalwâdhâ or Bâb-al-Baṣalîyah, later called Bâb-al-Khalaj (Modern Bâb-ash-Sharḳî).
20. Street of Bricks and Darb-al-Munîrah.
21. Abraz Gate of older Wall and Cemetery of the Wardîyah.
22. The Tâjîyah College.
23. Archway of the Armourers.
24. Street of the Canal.
25. Archway of the Artificer.
26. The Great Square and the Perfumers' Market.
27. Tomb of Abd-al-Ḳâdir Gîlânî.
28. The Persian Bastion.
29. The Azaj Gate.
30. The Zandaward Monastery.
31. The Bahâîyah and the Tutushî Hospital, in the Tutush Market.
32. The Niẓâmîyah College, Wharf, and Market.
33. The Tomb of Ma'rûf Karkhî.
34. The Barley Gate (Bâb-ash-Sha'îr).
35. Palace of 'Aḍud-ad-Dîn the Wazîr.
36. Shrine of 'Awn and Mu'în (site of the Modern Tomb of Zubaydah).
37. The Baṣrah Gate.
38. The Mosque of Manṣûr.
39. The Hospital of 'Aḍud-ad-Dawlah.

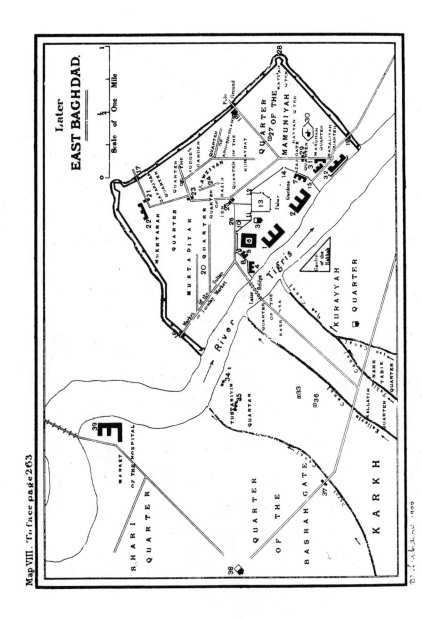

Map VIII. To face page 263

Later
EAST BAGHDAD.

Scale of One Mile

INTRODUCTION

The Framework of Inquiry

The period A.D. 950–1258—from the conquest of the ʿAbbasid capital by the Shiʿi Buyids to the Mongol invasions—has been viewed by modern scholarship as an age of transformation of Muslim societies.[1] After the Shiʿi conquest of the ʿAbbasid capital in A.D. 945, many characteristics of the classical ʿAbbasid world, with its magnificent caliphal empire and single political community, were gradually altered. During the fifth/eleventh century, a period often called the "Sunni revival," the main foundations of new forms of religious and social organizations were laid down in the central Islamic regions. Emerging social associations and frameworks were developed to teach the Islamic religious and legal sciences, apply religious law (the *shariʿa*), and harness mysticism. During the course of this century the four Sunni schools of legal interpretation (*madhahib*) were consolidated as scholarly establishments, the nuclei of the Sufi fraternities were formed, and the "law college" (madrasa) and Sufi hostel (*khanqah* or *ribat*) were founded, based on substantial pious endowments (*awqaf*). These developments took place against the background of the ʿAbbasid caliphate's disintegration and the subsequent rise to power of the sultanate of the Great Seljuks. In the politically divided, socially unstable, and unpredictable world created by the dissolution of the ʿAbbasid caliphate and the rise of the alien Turkish regime, stronger institutionalized forms were necessary to carry on the task of sustaining the communities' Islamic character and securing the essential unity of their heritage. Significantly, the city of Baghdad—which, more than any other Muslim city, suffered

1

from the instability and upheavals accompanying the collapse of the
ʿAbbasid empire—was a major scene in the crystallization of the
madhahib and the development of the madrasa into its "mature"
form.

To establish the madrasas and ensure their perpetuity, the
founders of madrasas—Seljuk officials, and later the sultans themselves—used one of the primary instruments at the disposal of
Islamic societies: the private law of the *waqf*. Bound by the terms of
legal documents (*waqfiyyas*), which established endowments principally for the study and transmission of the purely Islamic sciences
(to the exclusion of the so-called foreign or ancient sciences inherited
from the Hellenistic world), the advent and spread of the madrasa
marked an important phase in the movement toward conformity and
uniformity. The curriculum, if there was a curriculum in any useful
sense of the term, varied according to the stipulations of the founders
in the *waqfiyyas*, and, more importantly, in accordance with the
wishes and repertoire of the madrasas' teachers and directors.

Yet even if instruction in these new schools was not restricted to
Islamic religious law and other subjects elementary to a religious
education—Koran exegesis (*tafsir*), the prophetic traditions (*hadith*),
and Arabic grammar and syntax (*nahw*), as suggested by George
Makdisi and others—madrasas were considered to be the primary
focus of attempts to preserve the "transmitted" or "traditionalist"
learning, thereby formulate a more rigid and uniform curriculum.[2]
The new madrasas, in other words, represented an attempt to organ-
ize Islamic education to a degree hitherto unknown in its history,
and to define the boundaries of religious knowledge (*ʿilm*). As such,
they must have been intended to serve the cause of the movement
that pleaded a commonly accepted form of Sunni Islam.

Discussions on the renewed activity of Sunni Islam often reveal
disagreement on the nature of its origins. Should it be ascribed to
the elaboration and systematization of scholastic theology (*ʿilm al-
kalam*) by Ashʿarism, which not only renewed it, but also gave it new
direction in the great synthesis of al-Ghazzali? Or was it the product
of the forces of the "people of *hadith*" (*ahl al-hadith*)? Historians of
this period agree, however, that the process of Sunni self-definition
occurred independent of the Seljuks, ascribing it instead to internal
forces within Sunni Islam.[3] Indeed, there is no evidence at our disposal indicating that by founding madrasas and patronizing their
scholarly community, the Seljuk rulers and their viziers sought to
become involved in defining the content of "true" knowledge. Nor
are there any grounds to argue that they supported the madrasas

because they were fanatically anti-Shi'i. However, while it is true that members of the new ruling elite avoided the internal affairs of the 'ulama', it is also true that in order to put an end to the severe religious fomentation that might have led to the breakdown of the Islamic community, they lent their financial support to those 'ulama' who were considered representatives of the broad mainstream of Islam.

During the sixth/twelfth century, roughly one hundred years after the madrasa made its definite appearance, pressure for conformity and uniformity gained additional governmental support upon the establishment of two schools, the "House of Hadith" (*Dar al-hadith*) and "House of the Koran" (*Dar al-qur'an*). Raising the study of the prophetic traditions and the scripture to the same level as that of the study of the law, these new educational frameworks were designed by their founders to represent the shared tradition of the legal schools. Finally, in 631/1233, the Mustansiriyya Madrasa was founded in Baghdad to house all four legal schools, a further expression of a pan-Sunni policy.[4] Cultivation of a deeper spiritual life took the form of the Sufi organized, endowed, and supervised *khanqah*. Founded under the patronage of the Seljuks of the west during the last decades of the eleventh century, the *khanqah* spread throughout the Islamic lands.[5] Formed within the regular organization of Islam, the *khanqah*s were probably designed by their founders to replace the esoteric and mystical congregations which aroused the reaction of legal scholars, and to make Sufi associations more respectable.

Pressure for conformity and uniformity among Muslims was perhaps nowhere stronger than in the caliphal city of Baghdad, where the bitter disputes over proper Islamic creed and behavior reached a peak. During the "Shi'i century," as well as the period immediately after, the Hanbalis became the most vigorous and dynamic subfaction among the Sunnis of Baghdad. At the heart of the clashes between the Hanbalis and their rivals in the caliphal city was the old disagreement between *ahl al-hadith* and the *mutakallimun*, or "masters of opinion" (*ashab al-ra'y*) over the status of rational investigation. Fearing that rational inquiry into divine revelation would detract from the perfect integrity of the simple original faith, the Hanbalis led the movement of *ahl al-hadith*, which insisted on finding *hadith* solutions to legal and theological questions whenever possible. Hence, in addition to taking it upon themselves to persecute the Shi'a, Hanbali popular leaders and theologians were occupied in fighting rationalism of all shades, trying to enforce their rigid orthodoxy upon

Baghdadi society, and honing the boundaries between the religious groups.

During the second half of the eleventh century the Hanbalis of Baghdad fought against the Ash'aris, deriving their growing support primarily from among the city's lower classes. The violent reactions of the Hanbalis instilled fear in all those they considered responsible for "negative" innovations or sins such as drinking wine, singing, or playing musical instruments. The Hanbalis were even able to force conformity on those of their own allegiance who were sufficiently curious to listen to teachers of other intellectual traditions—the example of Ibn 'Aqil comes to mind.[6]

At first it may seem surprising that, while replete with descriptions of disputes in Baghdad during the eleventh century, the chronicles recording the significant events of the subsequent century seldom mention clashes between religiously defined factions. If the severe religious fomentation of the classical age began to fade away, this book contends it was not simply because the attention of the Muslim world was turned toward the invasions of the crusaders, but because, in a period of near anarchy, Muslim jurists and thinkers were determined to maintain a unified Islamic community by blurring the lines between their various intellectual traditions and delimiting a commonly accepted Sunni form of Islam. The phrase *ahl as-sunna wa'l-jama'a* ("the people of tradition and the community"), which refers to the broad mainstream of Islam, attests to the process of consensus-making in matters of proper Islamic creed and behavior, which began to set in the twelfth century. Conversely, we seldom find any reference to specific subfactions or theological streams, such as *ahl al-hadith* and *ahl al-ra'y*, in the sources pertaining to the twelfth century.

To be sure, scholars living during the period covered by this book still debated a considerable number of legal and theological issues. Islamic intellectual and religious life continued to flow in several, largely separate streams. Even jurists (*fuqaha'*) who felt bound to the teaching of their masters would exercise at least a limited degree of individual reasoning (*ijtihad*). Indeed, many considered themselves, and were considered by others, *mujtahidun*—such as the famous al-Ghazzali.[7] Rationalistic philosophical thought still posed a profound challenge to the normative form of Islamic belief and practice defined by scripturalist Islam, attaining its maturity in Muslim Spain. Although certain changes in its religious philosophy had begun, the original Mu'tazili school of *kalam* continued to be represented among "orthodox" circles and especially among Twelver, or *imami*, Shi'is, in central Asia.

One such representative was the famous Persian grammarian and Koran commentator az-Zamakhshari (d. 538/1144). The absorption of Muʿtazili ideas by Shiʿi scholars, and the comparative openness of their scholars to the external influences of philosophy, may explain why the religious and intellectual fomentation of the classical period continued in Shiʿism long after it came to an end in Sunni Islam. Equally important was the disappearance of the last *imam* (the doctrine of the *ghayba*), during the late third/ninth century, which allowed Shiʿi jurists and theologians a greater degree of independent thought.[8] Yet it was in Sufi Islam that the pluralism and fluidity of Islamic belief and practice during this period were revealed in their brightest light: sober Sufism existed alongside the old traditions of mild and extreme asceticism, while gnostic and popular forms of Islamic mysticism began to penetrate everywhere.

The high value ascribed to the acquisition of knowledge in Islamic tradition, specifically religious education, and the assumption that personal qualities are strictly connected to knowledge, continued to stimulate the evolution of Islamic scholarship. During what Franz Rosenthal called the "manuscript age" (from about the late ninth century), Muslim scholars in the various fields of learning set forth principles for the preservation of books, copying, citations, commentary, style, handwriting, and rules of editing and translation. Concerns ranged from precise instructions transmitted to contemporary and future scholars, to theoretical questions regarding the meaning of knowledge. Thus, along with the replication and interpretation of the literary productions of previous generations, there emerged a widespread literary criticism involving improvement of texts, corrections, a critical examination of classical works, and even special works of criticism.[9] Islamic learning during the eleventh and twelfth centuries was still imparted in a variety of study circles long after the foundation of cultural institutions for the preservation and propagation of accepted "knowledge." Nor did the old manner of learning, wandering from one place to another, fade from the Muslim world. Although the Islamic domains were ruled by autocratic regimes, political boundaries were vague and open. People and ideas moved freely from one place to another. Indeed, this social and intellectual flexibility assured the constant circulation of ideas, which, in turn, enabled the cultural flowering during the period from the Buyid conquests to the Mongol invasions, termed "the Earlier Middle Period" by Marshall Hodgson.[10] But for all the freedom and variety still evident in religious and cultural life, systematic expositions of Islamic thought had become more directed by the twelfth century.

The range of knowledge which would have been accepted in earlier centuries was probably narrowed.

I propose that the Sunni revival was not only a period when major steps were taken in the consolidation of Sunnism and the dissemination of its religious institutions, but was also a time when the fluid society of the "learned," the ʿulamaʾ, began to emerge as a more defined and exclusive group. The social implications of the Sunni revival, as reflected in the character of the Sunni ʿulamaʾ of eleventh-century Baghdad, are the main concern of this study. More specifically, its objective is to define the link between the cultural and social practices involved in the process of the transmission of Islamic learning, and the construction of social bonds and identities in a historical time and a specific place.

How were scholarly networks formed, and what were the bonds that made the loose associations of the ʿulamaʾ stronger? How, without the formal and stable institutions or corporations historians usually describe and expect, were the ʿulamaʾ able to guarantee their exclusive authority in transmitting legitimate knowledge and defining the boundaries of their group? By addressing these questions, this study undertakes to reconsider the characterization of all groups of ʿulamaʾ as fluid, unstructured groups, which was repeated in the scholarly literature about them.[11] While focusing on their lack of formal structure, scholars have overlooked the inner, informal mechanisms used by ʿulamaʾ in different periods and places to set limits to participation in the transmission of legal learning and bar inclusion in their ranks. An inquiry into these mechanisms, though focusing on the peculiar circumstances of one learned society in a specific historical setting, addresses a number of historiographical and methodological problems in the social history of eleventh-century Baghdad and the Islamic Near East as a whole.

Institutionalization and Social Change

Historians of Muslim societies have largely agreed that rigid institutionalization did not develop during the period following the collapse of the ʿAbbasid bureaucratic state. It was, in fact, hardly feasible in the vast conglomeration of disparate groups which the political elite of Turkish nomads and overlords had to govern. Rather, evidence points to the existence of networks of personal ties defined by family, ethnic origins, or sectarian homogeneity, or by a shared professional background. By replacing formal and stable institutions, these networks constituted the nucleus of the social, and sometimes even the political, order in the post-ʿAbbasid era.[12] In the world of the religiously learned, these personal networks evolved from the informal study circles which orbited around renowned masters (*shaykhs*) in the great cultural centers throughout the Muslim world. Yet despite these observations, several historians, when dealing with the transformation of Islamic societies in the eleventh century and the high medieval period, tend to concentrate on formal, institutional structures and processes as a category of historical explanation. While providing us with an insight into the origins and development of medieval Islamic forms of organization, the models they develop advance only partial explanations of the problem of social change.

The field of Islamic education is one of the principal subjects in surveys of Islamic societies in which particular attention was paid to institutions while highlighting their roles in the process of cultural and social change. Comprehensive surveys such as Henri-Irené Marrou's *Histoire de l'Education dans l'Antiquité* (Paris, 1948), whose primary interest is the link between education in its all its aspects— curriculum, methods, working through its problems, organization— and the civilization under study, have not yet been included in a survey of the history of Islamic education. Nor do we know much about Islamic learning before the rise and spread of the madrasas.

The advent of the madrasa during the late eleventh century, approximately one hundred years before that of the university in Latin Europe, and its rapid spread, have been discussed at length in Islamic and Middle Eastern studies in recent years. The model developed by George Makdisi and others is that of an educational institution par excellence, devoted purely to the instruction of Islamic religious law according to one of the four legal schools in Sunni Islam, whose appearance transformed Muslim education. The principal innovation, as most historians see it, lay in the large *awqaf* donated by the founders of madrasas, which ensured salaries for the teachers, and stipends and residence for the students. In this way, the madrasa was a sort of combination of a mosque (*masjid*), in which study was restricted as early as the tenth century to one of the *madhahib*, and the adjacent *khan*, where the students lived. All of these were given economic support to a degree unprecedented in the history of Islamic education.[13]

The madrasa very quickly became part of urban Muslim life, like the mosques and the rulers' palaces. The substantial *awqaf* donated by the rulers to the establishment, as well as the maintenance of the madrasa and the payment of teachers' salaries and students' living expenses, increased its attractiveness and eventually enabled it to develop as the principal forum of study in the Islamic Near East, similar to the university in the contemporary West. Almost anyone who sought an education—and, even more important, a chance for a religious or administrative position—during the high medieval period, turned to the madrasas scattered throughout the cities of Islam and the main cultural centers.[14]

A. L. Tibawi was the first to note that, for all the establishment of endowed and structured institutions of learning, Islamic education remained essentially informal, flexible, and linked to persons rather than to institutions.[15] Since then, several social historians have pointed out that the study circle (*halqa*) continued to serve as the basic framework in the world of the religiously learned, the 'ulama', long after the advent of madrasas.[16] Most recently, Jonathan Berkey has provided us with an extremely detailed and illustrative description of the informal character of Islamic education in Mamluk Cairo. He pointed out that madrasas far from monopolized or even dominated religious education.[17] Michael Chamberlain asserts that madrasas did not represent an institutionalized form of higher education and "had many uses that had nothing to do with education."[18] However, while questioning the importance of madrasas in the history of Islamic learning, scholars have generally agreed that the advent and dissemination of the new schools during the period of the Sunni revival marked a turning point in the social history of the religiously learned. Thus, several historians have concluded that madrasas served as centers for the recruitment of jurists and bureaucrats, thereby planting the seeds for the creation of a religious establishment incorporated into the state bureaucracy and dependent upon the military ruling elite.[19]

The main problem in this approach is that it discerns the roots of later developments in the early madrasa period, more precisely, the Ottoman period, from about the sixteenth century when the madrasa became an imperial institution in all respects. In other words, this approach assumes a high probability of historical continuity among societies distant in time and place. Moreover, it continues to view the madrasas as instruments of state power, intended to control institutions of learning, which would grant the political rulers influence over the 'ulama'. Contrary to this accepted view, this study asserts that the 'ulama' of Baghdad enjoyed an autonomous role in the city's public sphere throughout the Seljuk period. They acted independently of the political authorities in courts and madrasas, and were reluctant to become involved or assume positions in the official sphere. Moreover, the political rulers avoided the internal affairs of the ʿulamaʾ and were careful not to meddle in religious matters in general.

Other historians link the development of educational institutions with the consolidation of the *madhahib*, ascribing a crucial role in this process to the madrasas. The madrasas are thus considered to be centers around which the scholarly groupings, which formed the cores of the *madhahib*, crystallized and created their identities. Moreover, as the madrasa became the organized basis of the *madhahib*, the legal schools themselves developed into religious movements, extending their leadership to the masses.[20]

In a somewhat similar vein, the establishment of *khanqah*s by the Seljuks and their successors for the benefit of the Sufi devotees, where they were lodged, fed, and performed their rituals, is believed to be a major phase in the institutionalization of Sufism. Thus, parallel to the establishment of *khanqah*s, the loose Sufi associations yielded their place to organized systems (*turuq*) of initiation, instruction, and ritual, each developing a hierarchy of spiritual guides who derived their authority from a kind of apostolic succession bestowed upon them by the founder.[21] Needless to say, this interpretation of the social effects of the establishment of madrasas and *khanqah*s contradicts the repeatedly expressed description of the transmission of *ʿilm* and Islamic mystical learning (*maʿrifa*) as a highly personal process, one dependent upon the relationship between individual masters and their disciples.

In light of these observations, we must reconsider the problematic interrelationship between institutionalization and social change. What effect did madrasas have on the transition from "journeying" to the *madhahib* in Islamic cities where they proliferated? What importance did madrasas have in the social organization of the ʿulamaʾ? Did their appearance change the process by which individuals were recognized as scholars, gaining prominence among the ʿulamaʾ "class"? In sum, what was the contribution of the advent of the madrasa to the transformation of the ʿulamaʾ from loose associations into a better defined group in terms of membership and structure during the Sunni revival?

In respect to the Sunni *madhahib*, the study of their organization and consolidation should be taken further. Relatively little work has been done on the *madhhab* as a social and professional organization (as opposed to a body of legal doctrine). The inner structure of a *madhhab*, the ties that knit adherents to a *madhhab* together socially, and the extent to which men of religious learning were rigidly divided into the schools of law, each maintaining its identity and unity—these are but a few issues that must be pursued.[22] Likewise, we know little of how the legal schools fit into the general political and social life of medieval Islamic cities. Nor has contemporary scholarship as yet explored the dynamics of change in the character of the legal schools during their process of consolidation.

Rather than inquiring into the organizational and legal aspects of Islamic intellectual life—the law of the *waqf* as it pertained to madrasas, the *waqfiyyas* of specific institutions, the administration of madrasas—which have often attracted scholarly interest, this study explores these topics through an examination of the world of learning beyond its legal and organizational forms.[23] Similarly, I also propose shifting the focus from the institutions or frameworks related to the application and transmission of religious lore and knowledge to the cultural and social practices which grew up around them, from the content of learning to the learned society. The underlying assumption of this approach is that only by looking at how the universal practices involved in the transmission of Islamic learning were performed and understood by Muslim scholars of different periods and places can we bring their world to life. Moreover, it is by contextualization that these practices acquire their meaningfulness.

The nature of the sources about the 'ulama'—the kind of evidence they supply, their strategy of presentation, and the method applied for their use—is crucial to my discussion.

The 'Ulama' and the Problem of Self-Presentation

The 'ulama', perhaps more than any other social group, have captured the attention of modern historians studying Islamic societies. Frankly, they are the only group we know much about, compared to other groups in Muslim societies. This, as many have pointed out, should not be surprising, for the bulk of literary texts available to us—namely the biographical dictionaries which serve as a prime source for studies of social groups—was written by the 'ulama' for the 'ulama'.[24]

But it is perhaps because we know so much about them that they are so difficult to define. They appear in our texts as extremely learned "professional" scholars, and more frequently as part-time "semiprofessionals." Moreover, they seem to cut across almost every possible classification of groups within Islamic society. Added to this is the difficulty of defining a group of religious scholars of any one particular medieval Islamic city. How did the singularity of a city—its location, history, ethnic composition—shape the characteristics of this particular social group during a period in which scholars constantly wandered from one place to another? The cosmopolitan veneer of the medieval Muslim learned elites—the result of a common heritage and universal scholarly practices—stood in obvious contrast to the notion of affiliation with a particular city or the formation of local alliances between the local population and the religiously learned.

This problem of defining the ʿulamaʾ, their status and roles in the social and political life of Islamic cities in different periods and locales, has been addressed in studies by Ira Lapidus, Richard Bulliet, and Roy Mottahedeh.[25] Its explanation may lie, in several scholars' view, in the attitude of Islamic societies towards ʿilm, the "knowledge" that characterized the ʿulamaʾ. Due to the high value placed on the acquisition of knowledge and its transmission from one generation to the next, access to ʿilm must have been largely unrestricted and open to talent.[26] Yet if the names of a large number of people from widely different walks of life appear in the biographical dictionaries of the ʿulamaʾ, by which criteria can we identify the ʿulamaʾ and distinguish them from the rest of society?

Even when historians succeed in isolating the study of the ʿulamaʾ group from that of other parts of the socio-political body to which they belonged, they may still find the material in biographical dictionaries inadequate or insufficient in providing answers to many questions raised by today's research. Their limitations as a source of study of the various aspects in the group's history have usually been ascribed to the strategy of presentation by their compilers.

Recent research on biography and the medieval historian has discerned a profound change in the nature of biographies produced by Christian writers following the twelfth century, which transformed our access to medieval men. In the words of one of the historians: "After the time of William the Conqueror, the curtain, through which people appear to us only as cardboard figures in a pageant, is drawn aside, and we are presented not with a puppet show but with a live drama."[27] This change is attributed to the new spirit of "twelfth-century renaissance," a period during which the individual was discovered and humanism introduced into historical writing. It seems that the change in Islamic biographical literature is related to its criteria of inclusion, rather than to its strategy of presentation. Earlier biographical dictionaries (compiled during the ninth century) included broader groups of ʿulamaʾ—*hadith* transmitters, Koran reciters, legal scholars, and Sufis—as well as poets, men of letters, grammarians, physicians. During the tenth century, however, this encyclopedic-type biographical literature began to give way to works limited to subgroups. Two characteristic products of this period are the biographical dictionaries of members of a particular legal school, and those of scholars and famous men connected with a certain city or province. Compiled by local ʿulamaʾ, and often of enormous bulk, these local "histories" were probably modeled after the immense "History of Baghdad" (*Taʾrikh baghdad*) by al-Khatib al-Baghdadi (d. 463/1071).[28]

The change in the criteria of inclusion reflects broader religious and social trends in the so-called Earlier Middle Period. During this major phase in the consolidation of the schools of law, many compilers naturally devoted their biographical dictionaries to disciples and followers of a particular *madhhab*. While such works were designed to locate people in the genealogies of the legal schools, they most likely also served as a means of disseminating the teaching and behavioral patterns of their leading scholars, and enhancing a sense of solidarity among their followers. In a similar vein, the growth and maturity of urban Islamic communities gave rise to the genre of local "histories." In its turn, it served to educate the young to follow the example of their forefathers, thereby contributing to the consolidation of the community and to its distinct identity. That urban pride and identity were prime motivations sustaining these compilations is testified to by the inclusion of sections devoted to a description of the city's palaces, mosques, and quarters.

With the transition from all-embracing biographical dictionaries to those devoted to subgroups—defined by place of residence or by affiliation to a particular legal school—the data relating to the members of each group was extended and valuable information added concerning the biographees' professional background, course of studies, careers, and social positions. However, since the interest of the compilers remained focused on the professional lives of their subjects—the date of the first hearing (*samaʿ*), teachers and disciples, places visited while traveling for the sake of learning, intellectual competence, and reputation—the biographical notices fail to convey "a sense of personality." The biographees are often shown as little more than types, and their thoughts and private lives remain, for the most part, hidden.

Moreover, because biographical dictionaries were written by ʿulamaʾ for ʿulamaʾ—often members of the same legal school or city— they are replete with idealized descriptions of individual scholars, accounts shaped by long-enduring literary conventions further conceal the biographee's personality for the sake of depicting a role model. Finally, due to the method of the selection of material, the 'ulama' appear as an intellectual elite, representing the highly "canonized" culture and seldom affected by either the factor of time and place, or by adjacent "noncanonized" cultural strata.[29] Hence the question arises whether to accept the accounts and descriptions in biographical dictionaries literally, thus taking the 'ulama' at face value, or to search for more reliable accounts of them, complementary.

Social historians have stressed these difficulties and have offered various methods to deal with the social history of the 'ulama' class, which can only be briefly summarized here.[30] One such method, notably adopted successfully by Ira Lapidus for Mamluk Cairo and Syria, has been to gather all reliable accounts from the various literary genres—bibliographical dictionaries, chronicles, geography, legal documents—on political, cultural, or economic groups and institutions.[31] While exploiting all available complementary evidence in order to comprehend the 'ulama' as part of the entire socio-political order—how they mediated between all sectors of society and maintained an internal balance in the absence of state agencies or corporative bodies—this functionalist analysis tends to overlook important aspects of the complex reality of the 'ulama' in various historical contexts.

Aware of the informational aspects of the biographical dictionaries, a second method has been to use this literature for historical data. Because of the richness of its contemporary biographical dictionaries, the Mamluk period offers an ideal laboratory in which to analyze the 'ulama' class. The systematic use to which this genre can be put for the study of the 'ulama' during this period is clearly demonstrated in Carl Petry's study, *The Civilian Elite of Cairo in the Later Middle Ages*. Based on data in the biographical dictionaries, Petry's quantitative method permits the identification of several differentiated and specialized groups within the body of the 'ulama', such as bureaucrats, jurists, and religious functionaries, each drawing its personnel from distinct social and geographical backgrounds. The classification of the various specialized groups within the body of the 'ulama' has been derived from the language of modern social science, rather than from the self-description of what Petry labels the "civilian elite." Moreover, accounts and anecdotes have been ignored. The lives and concerns of individual 'ulama' whose names are included in biographical dictionaries remain hidden.

Since this study seeks to describe both the general and particular traits of the 'ulama' under consideration, its approach lies somewhere between quantitative and qualitative analysis. All information contained in biographical literature—places of origin, social backgrounds, fields of study, school affiliation, and office of over seven hundred ʿulamaʾ living in Baghdad during the eleventh and first half of the twelfth centuries (409/1018–549/1154)—was collected and analyzed. At the same time, the main emphasis was placed upon collecting and studying the "soft facts"—anecdotes illustrating how individual ʿulamaʾ thought and behaved in concrete situations, city descriptions, and accounts of major events—taken from the primary sources described below.

Undertaken in line with a growing body of research on both single individuals and groups of ʿulamaʾ using biographical literature as its principal source, my foremost objective is to integrate the study of this genre into the larger scheme of Islamic social and cultural history.[32] This objective rests on the premise that a close association exists between text and context; that the content of the biographies, like any other literary texts, the structure of their narrative, the methods of their transmission and preservation, were not determined solely by literary conventions, but by the concerns and expectations of those who simultaneously composed them, read them, or listened to them. Hence the importance of identifying and characterizing this community of text producers, reproducers, and receivers.[33]

Because of the need to verify the credibility of the authorities, the links in the chains of the transmission of religious lore and knowledge, the composition of biographical dictionaries was used, in its turn, as a means of preserving and disseminating the ideals of proper transmission, as well as constituting role models. If we bear in mind their edifying function, then the composition of biographies must be seen in the context of cultural reproduction, defined by Pierre Bourdieu as the tendency of society to reproduce itself by the transmission of its values, norms, or rules of behavior from one generation to the next.[34] In other words, these works served to nourish and reassert the ideals and values they mirror, and, as such, had social roles and uses.

Based on these observations, we must, as a point of departure, consider the strategy of presentation and methods of organization of the material used by authors of biographical dictionaries as essential to our capacity to interpret their accounts of the ʿulamaʾ.[35] Instead of dismissing the material in the sources as meaningless or unreliable, we should ask why certain aspects or "events" in a scholar's life are recorded while others are "forgotten." Why does it seem to have been much more important to record with whom one studied than where the studies took place, or even the texts transmitted? Why do biographers seldom depart from the formula: "who, when, where, scholarly achievements, reputation"? Why do they report the events in chronological order, following the scholar's life from cradle to grave; when and for what purposes do they depart from this order? Moreover, by interpreting the language in the sources, we can understand the cultural values and social norms that the idealized descriptions and the "other information" about the biographees attempt to convey.

Historical concreteness will not be sacrificed for the sake of setting up a general model for the comprehension of the ʿulamaʾ. Accordingly, it is not my intention to depict unitary cultural and social patterns that can readily be applied to other learned societies distant in time and place. Rather, this study seeks to reconstitute a society's description of itself, and to bring to life, as far as possible, the world of its subjects over a hundred-year period. I shall therefore begin by examining the peculiar environment of eleventh-century Baghdad in order to establish the milieu for its group of ʿulamaʾ.

Chapter 2 studies the formation of eleventh-century Baghdadi community of learning and knowledge. It points to a gradual passage from journeys to schools, placing this development in the wider context of migratory trends and the crystallization of local groups of ʿulamaʾ during the eleventh and twelfth centuries in the Islamic Near East as a whole. Together, chapters 1 and 2 provide an understanding of how the changing conditions of Baghdad under the Great Seljuks, and their policy of founding educational institutions and supporting religious scholars, led to an increase in the scholarly population of the city. Did the transition from a worldwide to a local basis of recruitment result in the emergence of a learned society with a strong local identity? Or did the cosmopolitan character of this society remain intact? This question may be examined through a study of the scholarly pursuits and self-image of the ʿulamaʾ connected with Baghdad during the eleventh and twelfth centuries.

Chapter 3 discusses the character of learning during the first century of the madrasa in Baghdad (between the late eleventh and mid-twelfth centuries). To what extent can the advent of the madrasa be perceived as a point of departure as far as the modes of scholarly communication and association are concerned? Did old frameworks of study, in which scholars of different schools of law and thought sat side by side as a matter of routine, yield their place to madrasas, where admission was restricted to members of a certain *madhhab*? The answers to these and other questions lie in the character and image of the madrasa as delineated by contemporary sources, causing us to reconsider the social significance of institutionalization.

After dealing with the scholarly networks in terms of chains of transmitters, chapter 4 studies the relationships between masters and disciples as social networks. The discussion revolves around the set of social relations among members of a study circle, and the ties which knit adherents of a *madhhab* together, so as to understand how the 'ulama' of this period in Baghdad constructed their identities and loyalties. While questioning the importance of the madrasa and the *madhhab* in the culture and society of the learned, the chapter contributes to our understanding of the social significance of the close, personal relationships between a master and his disciples, and the very personal nature of the *madhahib*.

Chapter 5 studies the composition of the 'ulama' of eleventh-century Baghdad according to socio-economic origins and occupation, defining a link between the movement toward conformity and uniformity, and the gradual trend toward greater exclusivity in the criteria of membership and leadership among the 'ulama'. This chapter argues that, while far from emerging as an institutionalized force represented, for example, by the Christian clergy, the Baghdadi 'ulama' of the Sunni revival made use of the system developed for the transmission of knowledge, as well as the madrasas supporting them, in order to reinforce the cultural and social distinctiveness of their groupings and ensure their self-perpetuation. An examination of the career opportunities and career patterns of the 'ulama' who taught or studied in the madrasas of Baghdad, reveals the contribution made by their establishment to this process.

After considering the 'ulama' themselves, the final chapter examines the web of relations which bound them to the larger society of eleventh-century Baghdad. More specifically, the chapter seeks to evaluate the status and role of the 'ulama' in the urban society of Baghdad following the breakdown of the 'Abbasid bureaucratic empire and the rise to power of an alien military elite. These trends, while involving constant upheavals, broadened the horizons of the public sphere in which 'ulama' could assume significant functions as a civilian elite, capable of providing communal services and lending a measure of social unity. The autonomy of the religious elite, composed of civil and religious officials, vis-à-vis the political authorities, the involvement of the political rulers in the internal affairs of the 'ulama', and the *madhahib* as social organizations are major topics raised and addressed. A study of these topics will show that, at the social and political levels, the 'ulama' can not be regarded as a single or unified group. Likewise, data on each of the schools, along with their different social and political outlooks, will force us to depart from the typical type of generalization about all Sunni groups. At the same time, such an inquiry will contribute to our understanding of the legal schools' process of consolidation during the Sunni revival.

When looking at the eleventh-century 'ulama' of Baghdad as a whole body, what will emerge is a gradual transformation from a heterogeneous society, open in its inclusion of various social groups, into a more defined and exclusive group. In the unstable and unpredictable world in which they lived, members of this learned society reinforced their collective identity and social distinctiveness and furnished new ideas of their place and roles in society.

A Note on the Sources

We are blessed with a rich biographical literature for Baghdad during the period under consideration, which is both primary and contemporary in nature.[36] Some of the sources described below were written by individuals about their contemporaries, associates, and intimates, thus offering a clearer view of subjects than similar literature from other periods provide. Others were composed by later authors who faithfully copied and continued their predecessors' work.

The works by two contemporary historians provide firsthand descriptions of the 'ulama' who resided in Baghdad during the eleventh century as well as accounts of 'ulama' of earlier centuries. Al-Khatib's history of Baghdad contains a description of the city and its buildings, as well as a voluminous biographical dictionary. Arranged alphabetically and covering the period from early Islamic times to 463/1071, the year of his death, al-Khatib's outstanding work provides far more biographical information of 'ulama' residing in or visiting Baghdad than any other, contemporary or later, source.[37]

Ibn al-Jawzi (d. 597/1200), the famous Hanbali preacher and writer, a native of Baghdad, is the author of the outstanding work, *al-Muntazam fi ta'rikh al-muluk wa'l-umam.* It is both a chronicle and a biographical dictionary, dealing in chronological order with the history of the world from its beginnings to the year 574/1178. At the end of each year, he provides biographies of all prominent people who died during that particular year: caliphs, viziers, judges, high officials, theologians, jurisconsults, and pious men. The *Muntazam* is also filled with anecdotes on the lives of Baghdadi ʿulamaʾ with whom the author was personally acquainted or about whom he had interviewed older friends and relatives.[38]

Another work compiled by a contemporary Baghdadi scholar is the diary by the Hanbali Abu ʿAli b. al-Bannaʾ, disciple of Ibn al-Jawzi. The singularity of Ibn al-Banna's work lies in his description of day-to-day socio-religious life of Baghdad, with the author concentrating his attention upon the local Hanbali community: its wealthy patrons, and its relationship with both the political rulers and the mass of the urban populace. Although it is only a fragment of his diary covering a little over a year (from August 461/1068 to September 462/1069), it contains an extraordinary picture of the daily activities of a "citizen" of the caliphal city, recording births, praying over the dead, interpreting dreams, observing what happened around him, and listening to others. Describing these activities in such a detail, Ibn al-Bannaʾ virtually takes us into the houses, orchards, and mosques of his heroes.[39]

Three universal histories compiled during the thirteenth and fourteenth centuries shed light on the political, religious, and intellectual life of Baghdad of the tenth, eleventh, and twelfth centuries. Sibt b. al-Jawzi (d. 654/1256) born in Baghdad in 581/1185, began his studies there under his grandfather, later continuing his education in Mosul and Damascus. A Hanafi, he adopted a different law school affiliation from that of his family, and became known as an outstanding preacher and authority on Islamic law. His famous work, *Mirʾat az-zaman fi taʾrikh al-aʿyan*, is a general universal history, providing an account of the major events of each year from creation to 654/1256. At the end of the events of each year he added biographies of important figures who died in that year. He also provides eyewitness accounts of his own time. For the tenth-eleventh centuries, *Miraʾt az-zaman* preserves several major lost works, copied without comment and with little alteration. The first part of this book exists in manuscript in various libraries in Europe. The published portion begins with an account of the year 448/1056, and extends to 654/1256, the year of the author's death. Both the unpublished and published portions were used in this study.[40]

Ibn al-Athir's famous work, *al-Kamil fiʾt-taʾrikh*, is another universal history written during the thirteenth century. It provides abundant accounts of the history of eleventh-century Baghdad. Covering the events of each year from the beginning of the world to 628/1231, the *Kamil* came to be regarded as a principal source by later Muslim historians, among them Ibn Kathir (d. 774/1372), the author of the great history of Islam, *al-Bidaya wa'n-nihaya*. A combination of a chronicle and a biographical dictionary, this work also provides valuable accounts on Baghdadi 'ulama' during the period under consideration.

As was mentioned above, as early as the tenth century there began a tendency to devote biographical dictionaries to members of a specific *madhhab*. However, the best-known biographical dictionaries organized on the basis of specific law schools were not written until the fourteenth century, a period when the universal, encyclopedic impulse reasserted itself. As-Subki (d. 771/1370), *mufti*, professor of Shafi'i law and *hadith* transmitter, compiled the Shafi'i biographical dictionary, *Tabaqat ash-shafi'iyya al-kubra*. He moved to Syria from Egypt, held numerous professorships in Damascus, and died in that city. Ibn Abi Wafa' (d. 775/1373), in *al-Jawahir al-mudi'ah fi tabaqat al-hanafiyya*, was the first scholar to collect the biographies of Hanafi scholars. He resided in Cairo and, like as-Subki, may never have visited Baghdad. Ibn Rajab (d. 795/1392) was born in Baghdad but migrated to Damascus, where he compiled a dictionary of the Hanbalis, *Dhail 'ala tabaqat al-hanabila*, a continuation of *Tabaqat al-hanabila* by the Baghdadi Hanbali historian, Ibn Abi Ya'la. These three biographical dictionaries provide a comprehensive picture of law school affiliation in eleventh- and early twelfth-century Baghdad. Later compilers of biographical dictionaries devoted to the Shafi'i and Hanafi schools, whose works were also employed in this study, relied on as-Subki and Ibn al-Wafa'.

Among the general biographical dictionaries of 'ulama' (as well as of people not in scholarly professions) that of Ibn Khallikan (d. 668/1282) *Kitab wafayat al-a'yan wa-anba' abna' az-zaman*, is possibly the most valuable. He was born in Iraq, and studied law and theology in Allepo, Damascus, and Cairo. The Mamluk sultan Bayrbas appointed Ibn Khallikan head judge of Damascus. Arranged alphabetically, his work contains over eight hundred biographies of famous persons from the entire Muslim world, beginning in early Islamic times, up to his own.[41] Ibn Shakir al-Kutubi (d. 764/1363) wrote the continuation of Ibn Khallikan's *Wafayat*, under the title *Fawat al-wafayat*. Three later authors provide additional, brief accounts of large numbers of 'ulama', particularly *hadith* transmitters. These authors are adh-Dhahabi (d. 748/1347), who wrote *al-'Ibar fi khabar man ghabar*, and *Kitab tadhkirat al-huffaz*;[42] as-Suyuti (d. 991/1583), who wrote *Tabaqat al-huffaz*; and Ibn al-'Imad (d. 1089/1678), who composed *Shadharat adh-dhahab*.

Put together, the few pieces of information in these works may well serve to document certain specifics, including a description of eleventh-century Baghdad and its involvement the worldwide networks of transmission of Islamic learning, an examination of the composition of its group of 'ulama' according to fields of study, school affiliation and origins, and an enumeration of official posts open to them. Even more meaningful for social historians are the anecdotes about individual scholars found in these sources. Whether true or false, these stories, written and preserved so as to survive to later generations, provide us with glimpses of the thoughts, values, and attitudes of medieval Muslims. Through them, the world of our subjects comes alive.

CHAPTER 1

❧

THE CITY

In a geographical treatise written in the late ninth century, the famous Arab geographer al-Ya'qubi explained why he began his geographical account with a description of Iraq and its capital, Baghdad:

> I begin with Iraq only because it is the center of this world, the navel of the earth, and I mention Baghdad first because it is the center of Iraq, the greatest city, which has no peer in the east or the west of the world in extent, size, prosperity, abundance of water, or health of climate, and because it is inhabited by all kinds of people, town-dwellers and country-dwellers.[1]

Al-Ya'qubi went on to describe the flow of luxurious goods carried to Baghdad by overland caravan trails and by river traffic from east and west. He describes, in great detail, the glorious "round city" founded by the 'Abbasid caliph, al-Mansur ("the victorious"), on the west banks of the Tigris in 140/757–758: its quarters, gates, arcades, walls, the caliph's palace, and the great mosque of al-Mansur surrounded by the houses of the caliph's officers and followers.[2] His description conveys the portrait of a well-established city, laid out according to a remarkable and carefully thought-out plan. So perfect was its plan that "it was as though it was poured into a model and cast."[3]

Approximately one hundred years later, the Arab geographer, al-Muqaddasi, described the characteristics of the various Muslim countries (*aqalim*):

Should anyone ask which of the numerous Muslim cities and provinces is the best, he will be provided with the following answer: . . . if he is devout and free from ambition, Mecca. If he seeks comfort, affluence, low prices, and fruits, he may be told: any country would serve you, or else, you have five capitals, Damascus, Basra, Rayy, Bukhara, and Balkh. . . . Choose whichever you please, for these places are the delights of Islam. It is said that Andalusia is a paradise, but the earthly paradises are four in number, the Ghuta of Damascus, the river of Ubulla, the Garden of Sughd, and Shaʿb Bawwan. Whoever desires commerce, should take Aden, ʿUman, or Egypt.

In regard to Baghdad, al-Muqaddasi added: "Know that Baghdad was great in the past but is now falling into ruins. It is full of troubles, and its glory is gone. I neither approve nor admire it, and if I praise it, it is mere convention."[4]

Al-Muqaddasi's account reflects profound changes in the conditions of Baghdad. By the early eleventh century, the caliphal city had long since lost the prestige of an imperial government it had enjoyed for nearly three hundred years, and was now forced to share its honors with cities such as Cairo, Cordoba, Ghazna, and Shiraz. Moreover, Baghdad had declined economically as a result of the loss of imperial revenues and income from the eastern trade, which by that time had shifted from the Persian Gulf route to the Red Sea route. In addition to its political and economic decline, the city suffered from sectarian differences fanned and incited by the Buyids, and from the turbulence of the ʿayyarun, gangs usually made up of young men.

However, even Baghdad's scholars, witnessing the collapse of the ʿAbbasids and lamenting over the devastation of their native city by the Shiʿi rulers, still portrayed their city as the most important center of Islamic thought. Al-Khatib al-Baghdadi's introduction to his famous work, *Taʾrikh baghdad*, is an excellent example of this sense of superiority: his view of Iraq as the "navel of the universe," and Baghdad as the geographical center of the Muslim empire and capital of a dynasty.[5] The introduction and the successive biographical entries, which comprise the remainder of the work, are evidence of the author's desire to convey the imperial splendor of the city's physical image and, more importantly, the intellectual climate created by its thousands of scholars and pious individuals.

The Coming of the Turks

The sense of turmoil and general decline characteristic of Sunni compilations on the conditions of the Muslim world, particularly in Baghdad under Buyid rule, was also conveyed by accounts of the Turkish influx into the central regions of Islam during the second half of the eleventh century. Contemporary writers described the Iraqis' fear and suspicion at the appearance of the Seljuks in Khurasan and their advance toward Iraq, and complained about the impoverishment of their native cities by the Turkish nomads. Sibt b. al-Jawzi wrote that in 442/1050, as a result of the arrival of the Ghuzz east and southeast of Iraq, people from Basra and Wasit fled to Baghdad.[6] According to the chronicler, the arrival of the Seljuks in Baghdad in 447/1055 worsened the situation. More people fled to the city from the surrounding areas, and bands ruled by the Seljuk chieftain, Tughril Beg, found quarters in homes in the eastern areas of Baghdad, forcing the inhabitants to supply them with food.[7] The scarcity of food supplies resulted in epidemics and death increased rates. Ibn al-Jawzi related that a large number of men and women died daily, until few people were to be seen in Baghdad's streets.[8] Natural catastrophes added to the dreadful situation, the most serious, known as "the year of the flood," taking place in 466/1073. The Tigris rose an unprecedented thirty cubits that year, destroying property and lives. According to Ibn al-Athir, the extraordinary phenomenon was that people attributed the terrible flood to malicious deeds among the populace (namely wine-drinking and prostitution), perceiving the disaster as the wrath of God.[9]

These sources are replete with descriptions of human suffering as well as comments on the poor conditions in the city. When asked about these conditions, the famous Hanbali scholar, Ibn ʿAqil (d. 513/1119) replied: "I will not describe to you what you might find hard to believe, but will simply give you a description of my city."[10] His account expresses a keen sense of pride in his city. Yet at the same time it reveals the sorrow felt by the Baghdadis at their first sight of the city's caliphal palaces in ruins, and the loss of its imperial splendor, which they ascribed to the disappearance of the ʿAbbasid central authority and the lack of the people's piety.

However, a closer examination of contemporary reports of the mid-eleventh century indicate that, beneath the stormy surface, signs of relative peace and prosperity had begun to appear.[11] The Seljuks began to restore order and rebuild the city immediately after the suppression of the Basasiri revolt in 451/1059. In the same year, Sultan Tughril Beg appointed Abu al-Fath al-Muzaffar to the post of the provincial governor (*ʿamid*), who immediately began rebuilding the city's economy. He restored the marketplace of al-Karkh quarter, ordering its inhabitants, who had fled to *Dar al-khilafa* (the official residence of the ʿAbbasid caliphs) during the disturbances, to return. The marketplace soon recovered its former activity. The governmental residence, or *Dar al-mamlaka* (constructed by the Buyids in the eastern part of the city, north of *Dar al-khilafa*) was reconstructed and renamed *Dar as-saltana as-saljukiyya*; new buildings were also constructed in both east and west Baghdad. The governor, who supervised the construction activity, is said to have exhibited great concern for the city's welfare, winning the esteem of its inhabitants.[12] *Dar al-ʿilm*, the famous library founded by the Buyid vizier al-Sabur b. Ardashir, was also restored at this time. The library had been burnt several times, and many of its books plundered. Fearing that Baghdad's repository of knowledge might disappear, the governor ordered that the thousand volumes, rescued and sent to Khurasan, be returned to the city.[13]

Upon Tughril Beg's death in 455/1063, his nephew and heir, Sultan Alp Arslan, expanded the Seljuk empire until it included all the lands from the Mediterranean to the confines of eastern Iran. His vizier, Nizam al-Mulk (d. 485/1092) restored the peace and relieved Baghdad of external threats. Especially important to Baghdad was the destruction of the power exercised by the seminomadic Arab and Kurdish petty dynasties which had established themselves in the Jazira and had interfered with the grain trade.[14] Within the city itself, older buildings, destroyed by the floods, were rebuilt and east Baghdad extended; new markets, palaces, mosques, and educational establishments were founded by Seljuk officials. Among these were the madrasas and the *ribat*s.

Relations between Sunnis and Shiʿis also improved. Ibn al-Jawzi reported a number of clashes which broke out between the Shiʿis concentrated in al-Karkh and Bab at-Taq quarters, and the militant Hanbalis who gathered in the Bab al-Basra quarter. In 488/1095, however, the two factions reached a settlement, and the rival quarters, once kept locked, were reopened. Ibn al-Jawzi recalled: "the people of the two quarters began to exchange visits, to trust each other, and to drink in each other's company," a phenomenon he called "one of the remarkable (*ajaʾib*) events."[15] Clashes between adherents to the various *madhahib* early in the twelfth century are also rarely mentioned.

During the twenty years following the great flood of 466/1073, Baghdad enjoyed tremendous prosperity, reflected in an exceptional plenitude and low food prices. It is no wonder that Sultan Malikshah chose Baghdad as a place of relaxation after strenuous campaiging in 480/1087.[16] Four years later, during his last visit to Baghdad, which coincided with his birthday, a great number of people gathered on the banks of the Tigris to welcome him. The sultan marked the occasion by building a new mosque adjacent to the sultan's palace in *Dar as-saltana as-saljukiyya*. The mosque, known as "Jami‘ as-Sultan," is often mentioned in the chronicles as one of the great congregational mosques in east Baghdad, where the Friday prayers continued to be said until the extinction of the caliphate. At the same time, Nizam al-Mulk and some other high ranking officials built houses in the city.[17] Yet accounts of the reconstruction and building of mosques, palaces, and houses are usually brief, whereas the sources yield a veritable wealth of detailed information on the foundation of madrasas.

The Appearance of the Madrasa

Construction of madrasas in Baghdad began during the late eleventh century on a scale that increased during the course of the next century. During this period, madrasas were built for the three dominating schools of law: Shafi‘i, Hanafi, and Hanbali (Figure 1.1, below). Of the twenty-four madrasas whose location, founders and beneficiaries are known, ten were built for the Shafi‘i school—all were erected in the quarters on the eastern side of the city, at first by the sultans' Iranian-Shafi‘i ministers and later by the caliphs. The famous Nizamiyya Madrasa, the first to be constructed, was located in the middle of Suq ath-Thalatha, adjacent to *Dar al-khilafa*. All other madrasas established for the Shafi‘i school were situated either directly on the east bank of the Tigris or near the riverbank in one of the eastern quarters, often in main marketplaces, which served as the main street or highway at that time.

Madrasas for the Hanafi school were built as early as 459/1066, the same year the Nizamiyya Madrasa was founded, but most were constructed during the late eleventh and first half of the twelfth centuries. The first Hanafi madrasa was constructed adjacent to the tomb of Abu Hanifa, in Bab at-Taq, a quarter which, though populated by Shi‘is, was the center of the Hanafi school. The Hanafi madrasas were founded by the Seljuk sultans, members of the royal household and its entourage—all Turks affiliated with the Hanafi *madhhab*. Moreover, the madrasas were built in quarters adjacent to the east bank of the Tigris, the sites of palaces belonging to the patrons of both the Shafiʿi and Hanafi schools.

This preferred area was not accidental; most of the founders were members of the ruling class, hence madrasas were often constructed in the quarters adjacent to the palaces in *Dar as-saltana* and *Dar al-khilafa*. Anyone of standing could sail up and down the river, ogling the great mosques, palaces, and madrasas which added glamor to the caliphal city. Designed as great enclosed spaces, the madrasas were viewed as fortresses of learning, symbolic of the Seljuk dynasty's role as defender of Sunni Islam and patron of the ʿulamaʾ.

Female members of royal families also played a prominent role as patrons of religious learning and the ʿulamaʾ during the eleventh century and the high medieval period in general. The allocation of private property to a religious or charitable purpose was one of the few public acts in which, in accordance with Islamic religious law itself, men and women could equally participate. Muslim women could own, inherit, and dispose of property. It is therefore no wonder that pious women—susceptible to the same concerns which encouraged Muslim men to support religious institutions—participated in the public act of religious charity by committing a significant portion of their wealth to the construction and endowment of a school of higher learning.[18] Seljuk women, and women who married into the Seljuk family, possessed their own assignments, pensions, and landed estates, and were sometimes able to transmit these by inheritance. Some of these gifts, as evidenced by their charitable benefactions, were considerable.[19]

At least two madrasas, owing their endowment to female members of the Seljuk family, were established in Baghdad during the Seljuk period. The first, Madrasa Terken Khatun (princess of the Turks), a Hanafi madrasa, was endowed by the wife of Malikshah and mother of Sultan Mahmud, and was named after her. A woman of substance, she played an active role in the struggle of succession after her husband's death.[20] Her daughter founded another Hanafi madrasa, the Madrasa al-Waqfiyya. During the late twelfth century, female members of the caliphal family also became involved in the construction and endowment of schools of higher religious education. As-Siyada Binafsha, wife of the caliph al-Mustadiʾ, founded a school for the Hanbalis, assigning the post of the professor of law (*mudarris*) to Ibn al-Jawzi.[21] More important were the two schools endowed by

Zumrad Khatun, mother of the caliph an-Nasir li-Din, which taught classes in Shafiʿi law.

The Hanbalis were at first reluctant to adopt the madrasa as a center for their teaching activities; thus the teachings of the *madhhab* appear to have been conducted in the mosques and private homes long after the spread of the madrasa "system" in Baghdad and in other Islamic cities.[22] What appears to have been their first madrasa dates from the beginning of the twelfth century, nearly half a century after the first Shafiʿi and Hanafi madrasas made their appearance in the city: the Madrasa of Mukharrimi (d. 513/1119), named for a Hanbali jurisconsult and Sufi who presented the celebrated ʿAbd al-Qadir al-Jilani with the Sufi cloak, or *khirqa*. Al-Jilani assumed leadership of the madrasa after his teacher's death, and expanded it. The madrasa stands in Baghdad to this day, an object of pilgrimage, as is al-Jilani's tomb.

Seven other Hanbali madrasas were founded during the twelfth century; most of them were purely private establishments in the sense that they were built by Hanbali scholars themselves. Six of them were located in East Baghdad, particularly in Bab al-Azaj quarter, south of *Dar al-khilafa*. Although generally considered to be a Hanbali section of town, a Hanafi madrasa was established in this quarter by a grandson of Malikshah. Only one madrasa was built in the western part of the city, in Bab al-Basra, which was heavily populated by adherents to the school, and where the Mosque of al-Mansur, their stronghold, stood. This madrasa, the Madrasa al-Wazir, was founded for the Hanbalis by Ibn Hubayra, the Hanbali vizier of the caliphs al-Muqtafi and al-Mustanjid (d. 560/1165).

There are no deeds of *waqf* for the madrasas founded in Baghdad during the late eleventh and twelfth centuries, with the exception of a single document setting forth the budget for the Nizamiyya Madrasa and its beneficiaries. The deed of this glorious madrasa was read in public in April 1070, about three years after its inauguration, at a special gathering of the chief *qadi* and other dignitaries. It designated the members of the Shafiʿi school of law as beneficiaries of the endowment, and named Nizam al-Mulk, and his sons after him, as the administrators. Its *waqf* provided for the appointment of a *mudarris*, a preacher and teachers of the Koranic science and grammar, as well as a librarian; it also specified the portion of endowment revenue to be received by each one.[23] During his last visit to Baghdad in A.H. 480, Nizam al-Mulk held a session for dictating prophetic traditions in the library of the Nizamiyya.[24]

Figure 1.1
The Madrasas Founded in Baghdad in the
Late 5th/11th and 6th/12th Centuries

MADRASA	DATE OF INAUGURATION	BENEFICIARIES	FOUNDER	LOCATION
Al-madrasa an-nizamiyya	459/1066	Shafi'is	Nizam al-Mulk	east Baghdad - Suq ath-Thalatha
Madrasa Abu Hanifa	459/1066	Hanafis	Abu Sa'd al-'Amid	east Baghdad - Bab at-Taq
Al-madrasa at-tutushiyya	469/1076	Hanafis	Khimar Takin - mamluk of at-Tutush, brother of Malikshah	east Baghdad - Dard Dinar
Madrasa at-tajiyya	482/1089	Shafi'is	Taj al-Mulk al-Mustawfi (the treasurer)	East Baghdad - Bab Abraz
Madrasa Terken Khatun	unknown	Hanafis	Terken Khatun - the wife of Malikshah	east Baghdad
Al-madrasa al-baha'iyya	unknown	Shafi'is	unknown	east Baghdad, close to the Nizamiyya
Al-madrasa al-waqfiyya	unknown	Hanafis	Daughter of Malikshah	east Baghdad - Darb Zakha (on the bank of the Tigris)
Madrasa as-sultan	unknown	Hanafis	Malikshah (d. 485/1092)	east Baghdad
Madrasa al-mughaithiyya	unknown	Hanafis	Mughaith ad-Din Mahmud b. Malikshah (d. 487/1094)	east Baghdad
Madrasa al-Amir Sa'ada	unknown	Hanafis	Al-Amir 'Izz ad-Din Sa'ada (d. 500/1106)	east Baghdad
Madrasa ash-Shashi	unknown	Shafi'is	Abu Baker ash-Shashi ash-Shafi'i (d. 507/1113)	east Baghdad Qarah Zafar
Madrasa ath-thiqatiyya, or Madrasa Thiqa ad-Dawla	unknown	Shafi'is	Abu al-Hasan al-Anbari (d. 549/1154), husband of Shuhda al-Katiba (Fakhr al-Nisa')	east Bahgdad

MADRASA	DATE OF INAUGURATION	BENEFICIARIES	FOUNDER	LOCATION
Madrasa Ibn Sa'd al-Mukharrimi, or Madrasa 'Abd Qadir al-Jilani	unknown	Hanbalis	Ibn Sa'd al-Mukharrimi (d. 513/1119)	east Baghdad - Bab al-Azaj
Madrasa Ibn Hubayra, or Madrasa al-wazir	557/1161	Hanbalis	Ibn Hubayra (d. 560/1164)	west Baghdad - Bab al-Basra
Madrasa al-kamiliyya, or Madrasa Hamza b. 'Ali	535/1140	Shafi'is	Hamza Ibn 'Ali b. Talha, the treasurer	east Baghdad - Bab al-'Amma
Madrasa Ibn al-Abradi	unknown	Hanbalis	Ibn al-Abradi al-hanbali az-zahid (d. 531/1137)	east Baghdad
Madrasa Ibn Dinar	unknown	Hanbalis	Abu al-Hakim b. Dinar al-hanbali (d.556/1160)	east Baghdad - Bab al-Azaj
Madrasa Ibn al-Jawzi	570/1174	Hanbalis	Ibn al-Jawzi, the famous Hanbali historian	east Baghdad - Darb Dinar
Madrasa darb al-qiyar	unknown	Hanbalis	Ibn Bakris al-Hammi al-hanbali (d. 573/1177)	east Baghdad - Darb al-Qiyar
Madrasa Binafsha	570/1174	Hanbalis	As-Siyada Binafsha - wife of the caliph al-Mustadi'	east Baghdad - Bab al-Azaj
Madrasa an-Najib as-Suhrawardi	unknown	Shafi'is	Ash-shaykh an-Najib al-Suhrawardi (d. 563/1167)	east Baghdad
Madrasa al-fahriyya, or Dar dhahab	unknown	Shafi'is	Fahr ad-Dawla al-Wazir (d. 578/1182)	east Baghdad
Madrasa Zumrad Khatun	589/1193	Shafi'is	Zumrad Khatun - mother of the caliph an-Nasir li-Din	east Baghdad
al-Madrasa al-qaysariyya	unknown	Shafi'is	Zumrad Khatun	east Baghdad

Notes:
1. For the location of the madrasas, see Map 2.
2. When the date of inauguration is unknown, the death date of the founder is indicated.

Descriptions of inauguration ceremonies further reflect the importance attributed to the new madrasas by contemporary observers
and later writers, highlighting the good fortune of those legal scholars
who assumed the chair of *mudarris*. Such ceremonies, which delighted
the public, usually included an inaugural lecture or lesson by the
appointee, and were attended by government and scholarly dignitaries. A typical example is the inauguration of the Iqbaliyya Madrasa,
founded in Baghdad in the early thirteenth century. The historian
Ibn Kathir, without naming the appointee, reported that the inaugural lecture was attended by a large crowd, including noted legal
scholars of the different *madhahib*. Sweetmeats were prepared for
all the guests, and sent to the other madrasas and *ribat*s of the city,
and robes of honor were bestowed on the new appointee, his assistants, followers (*ashab*), and pupils (*talaba*).[25]

By the thirteenth century, the madrasas proliferated to such an
extent that they appeared in descriptions by chroniclers and travelers
as an almost integral part of the city, together with the rulers' palaces,
mosques, and bazaars. The famous Magribi traveler Ibn Jubayr
visited Baghdad in 580/1184, making note of no less than thirty
madrasas in the eastern part of the city. The most famous were
the Nizamiyya and the madrasa of Abu Hanifa (founded by the
head of the Sultan's tax bureau, Abu Saʿd Muhammad b. Mansur al-
Khwarizmi, Sharf al-Mulk).[26] Ibn Jubayr noted that the Nizamiyya's
endowments, derived from domains and rents belonging to the
madrasa, were enough for teachers' salaries, building maintenance
and support for poor scholars.[27] By Ibn Jubayr's time, the Great
Seljuk empire had long been dissolved and Baghdad had been
reduced to the mere capital of Iraq. Yet his account of east Baghdad,
with its magnificent caliphal palaces and gardens, excellent markets
and over thirty madrasas, all housed in excellent buildings with
plenty of charitable endowments for their upkeep and for students'
expenses, implies that for all its political decline, the caliphal city
still enjoyed a considerable economic and cultural prosperity.

Marshall Hodgson has convincingly argued that in this confused
and unstable world, the result of the loss of the caliphate's political
framework and the decline of Baghdad's central role, a more institutionalized educational framework was required to meet the old threat
of disintegration.[28] The importance of the madrasa to contemporary
writers, and their perception of it as a fortress of learning, designed
to disseminate the community's Islamic heritage, is underlined by
the Baghdadi poet Abu Jaʿfar al-Biyad. Entering the magnificent
shrine college of Abu Hanifa on the day of its inauguration, the poet

wondered at the beauty of the building and the considerable equip-
ment placed at its disposal: "Knowledge (*ilm*) was about to vanish,
until the revelation of this hidden (*mughayyab*) person who gathered
it in this tomb. This country, too, was declining, until this prominent
amid [Abu Sa'd Sharf al-Mulk] appeared and brought it back to
life."[29]

Did the madrasas come to dominate religious learning in
Baghdad as envisioned by the Baghdadi poet? Or were madrasas
only glorious buildings signifying the role of the Great Seljuks as the
protectors of "true" religion? This is a question central to the understanding of the world of learning during the early madrasa period in
Baghdad.

CHAPTER 2

∾

FORMATION

"The seeking of knowledge is a *fard*
incumbent upon every Muslim."

Ibn Majah, *Sunan*, 1, no. 224

Inter-Islamic migrations and population shifts, which displaced a great number of Muslims and contributed to the fusion of the Islamic societies' diverse elements, became one of the visible phenomena of medieval Islam. Though available sources do not allow us to study the precise dimensions of the migratory movements, nor do they always specify the destination of the migrants, distinctions between the various migratory patterns and categories of migrants can be made. The first is a differentiation between the population movements of tribal societies into Islamic domains and inter-Islamic migrations; the movement of the Turcoman nomads into the Middle East during the first decades of the eleventh century was no doubt different from the inter-Islamic migrations that took place during the same period not only in terms of scale, but also in terms of its political consequences and influences on the economies and societies that the nomads penetrated.

When dealing with inter-Islamic migrations a distinction should be drawn between the various types of waves. The first is a massive flight of people—sometimes sudden, sometimes over a long period—who are compelled to leave their countries as a result of natural disasters, government oppression, or pressures from the outside. The second is that of individuals or small groups of people seeking adventure or an improvement in standard of living. Merchant families trying to expand their markets and establish a foothold in more prosperous areas are a good example of this category.[1] But scribes and scholars—including religious scholars, physicians, and poets—who left their native towns in search for better opportunities in administrative careers and intellectual achievements, also belong to this category.

The phenomenon of migration and wandering was, of course, not unique to medieval Muslims. Beginning in the mid-eleventh century, medieval Christians too were not content to remain in one place. Notwithstanding the severe pressures which held medieval Christians to their native regions—the constraints of feudalism which sought to tie down essential personnel, religious traditions which were opposed to wandering, or indeed to any earthly movement which kept men from seeking heaven—demographic expansion itself forced ever-growing numbers of individuals and groups to abandon their homes, their countries, and their accustomed milieu and seek new horizons. Wandering, then, became a need, a habitual practice, and, indeed, an ideal for almost all classes of the Christian world from the mid-eleventh to the thirteenth century. Peasants left the lands of their feudal lords and traveled to new places in search for room to breath, to learn new ways of earning their living; knights rode off in search of glory—or at least to find relief from boredom. Exile and wandering became a way of life for many students who flocked to join both new schools and famous old universities. And of course there were the merchants, profiting from the resurgence and growth of overland and marine trade.[2]

Yet despite these similarities, there were clear differences. In Europe wanderers ran up against social boundaries. Social mobility was liable to undermine the traditional patterns of their social structure. The ruling classes sought to avoid granting freedom and privileges to peasants settling in new lands. There arose a trend in cities to regulate migration so as to keep economic and political power in the hands of a small group of families, including the wealthier merchants and the heads of the larger corporations. The lack of formal and stable groups comparable to the feudal manor and the European trade guild, or the corporation in medieval Islamic societies benefited newcomers in Islamic cities. Freedom of physical and social mobility characterized Islamic societies from their very beginning, and became commonplace during the tenth and eleventh centuries. Indeed, one of the most beneficial effects of the breakdown of the monolithic ʿAbbassid state was the greater freedom of social mobility and intellectual expression. Instead of a single imperial court, many small courts arose throughout the Muslim world during the fourth and early fifth Muslim centuries, courts that endeavored to develop their capitals into economic and cultural centers. In an environment which offered abundant opportunities for patronage and recognition, people engaged in commercial, professional, and scholarly pursuits moved freely from one urban center to another, profiting from their talents and reputation, and maintaining their privileged status.[3] Some settled permanently in new locales, while others continued to travel, eventually returning to their places of origin.

Merchants and religious scholars, prominent among these "cosmopolitan elite" and bearers of culture, had much in common. Both belonged to the social category of the *a'yan*, the most eminent men of urban community who attained their social prestige through wealth, piety, and learning. Imbued with a spirit of enterprise, they were relatively free to move from one Islamic land to another with profession and status unchanged. Many merchants engaged also in the study and transmission of the prophetic traditions, while many 'ulama' were part-time religious scholars who engaged in secular occupations, often trade. Yet when we encounter difficulties in distinguishing between the pursuits of men belonging to various social categories, it is because travel in all its myriad forms—migration (*hijra*), pilgrimage (*hajj*), trade, scholarship, adventure—is often explained by biographical dictionaries in terms of a "journey in the search of knowledge" (*rihla fi talab al-'ilm*). The next discussion examines the frequency and manners with which the 'ulama' in eleventh-century Baghdad pursued the universal practice of the *rihla*, and its effect on the formation of the city's scholarly community.

The Baghdadi 'Ulama' and Worldwide Scholarly Networks

During the eleventh century Baghdad emerged as a major link in the worldwide chains of the transmission of Islamic learning. Many 'ulama' traveled from their homes to centers of religious learning around the Muslim world in order to study under the most celebrated teachers of their generation, to acquire teaching experience, and to establish their scholarly reputation. Baghdadis who left the city in search of better opportunities abroad spread the teachings and legal doctrines of their schools, while other scholars came to Baghdad from all parts of the Muslim world from as far as Spain and Transoxania. Some adopted the city as their home; others resided in Baghdad for a while, later returning to their homes or moving to other cities where they pursued their scholarly careers and contributed to intellectual life.

Data on 265 immigrant, transient, and emigrant ʿulamaʾ who lived in eleventh-century Baghdad for most of their careers, and for whom we have places of birth and death (figures 2.1 and 2.2), show how the city was incorporated into this universal scholarly scene. It is important to note that migration is determined by references on individual ʿulamaʾ who are explicitly reported to have left their places of origins and settle in the city, rather than the geographical *nisba*—the adjective denoting descent or origin. The verbs usually employed in these sources to denote immigration are *intaqala* (form III): to change locality, change one's residence; *qadima* (form I): to arrive at a place when it appears in conjunction with *nazala* (form I);

Figure 2.1
**The Geographical Origins of Immigrant and Transient
5th/11th–Century ʿUlamaʾ of Baghdad (409/1018–549/1154)**

(Total: 231)

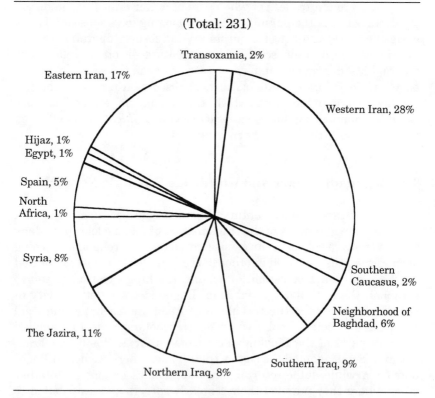

Note: The assumption is that the average ʿalim lived 70–75 years.

Figure 2.2
Places of Destination of 5th/11th–Century Emigrant 'Ulama'
of Baghdad (409/1018–549/1154)

(Total: 34)

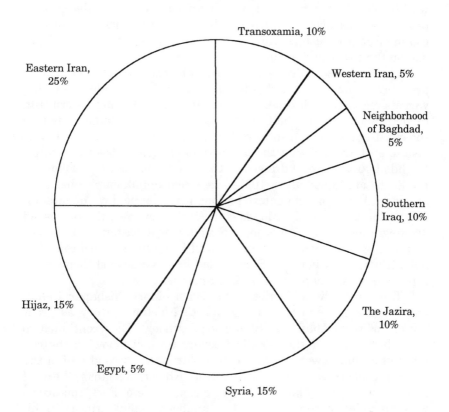

and *sakana* (form I): to remain in order to live, dwell, inhabit. Occasionally we are also told that a certain individual residing in the city ("*al-muqim al-an*") originally belonged to the people ("*kana min ahl*") of another city or town. Taking into account, however, the difficulty of determining the exact date of migration, the figures below attempt to point to general trends only.

The data on migration indicate the general trend of a huge movement westward, which began in the eleventh century and continued in the later medieval period. Figure 2.1 shows that the greatest number of immigrant and transient 'ulama' came to Baghdad from the Iranian cities, and that religious scholars from the Jazira and Syria formed the next largest group. Scholars from Egypt, the Hijaz, and the peripheral areas of North Africa, Transoxania, and Rum were less numerous. Because of its location and political history, Baghdad was, in some ways, always caught between the Persian and Arab worlds. The Khurasan Road, which linked the city to the eastern provinces, was also a principal pilgrimage road; hence transients coming from the eastern provinces were likely to pass through Baghdad on their way to the *hajj.*

The data also reflect a hierarchy of learning centers which was probably influenced by the political and economic conditions in the various regions. While 'ulama' coming to Baghdad from western Iran tended to stay, nearly half of the total number of 'ulama' drawn to the city from eastern Iran were transients (figure 2.3 below). It was also to eastern Iran that the majority of emigrant eleventh-century Baghdadi 'ulama' were drawn. At the end of this century—following the death of Malikshah in 1092—the Great Seljuk empire began to break up. Western Asia entered a long period of political disintegration, culminating in the Mongol invasions. However, the process of disintegration was not uniform, and conditions in eastern and western Iran in the late eleventh and early twelfth centuries varied considerably. Khurasan, where the Seljuks had first established themselves, remained relatively peaceful and prosperous.

The four traditional cities of the region—Marv, Nishapur, Balkh, and Herat—had emerged in the fourth Muslim century as great centers of the Hanafi and Shafi'i legal schools. They continued to flourish throughout the period of severe turmoil following the collapse of Seljuk power in eastern Iran during the second half of the twelfth century, and the rise of the Khwarizmshahs.[4] West of Khurasan, in particular in the adjacent province of Fars, conditions were much less encouraging, as the number of Seljuk princes diminished and a growing number of Seljuk officers seized power in the region, fighting endlessly among themselves. As a result, the cities of western Iran, primarily Shiraz, suffered from continuous turmoil and economic decline.[5]

The data on the destinations of emigrant eleventh-century Baghdadi 'ulama' also show that representatives of the Baghdadi traditions of *hadith* and law were present in Syria and the Jazira. However, the number of immigrant 'ulama' drawn to Baghdad from these regions outnumbered those leaving Baghdad for the same places (figure 2.3). These regions were not prosperous during this period, and their cities had not emerged as great centers of learning to the

Figure 2.3
Migration and Movement of 5th/11th–Century ʿUlamaʾ of Baghdad (409/1018–549/1154)

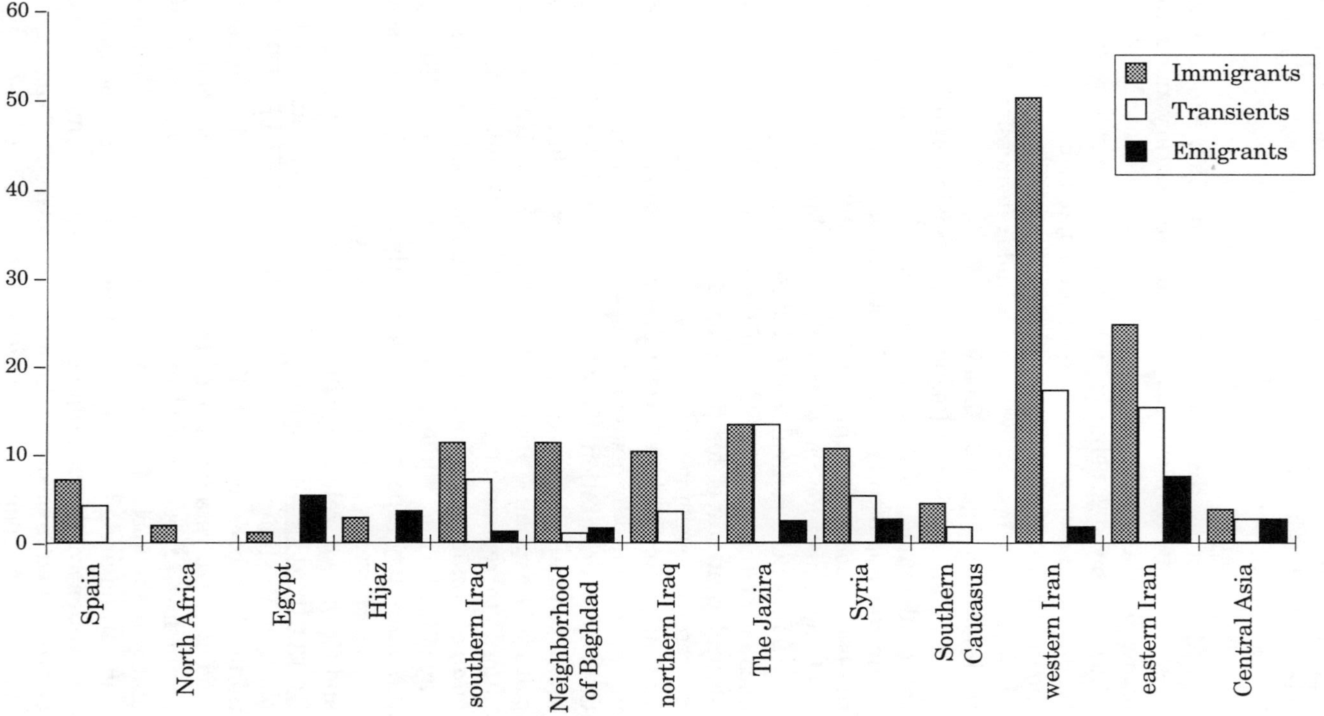

same degree as Baghdad and the cities of eastern Iran. It was only during the late twelfth century, with the rise of the Ayyubids, that Syrian cities, particularly Damascus, became important centers of learning.

Although by the sacred cities of the Hijaz had long since lost their political significance by the eleventh century and declined economically, they continued to represent the common Muslim heritage which bestowed kinship on all Muslims, regardless of birthplace. Baghdadi 'ulama' who moved to the Hijaz comprised 15 percent of the total number of emigrant 'ulama' (figure 2.2), and were described as pious men engaged in the study and transmission of the prophetic traditions (see figure 2.6, below).

Scholars coming to Baghdad from Spain comprised 5 percent of the total number of transient and immigrant 'ulama'. Conversely, Spain did not attract any religious scholars from Baghdad during the period concerned (figures 2.1, 2.2, and 2.3). In his comparative study on travel for the purpose of learning, Sam Gellens describes the *rihla* as the central feature of Spanish Muslim intellectual life. Located at the western edge of the medieval Islamic world, it was natural that travel for the sake of study should achieve its most impressive development in Spain. More important, in his view, is the fact that from the late eleventh century, Muslim Spain was increasingly threatened by a militant crusader movement, fervently Spanish-Catholic in orientation. Hence, Spanish Muslims had every reason to seek spiritual refreshment in areas where Islam was the majority culture. Egyptians, Iraqis, or 'ulama' in the Iranian cities could "afford" to remain at home, whereas for Spanish Muslims, *rihla/ talab al-'ilm* meant the survival of Islam as a coherent, *shari'a*-based way of life.[6] Thus, while all Muslim regions embraced the practice of the *rihla*, they experienced it differently for a variety of reasons.

The Koran was consolidated as central to the definition of Islam, and the core of religious education during the first Muslim century. By the third Muslim century, *hadith* had also achieved a central place in Muslim religious life, and the basic canons of the prophetic Sunna had been codified. During the fourth Muslim century, following the crystallization of the interpretive methods of the four Sunni law schools, a distinction began to be drawn between the ability to memorize *hadith*s by note (*riyawa*) and the loftier ability to understand and utilize them so as to interpret religious law (*diraya*). Consequently, the biographical notes began to include distinctions between men involved in the oral transmission of *hadith*, and those expert in the legal sciences (*'ilm al-fiqh wa-usul al-fiqh*).[7] Forming one of the bases—in many ways the most important one—of Islamic law, the serious study of the prophetic traditions constituted an essential element in any jurisconsult's religious education. It is no wonder that many legal scholars are also labeled *muhaddithun* in biographical dictionaries, while *hadith* experts are said to have acquired legal learning. As the Hanbali and Shafi'i interpretations stressed the importance of *hadith* in deriving legal rulings, it is primarily in the *tabaqat* of their schools that we find the biographies of many 'ulama' known for their profound scholarship in *hadith*.

Beginning in the fourth Muslim century, references to a man's legal school affiliation often appear in biographical literature. References to the theological beliefs of a great number of 'ulama', however, are much rarer. The majority of the 'ulama' during this period adhered to one of the legal schools, but only a few defined their theological inclinations. Therefore, the most that can be said about the relationship between law and theology is that, for the most part, Ash'ari theology appealed to the Shafi'is, while those who inclined toward Mu'tazili dogmatic theology were more likely to be Hanafis. This is why Ibn al-Jawzi, in his account on theological tendencies of the Hanafi *qadi* Abu Hasan as-Simnani, found it odd that he adhered to Ash'arism, since many Hanafis in Baghdad were *ashab al-ra'y* ("masters of opinion")—that is, Mu'tazilis.[8]

These observations allow us to examine the composition of the eleventh-century 'ulama' in Baghdad according to school affiliation and areas of study (figures 2.4, 2.5, 2.6, and 2.7, below). More than half the transient 'ulama' drawn to Baghdad were *muhaddithun*. Eager to hear as large a number of prophetic traditions from as many qualified transmitters as possible, these men truly interested in *hadith*, keenly preserved the practice of the *rihla*. We often find the following phrase in the biographies of these transient scholars: "He was one of those who wandered in the remotest parts of the earth" (*wa-kana min al-jawalin fi'l-afaq*). From the beginning, the transmission of *hadith* took place in the 'Abbasid capital, and during the period under review many *muhaddithun* were still coming from all parts of the Muslim world to learn the *hadith*s of the Baghdadi tradition. Since the science of *hadith* required an accurate understanding of the prophetic accounts, many *muhaddithun* also engaged in the science of language (*lugha*), in particular grammar (*nahw*).

Experts on the Koran appear to have traveled less than *hadith* transmitters. The teaching of the Koran often took place in private homes, small mosques, and in unendowed neighborhood schools which provided early education. Because the accurate recitation and

Figure 2.4

The Composition of 5th/11th–Century Immigrant 'Ulama' according to School Affiliation and Fields of Study

	SPAIN	NORTH AFRICA	EGYPT	HIJAZ	SYRIA	JAZIRA	NORTHERN IRAQ	SOUTHERN IRAQ	NEIGHBORHOOD OF BAGHDAD	SOUTHERN CAUCASUS	WESTERN IRAN	EASTERN IRAN	CENTRAL ASIA	
Muhaddith	1			1	3	2	2	2	2	1	15	1	2	
Muahddith, Qari'				1					1					
Muhaddith, Nahwi	1				1	1				1				
Muhaddith, Nahwi, Qari'	1													
Muhaddith, Zahid			1								2	1		
Muhaddith, 'Abid						1								42
Qari'					1			1	1					
														3
Hanafi					2	1		2	3		3	3		
Hanafi, Muhaddith, Nahwi, Qari'			1											
Hanafi, Muhaddith, Zahid												1		
Hanafi, Muhaddith, Qari'					1				1					
Hanafi, Nahwi							1							
Hanafi, Mu'tazili							1	1				1		
Hanafi, Ash'ari											1			23
Hanbali	1					2		1			2			
Hanbali, Muhaddith						2	2	2	2		4		1	
Hanbali, Muhaddith, Qari'								1	2					
Hanbali, Qari'				1			1							
Hanbali, Muhaddith, Zahid							1							
Hanbali, Muhaddith, 'Abid							1							26
Shafi'i						2	2	2		2	10	6		
Shafi'i, Muhaddith	1					1				1	6	1	1	
Shafi'i, Muhaddith, Qari'					1						1	1		
Shafi'i, Muhaddith, Nahwi											1	1		

	SPAIN	NORTH AFRICA	EGYPT	HIJAZ	SYRIA	JAZIRA	NORTHERN IRAQ	SOUTHERN IRAQ	NEIGHBORHOOD OF BAGHDAD	SOUTHERN CAUCASUS	WESTERN IRAN	EASTERN IRAN	CENTRAL ASIA	
Shafiʿi, Muhaddith, Zahid											1			
Shafiʿi, Muhaddith, ʿAbid		1			1									
Shafiʿi, Ashʿari					1	1					4	5		
Shafiʿi, Zahid												1		
Shafiʿi, Sufi												2		54
Malki		1												1
Zahiri	2													2
Sufi											2	1		3
														154

Figure 2.5
The Composition of 5th/11th–Century Transient ʿUlamaʾ in Baghdad according to School Affiliation and Fields of Study

	SPAIN	SICILY	SYRIA	JAZIRA	NORTHERN IRAQ	SOUTHERN IRAQ	NEIGHBORHOOD OF BAGHDAD	SOUTHERN CAUCASUS	WESTERN IRAN	EASTERN IRAN	CENTRAL ASIA	
Muhaddith	4	4		5	1	3			9	8	1	
Muahddith, Qariʾ					1						1	
Muhaddith, Nahwi										1		
Muhaddith, Zahid				2	1							40
Hanafi						1						
Hanafi, Muhaddith										1		
Hanafi, Muhaddith, Qariʾ						1					1	3
Hanbali, Muhaddith						1						
Hanbali, Muhaddith, Nahwi, Qariʾ				2	1							4
Shafiʿi	1		1	4		1	1		4	4		
Shafiʿi, Muhaddith			1							1		
Shafiʿi, Muhaddith, Qariʾ									1			
Shafiʿi, Muhaddith, Nahwi						1						
Shafiʿi, Ashʿari								1	1	1		
Shafiʿi, Sufi								1	2			27
Maliki		1				1						2
Sufi												1
												77

Figure 2.6

The Composition of 5th/11th–Century Emigrant ʿUlamaʾ of Baghdad according to School Affiliation and Fields of Study

	EGYPT	HIJAZ	SYRIA	JAZIRA	SOUTHERN IRAQ	NEIGHBORHOOD OF BAGHDAD	WESTERN IRAN	EASTERN IRAN	CENTRAL ASIA	
Muhaddith	1		1			1	1	1	1	
Muahddith, ʿAbid		2			1		1	1		11
Hanafi						1	1		2	4
Hanbali				1	1					
Hanbali, Muhaddith	1	1	1							9
Hanabali, Muhaddith, Zahid, Qariʾ	2	1		1						
Shafiʿi	1		2					3		
Shafiʿi, Ashʿari								1		9
Shafiʿi, Zahid								2		
Maliki	1									1
										34

Figure 2.7
The Composition of 5th/11th–Century Native-Born 'Ulama'
Residing in Baghdad according to School Affiliation
and Fields of Study

Muhaddith	216	
Muhaddith, Qari'	29	
Muhaddith, Nahwi	7	
Muhaddith, Zahid	6	
Muhaddith, 'Abid	5	
Muhaddith, 'Abid. Qari'	3	266
Qari'	23	
Qari', Muhaddith	1	
Qari', Nahwi	2	
Qari', Zahid	2	
Qari', 'Abid	1	29
Hanafi	20	
Hanafi, Muhaddith, Azhid	1	
Hanafi, Mu'tazili	2	
Hanafi, Ash'ari	1	24
Hanbali	12	
Hanbali, Muhaddith	50	
Hanbali, Muhaddith, Qari', Nahwi	3	
Hanbali, Muhaddith, Qari'	11	
Hanbali, Muhaddith, Zahid	13	
Hanbali, Muhaddith, 'Abid	1	
Hanbali, Sufi	1	91
Shafi'i	19	
Shafi'i, Muhaddith	17	
Shafi'i, Sufi	2	38
Maliki	4	
Maliki, Muhaddith, Qari'	1	5
Zahiri	1	
Zahiri, Zahid	1	2
Zahid	5	5
Sufi	2	
Sufi, Muhaddith	9	11
		471

understanding of the Koran was considered essential for the process
of religious training, 'ulama' directed their travels toward visiting
famous Koran experts. One such expert was Abu al-Hasan al-
Hamami (d. 417/1026), who lived for most of his life in east Baghdad
though his family was from Hama (Syria). As his fame as an expert

in the seven "canonical" variant readings of the Koran spread, he attracted a circle of scholars from around the Muslim world. Ibn Fawaris, one of the eminent Hanbalis of the day, said of him: "If one were to travel all the way from Khurasan in order to recite the Koran under him, the journey would not be in vain."[9]

Shafiʻis constituted the largest group of transient and migrant legal scholars. The number of these Shafiʻi scholars present in eleventh-century Baghdad was more than double the number of native-born members of the school residing in the city (compare figures 2.4, 2.5, and 2.7). Originating outside the city, the mainstream of Shafiʻi scholarship was continually augmented by the international ties between native-born and foreign scholars moving to Baghdad, primarily from western Iran and Khurasan. These immigrant and transient scholars included both aspiring students and accomplished ʻulamaʼ who had established their reputation elsewhere. The Iranian provinces, which had become scholarly centers of special importance to Baghdad, also sent a considerable number of Hanafis and Sufis to the city. Transoxania, particularly Bukhara, became another important source of Hanafi immigration. Approximately one half of the Hanafis present in eleventh-century Baghdad were immigrants and transients (compare figures 2.4, 2.5, and 2.7). The great number of transient and immigrant Shafiʻi and Hanafi scholars was apparently connected with the establishment of Shafiʻi and Hanafi madrasas in the city during the late eleventh and early twelfth centuries. Similarly, the proliferation of madrasas in Damascus and Cairo during the second half of the twelfth century attracted members of the two legal schools to these cities.

By the eleventh century, Baghdad had become a major center of Hanbali law and theology. The Hanbali school was the only one in medieval Islam which did not have a territorial basis, but established itself in urban centers, particularly Baghdad, Damascus, Harran, Jerusalem, and Nablus. During the eleventh and twelfth centuries, Baghdadi Hanbalism was dominated by native-born ʻulamaʼ (compare figures 2.4, 2.5, and 2.7). School adherents confined their educational and professional pursuits to Baghdad–Jazira–Syria axis. As discussed above, the first Hanbali madrasa was only established in Baghdad in the first half of the twelfth century, nearly a half-century after the establishment of the first Shafiʻi and Hanafi madrasas in the city. But the school's teachings occurred primarily in the great mosques of Baghdad, notably the mosque of al-Mansur, as well as in study circles convened in the smaller mosques which attracted a great many aspiring students to the city (figures 2.4 and 2.5). At the same time, Ibn Hanbal's companions spread the school's legal and theological doctrine to cities in northern Iraq, the Jazira and Syria which, during the late eleventh century, emerged as important centers of Hanbali law and thought.

During the eleventh century the Maliki school had its main centers in North Africa and Spain. Despite the fact that they were a small minority in Baghdad, the Malikis had their own professors and mosques in the city. The intellectual pursuits of the Maliki *fuqaha'* still present in eleventh-century Baghdad were, however, reduced for the most part to jurisdiction (*qada'*) and the issuing of legal opinions required by the small Maliki community. Abu Muhammad al-Maliki (d. 422/1031), the most famous Maliki *qadi* during the early part of the century, was obliged to move to Egypt toward the end of his life because he could not find adequate means of living in Baghdad, the city of his birth, though he was greatly respected. The day he left, he was escorted out of the city by the most distinguished men of the regime and the great religious leaders of other schools.[10] Only a few Maliki scholars remained in Baghdad after his departure.

Another of the small schools still present in eleventh-century Baghdad was the Zahiri school. Founded by Daud b. Khalaf az-Zahid (d. 269/882) about the same time that the movement of *ahl al-hadith* gave rise to the Hanbali school, the Zahiri school's importance gradually waned in the caliphal city. Its most important *'alim*, Ibn Hazm (d. 456/1064), resided in Cordoba. There were, however, a few of the school's representatives in Baghdad during the eleventh and early twelfth centuries. Some were Baghdadi in origin, others were recruited from western Iran, Jerusalem, and Majorca.[11] Abu 'Amir al-'Abdari (d. 534/1130) was the last Zahiri of Baghdad mentioned by the sources. This *hadith*-transmitter and *faqih*, who came to Baghdad from Majorca, is praised by authors of biographical dictionaries for his ascetic life as well as for his profound knowledge of the prophetic traditions.[12]

The data on school affiliation and fields of study of the *'ulama'* show that the majority of those who bear the epithets *zahid* (ascetic), *'abid* (pious), and Sufi were also legal scholars and *hadith* transmitters. These three appellations represent the three currents which contributed to the formation of Sufism—asceticism (*zuhd*), pietism (*'ibada*), and mystic speculation (*tasawwuf*), although the last term, to some extent, includes the other two. The field of mysticism, as the field of theology, had no formal identification with a specific school of law. Most of the Sufis whose legal affiliation is identifiable, however, were Shafi'is. As for the Hanafis, their devotion to legalism as well as their rationalist tendencies naturally made them the antagonists of mysticism; no Hanafi *faqih* is mentioned as being a Sufi. While some Sufis assimilated into the Shafi'i school and cultivated Ash'ari theological doctrines, others found their home in antirationalist Hanbalism.[13] These Sufis can be identified in the biographical dictionaries through the appellations of *zahid*, *'abid*, and *salih* (ascetic, pious, worshiper). The majority of the Hanbalis who bear the epithets associated with Sufism were native Baghdadians, unlike most of the Shafi'is labeled as Sufis who were immigrants and transients, drawn to the city from Khurasan and other Iranian provinces (figures 2.4, 2.5, and 2.7).

If we bear in mind the growing rapprochement between orthodoxy and Sufism, as well as the internal differentiations and nuances within each of the religious and intellectual traditions in Islam, it should not be surprising to find legal scholars bearing appellations often associated with Sufism. Biographical dictionaries are replete with descriptions of pious individuals characterized as mild ascetics, men known for their self-control, and who shared with the Sufis a similar critique of materialism and worldliness. Conversely, Sufis at least the sober Baghdadians, worked for their living, prided themselves on being experts in *hadith*, and taught the Koran and the *hadith* in the great mosques of Baghdad. A man could be "orthodox" in the legal domain, and *zahid* or Sufi in his private conduct, ethical posture, and even his social affiliation, a point to which we shall have occasion to return.

Yet despite these overlapping tendencies, Sufism had an inner life and organizational form of its own, the *ribat*. The first famous *ribat* founded in Baghdad was the Ribat az-Zauzani, located on the western side of the city facing the Mosque of al-Mansur and named after its founder, Abu al-Hasan az-Zauzani (d. 451/1059), a native-born Sufi and Hanbali *faqih* and the *shaykh as-sufiyya* of Baghdad.[14] The second most famous *ribat* was that of Abu Sa'd as-Sufi (d. 477/1084), an immigrant from Nishapur, who, upon the death of az-Zauzani, became *shaykh as-sufiyya* in Baghdad. As a Sufi of Iranian origin, his *ribat* hosted many foreign Sufis, as well as legal scholars drawn to the city from the eastern provinces, which had become a major source of Sufi recruitment.[15] As the flow of immigrant and transient Sufis increased, many other *ribats* were founded throughout the city. Originally places of worship and asceticism, the *ribats* of Baghdad gradually became centers of learning where a variety of cultural and social activities took place.[16]

From Journeys to Schools

An extensive survey of biographical literature enables us to identify the leading legal scholars, or *fuqaha'*, of the three law schools
which dominated legal studies in eleventh-century Baghdad: the
Hanbali, Hanafi, and Shafi'i schools. Their names are included in
almost all the biographical dictionaries reviewed in this work, together
with information on a large number of students who studied with
them. A survey of their scholarly pursuits provides us with further
insight into the participation of the 'ulama' associated with eleventh-
century Baghdad in the worldwide system of Muslim scholarship,
and the formation of the learned Baghdadi community.

Six great Hanbali scholars of eleventh-century Baghdad played
major roles in the scholarly development of Hanbalism. The first
great Hanbali *faqih* of the period recorded by the sources was Abu
'Abd Allah b. Hamid (d. 403/1012), a native Baghdadian who excelled
in both the science of *hadith* and law, and whose scholarly *isnad* goes
back to the famous Hanbali jurisconsult of the fourth Muslim century,
al-Khiraqi. An outstanding, pious man, Ibn Hamid made several pil-
grimages, taking advantage of the *hajj* to meet other scholars who
flocked to Mecca from all over the Muslim world. In order to illustrate
his outstanding pietism, his biographers relate that he refused to
drink water during the *hajj*, insisting that his time should be devoted
entirely to the worship of God. Ibn Hamid was killed by Bedouins on
his last journey to Mecca.[17]

Ibn al-Hamid's closest disciple, al-Qadi Abu al-Ya'la (d. 458/
1066), is described by Hanbali writers as the leader of the Hanbali
school in Baghdad, and bears the epithet of *shaykh al-hanabila*. He
began his studies at the age of five, learning the prophetic traditions.
Unlike his father, a Hanafi, he became affiliated with the Hanbali
school, and continued his studies under Ibn Hamid. Upon the death
of his mentor, the young Abu Ya'la began his long career as a teacher,
mufti, and the *qadi* of *Dar al-khilafa*. His son, the historian Ibn Abi
Ya'la, relates that he made several journeys to Mecca, Damascus,
and Allepo, studying the Koran and the *hadith*, and teaching the
doctrine of his *madhhab* at the same time. Large numbers of native
and foreign students came to hear the *hadiths* he dictated, and to
attend his lectures on *fiqh* held in a mosque in Bab ash-Sha'ir.[18]

Two of his many disciples played prominent roles in the spread
and consolidation of the Hanbali school abroad: Abu al-Fath al-
Baghdadi al-Harrani, known as Qadi Harran (d. 476/1083), and Abu
al-Faraj ash-Shirazi (d. 486/1094). Having completed his studies of

law, Abu al-Fath was sent by his master to Harran, where he assumed
the post of the local *qadi*, serving at the same time as a *mufti*, preacher
(*wa'iz*), and teacher of Hanbali *fiqh*.[19] The propagation of Hanbali legal
and theological doctrines in Jerusalem and Damascus is attributed to
Qadi Abu Ya'la's other disciple, ash-Shirazi, considered by the Hanbali
biographer Ibn Rajab to be the greatest Hanbali scholar of his time in
Syria.[20]

Ya'qub al-Barzabini (d. 486/1093) and Abu al-Khattab al-
Kalwadhani (d. 510/1116)—two other famous disciples of Abu al-
Ya'la—came from towns near Baghdad. Both were versed in *hadith*
and *fiqh*, and are said to have taught a great number of students.[21]
Al-Kalwadhani was so learned and highly regarded that some even
called him *mujtahid al-'asr*, the "renewer" of Islam of his era.[22] As
the number of accomplished Hanbali masters grew, more students of
the *madhhab*, as well as of *hadith*, were attracted to the city. The
flourishing study of Hanbalism in eleventh-century Baghdad thus
not only contributed to the development of the school within the city,
but also inspired its development abroad.

Three great *fuqaha'* dominated the Hanafi school in eleventh-
century Baghdad prior to the appearance of the first Hanafi madrasas
in the later part of the century: al-Quduri (d. 428/1037); as-Saimari
(d. 436/1045); and Abu 'Abd Allah ad-Damaghani (d. 478/1085).
While al-Quduri was a native of Baghdad, the two other were raised
elsewhere.[23] The career of Abu 'Abd Allah ad-Damaghani, head of
the famous family of *qadi*s and chief *qadi*s which was to flourish in
Baghdad for two centuries, is perhaps one of the best examples of
the worldwide system of Muslim scholarship and its social aspects.
Born to a poor family in Damaghan (in the province of Jibal, western
Iran) where he began his studies of law, ad-Damaghani moved to
Baghdad at the age of twenty-one, continuing his studies of *fiqh* and
hadith under al-Quduri and his disciple as-Saimari, whose scholarly
chains of authorities (*isnad*s) extend as far back as Abu Bakr ar-
Razi, the great Hanafi jurist of the tenth century. In order to finish
his studies he was forced to work as a night guard, resorting to
reading in the streets at night as he could not afford to pay the price
of candles. However, his position soon improved. Upon the death of
the Shafi'i chief *qadi*, Ibn Makula in A.H. 447, ad-Damaghani was
appointed to the post of chief judge, which he held to his death in
A.H. 478. Before his prestigious nomination, he married his daughter
to the Hanafi-Ash'ari scholar Abu al-Hasan as-Simnani, whom he
later nominated as a *qadi* of the Bab at-Taq quarter, and whose
brother was one his closest disciples in *fiqh*.[24] This marital alliance

tightened the bonds between the two Hanafi families and helped the Damaghanis to establish roots in Baghdad. As chief judge and renowned teacher of *fiqh*, ad-Damaghani laid the foundation for a strong line of judges and a network of Hanafi scholars whom he eventually appointed as judges and professors in the Hanafi madrasas of Baghdad.

The line of the leading Shafi'i masters in eleventh-century Baghdad commenced with Abu Hamid al-Isfara'ini (d. 406/1016), who, early in the eleventh century, instituted the Baghdadi method or system (*tariqa*) of Shafi'i law and "filled the earth with partisans of ash-Shafi'i opinions."[25] Born in Isfara'in (in the province of Khurasan), al-Isfara'ini arrived in Baghdad at a young age and studied *fiqh* under Abu al-Hasan al-Marzuban and Abu al-Qasim ad-Daraki, the two renowned Shafi'i scholars of his time. Like many other Shafi'i jurisconsults of his generation, al-Isfara'ini acquired a profound knowledge of the prophetic traditions, studying the science of *hadith* under the famous *muhaddith* ad-Daraqutni. Because he came from a humble family, he supported himself by working as a gardener. However, after he became well-versed in the legal doctrine of his school and the issuing of legal opinions, he assumed the leadership (*riyasa*) of his *madhhab*, teaching its law in the mosque of al-Mubarak, located in Qati'at ar-Rabi in al-Karkh quarter. His name soon became well known in Baghdadi circles. His study group is said to have numbered seven hundred law students, a very unusual number for a course in law. He was highly regarded, not only by members of his own *madhhab*, but by *fuqaha'* of other schools, as well as by political figures and common people.[26]

Among al-Isfara'ini's most celebrated disciples were Abu al-Hasan al-Mawardi of Basra, and Abu at-Taiyib at-Tabari, who, upon the death of his master, succeeded him as the leader (*imam*) of the Shafi'i school in Baghdad. Among the other school's adherents attending al-Isfara'ini's study circle were Abu al-Hasan al-Mahamili (d. 415/1024), a native of Baghdad and the son of a court witness (*shahid*),[27] and Abu al-Fath Sulaim ar-Razi (d. 447/1055). Moving to Baghdad from his native Rayy, ar-Razi began his studies of *fiqh* under al-Mahamili's father and later became one of al-Isfara'ini's closest disciples. Upon his master's death, he succeeded to his chair in the mosque of al-Mubarak. Shortly afterward, however, he left Baghdad and moved to Tyre in order to spread the teachings of the Shafi'i school there, leaving behind his disciples and his position at the mosque.[28] The celebrated Shafi'i *faqih* Nasr al-Maqdisi studied *fiqh* in Tyre with him before moving to Damascus.[29] Thus, ar-Razi became a major link in the worldwide network of Shafi'ism.

Like many other Shafi'i scholars, Abu at-Taiyib at-Tabari (d. 450/1058) maintained contacts all over the Muslim world. He first studied *fiqh* in his native town in the province of Tabaristan (western Iran), and later journeyed to Jurjan and Khurasan. Moving to Baghdad, he joined al-Isfara'ini's study circle, and upon his masterís death, formed his own study circle, beginning a long career as a *mufti, qadi* of the al-Karkh quarter, one of the most prestigious positions in Baghdad, and professor of law.[30] The poet Abu al-ʿAlaʾ al-Maʿarri told him: "Though possessing little worldly wealth, you are rich in treasured science. . . . The earth is proud to bear you on its surface."[31] Like that study circle of his predecessor, al-Isfara'ini, at-Tabari's study circle consisted of native-born and foreign students. His two most prominent disciples were Abu Ishaq ash-Shirazi (d. 476/1083), an immigrant from Firuzabad in the province of Fars (western Iran) who became the first professor of the Nizamiyya Madrasa, and Abu Nasr b. as-Sabbagh (d. 477/1084), Baghdadi in origin, who is renown for his famous treatise on jurisprudence, entitled the *Kitab ash-shamil fiʾl-fiqh*. After having completed their course of legal studies, these two famous Shafi'i *fuqahaʾ* formed their own study circles, attracting great numbers of students, both native-born and foreign.[32]

Among them was Abu Bakr ash-Shashi (d. 507/1114), who was born in Mayyafariqin in the Jazira, though his family belonged to Shash, a town in Transoxania. He arrived in Baghdad after studying the legal doctrine of the *madhhab* with the *qadi* Abu Mansur at-Tusi (a disciple of the eminent Shafi'i *faqih* and Ashʿari theologian, Imam al-Haramain, al-Juwaini), and attached himself to both ash-Shirazi and as-Sabbagh, reading the *Shamil* under its author's direction. Upon the deaths of his two masters, he became the most famous Shafi'i scholar of his generation in Baghdad.[33]

The last leading Shafi'i scholar of eleventh-century Baghdad was Abu al-Fath b. Barhan (d. 518/1124), a native of the capital city. He adhered to Hanbalism at first, but later changed affiliation to the Shafi'i *madhhab*, studying under the direction of both ash-Shashi and the famous al-Ghazzali (d. 505/1111), as well as under ʿAli at-Tabari al-Harrasi, known as al-Kiya al-Harrasi (d. 504/1110). The latter is a good example of a scholar who had established his reputation before settling in the city. Born in Tabaristan where he began his studies, al-Harrasi moved to Nishapur, continuing his studies of

Islamic law under Imam al-Haramain. He then traveled to Baihaq where he taught the doctrine of the *madhhab* for several years. Eventually he reached Baghdad where he remained for the rest of his life.[34] He was a Shafiʾi-Ashʿari scholar, but unlike his contemporary, al-Ghazzali, he specialized in the prophetic traditions as a distinct subject of learning; some of the noted Baghdadi *hadith* scholars are said to have studied under him. His argument that the *hadith* should be elevated over individual reason is clearly revealed by the saying attributed to him: "When the horsemen of the traditions gallop about in the battlefield, the heads of analogical deductions are struck and carried off by the wind."[35]

Al-Ghazzali's remarkable journeys throughout the Muslim world are the best illustration of the sense of community in the sphere of Islamic learning. After studying law in Tus, Jurjan, and Nishapur with Imam al-Haramain, he was sent by Nizam al-Mulk to teach at the Nizamiyya Madrasa in Baghdad. While in Baghdad he experienced his famous "conversion" to Sufism and made the pilgrimage to Mecca. Before he returned to his native town of Tus, he traveled to Damascus, Jerusalem, and Egypt. Although his stay in Baghdad was short, he was no doubt the most celebrated transient scholar to influence religious thought in the city.[36]

Sufi fraternities (*turuq*) first appeared in Baghdad and other great Islamic centers of learning in the course of the late twelfth and early thirteenth centuries. Most prominent, and eventually the most wide spread of all fraternities, was the Qadariyya, named after ʿAbd al-Qadir al-Jilani (d. 561/1166). With this Hanbali Sufi, considered the *qutb* ("spiritual axis") of his age, begins the Sufi tradition which holds one particular great man or saint to be the founder of a "way" (*tariqa*) shared by a group of Sufis. Al-Jilani was born into a family of *sayyids*, the alleged descendants of ʿAli, in the south of the Caspian Sea, and like many *sayyids* he was encouraged to take up religious studies. As a youth, he was sent to Baghdad for further religious training. He received his Sufi cloak (*khirqa*) from the Hanbali Sufi, Abu as-Saʿd al-Mukharrimi (d. 513/1119), a native of Baghdad, whose Sufi genealogy goes back to Junayd. After twenty-five years of ascetic wandering in the Iraqi desert, al-Jilani's preaching so impressed the people of Baghdad that they built a *ribat* for him outside the city walls. He was also given a madrasa which had to be enlarged, so popular he had become, and he took to preaching in the prayer grounds outside the city, normally reserved for mass worship during religious celebrations. Visitors to Baghdad made a point of attending his public sermons, and *fatwas* were addressed to him from distant lands. Although there is no evidence he had ever intended his "way" to be perpetuated, a great Sufi fraternity developed around his personality, and a large number of miracles (karamat) were attributed to his spiritual powers. As a result of al-Jilani's worldwide ties, as well as the efforts of his disciples and family, the Qadiriyya spread to other major cities such as Damascus, during the late twelfth and thirteenth centuries.[37]

These individuals exemplify the roles played by eleventh-century 'ulama' in Baghdad in the worldwide networks of Islamic learning. These men acquired profound knowledge in the realms of law, hadith, theology, and Sufism, passing on to succeeding generations. They are, however, merely a few of the more than seven hundred scholars who comprised the learned society taking shape in Baghdad during the eleventh and twelfth centuries, and upon whose lives and careers the general conclusions of this study are based.

The early twelfth century witnessed a rise in the number of Baghdad's resident scholars (figures 2.8 and 2.9, below). Thus, while the number of transient 'ulama' outnumbered those who resided in the city throughout the first few decades of the eleventh century, a conspicuous change in this ratio took place during the second half of the century, with an increasing number of immigrants moving to the city. As the number of resident scholars grew, a local group of 'ulama' began to consolidate. One of the visible expressions of this process of consolidation was the growing number of families of 'ulama', both native-born and immigrants.[38]

This noteworthy change toward a local basis of recruitment should not be regarded as a source artifact. Changes in the conditions of Baghdad under the Great Seljuks, and their policy of founding madrasas and sponsoring religious scholars to teach and study in them, must have made the city a more attractive place, and contributed to the growth of its learned society.[39] Figure 2.9 shows that immigration of 'ulama' to Baghdad reached its peak during the second half of the eleventh century, the peak of the Seljuks empire, the period in which they began to found madrasas and ribats throughout the city. Seventy-nine 'ulama' immigrated to Baghdad during this period, constituting 43 percent of the total number of 183 immigrants. The number of immigrants decreased in the first half of the twelfth century, dropping to twenty (11 percent) during the second half.

A scholarly traveler of the type described by the biographical dictionaries might eagerly contact local 'ulama' wherever he went, but would tend to settle in places where he would be best rewarded.

Figure 2.8
Native Born 'Ulama' Residing in 5th/11th–Century Baghdad
(409/1018–549/1154)

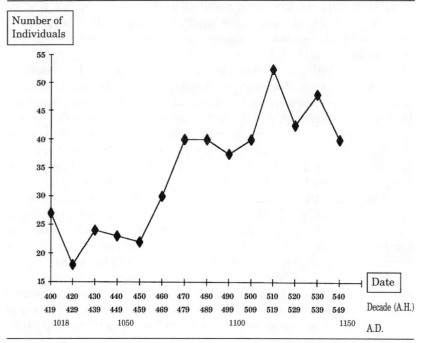

Notes:
1. The year listed is the year of death.
2. Included are individual 'ulama' whose families, according to their geographical *nisbas*, originated in other places, but they themselves were born in Baghdad.

Even 'ulama' from the cities of eastern Iran, such as Nishapur and Tus, who had their own madrasas founded by the Seljuks, were attracted to the madrasas of Baghdad, in particular the prestigious Nizamiyya Madrasa—the example of al-Ghazzali comes to mind—where they could gather more credentials and be best rewarded. Similarly, the decrease in the number of immigrants to the city, which began during the first half of the twelfth century, must have been sparked by the disturbances caused by the intensification of political struggles during the period of the dissolution of the Seljuk empire, as well as a new wave of natural disasters. Equally impor-

Figure 2.9
Immigration of 'Ulama' to Baghdad in the Period
Beginning in the Early 5th/11th Century
to the End of the 6th/12th Century

Number of Individuals

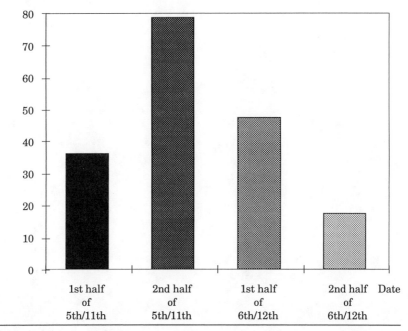

Note: In cases where the date of immigration is not mentioned, the supposition is that it took place around twenty years before the date of death.

tant, however, appears to be the rise of other scholarly centers in the high medieval Middle East, primarily Damascus and Cairo, affecting the trends of 'ulama' migration. In their attempt to restore Sunnism to Syria and Egypt, and to develop their capitals as scholarly centers, the Ayyubids followed in the footsteps of the Great Seljuks by founding a number of madrasas and ribats which provided a major stimulus for the immigration of 'ulama' to both Damascus and the great cities of Egypt.[40]

To what extent did the rise of the madrasa lead to the disappearance of the free-floating world of Islamic learning—that is, the wandering from teacher to teacher, the worldwide networks of masters and disciples? Did the gradual consolidation of a local group in Baghdad bar acceptance of newcomers into the ranks of the Baghdadi ʿulamaʾ? Or were new arrivals fully accepted because of their international reputation, achievements, and connections? These are some of the questions upon which the discussion of the social consequences of the advent and spread of madrasas will focus.

CHAPTER 3

LEARNING

Abu b. Malik reported that the Prophet said: "Those who go out in
search of knowledge will be in the path of God until they return."

at-Tirmidhi, *Sunan*, 3: 2

One of the most curious phenomena is that biographies of
eleventh- and twelfth-century Baghdadi scholars make almost no
mention of the madrasa, although it was already well-known at the
time the biographical dictionaries were written, and despite evidence
that the authors of the dictionaries themselves studied or taught in
those schools.[1] Instead, these biographies feature long lists of teachers
with whom the respective scholars studied and who conferred upon
them the *ijaza* or the certificate entitling them to pass on the "knowledge" they attained. The actual location where the studies took place
must be reconstructed from the context. One method is to study the
biographies of the *mudarrisun*, which occasionally note their appointments to teach at a certain madrasa. Another is to study the chronicles documenting the establishment of madrasas by the rulers and
the appointment of teachers. At the same time, however, this reconstruction shows that traditional patterns and frameworks of study
did not fade away with the appearance of the madrasa.

Travel and Worldwide Scholarly Connections

Data regarding the places and dates of deaths of 332 immigrant and
transient ʿulamaʾ indicates a reduction in the number of transients
in Baghdad during the first half of the twelfth century,[2] while other

evidence points to an increase in the number of resident scholars in the city (figure 2.9, above). However, an examination of the scholarly pursuits and self-description of the learned society taking form in Baghdad yields a picture more complex than the data might initially suggest. In other words, while the transition from a worldwide basis of recruitment to a local one began to occur as early as the late eleventh century, Baghdad's learned society took on its strong local identity more slowly.

The scholarly connections that cut across geographical and political frontiers remained strong for a relatively long period after the advent of the madrasa, and ʿulamaʾ—both those indigenous to Baghdad and those who eventually settled there—continued to travel throughout the Muslim world. As a result, the cosmopolitan character of Baghdad's learned society remained intact throughout the eleventh and twelfth centuries. Authors of biographical dictionaries frequently provide extensive descriptions of the travels of ʿulamaʾ living during this period, stressing the extensive connections and the esteem shown to renown scholars journeying to various Islamic towns and cities by both their learned colleagues and the common people.

One of the most telling examples relates to the journey of the celebrated Shafiʿi jurist Abu Ishaq ash-Shirazi. Traveling to Khurasan as the envoy of the caliph al-Muqtadi, ash-Shirazi was enthusiastically welcomed everywhere, with people gathering the dust of his mule and his parcels, preserving it as a relic of great virtue, and craftsmen of every town and village offering him their products. Arriving in Nishapur, he took the opportunity to discuss legal questions with Imam al-Haramain who welcomed him with great honor and respect.[3] Summing up his visit, ash-Shirazi prided himself on having a great number of disciples flocking round him wherever he went: "I traveled through Khurasan, and there was not a *qadi*, a *mufti*, or a *khatib*, or preacher in any town or village who had not been among my students or followers (*ashab*)."[4]

Having its justification in Islamic tradition which enjoined Muslims to seek learning wherever it was to be found,[5] the practice of the *rihla* still constituted a main characteristic of the transmitting process during the first century of the madrasa. *Muhaddithun* in particular preserved the practice of the *rihla*, visiting many towns large and small to hear Islamic teachings directly from reliable authorities, each linked in an unbroken chain (*isnad*) extending back to earlier generations of teachers and transmitters. The greater the number of *hadiths* heard by the student from various authorities, and the fewer the links between these authorities and the Prophet himself, the more the student was still viewed as a reliable source for future generations. Ibn Khallikan summed up the accomplishments of Abu Hafs al-Mu'addib one of the noted Baghdadi *hadith* scholars (d. 606/1210):

> The traditions which he had received by oral transmission were remarkable as coming from the highest authorities, and as he traveled through various countries teaching [them] to others, he became the link which connected the rising generation of traditionalists to the past. He filled the earth with the certificates (*ijazat*) which he gave to those who heard him deliver traditions and with licenses to teach, which he granted to his disciples.[6]

Indeed, this image of scholars, especially *muhaddithun*, as living links in the chains of authorities extending backwards into the past, and forwards into the future through their students, is a common thread in descriptions of their professional lives.

Sufis also appear as wanderers. Although the Sufi fraternities date from a later period, one of their essential features, the *silsila*, the feature of the genealogy of spiritual authority, goes back much earlier.[7] Aspiring to learn the *shaykh's tariqa* and enter the *silsila* through him, Sufi disciples during the eleventh and twelfth centuries would follow the *shaykh* as he traveled through the lands ruled by Islam and to countries far beyond. As the belief in the spiritual powers of the Sufi saints (*awliyya*') spread, visiting the tombs of venerated Sufi saints (*ziyara*) became another important motive for Sufis, as well as ordinary people, to travel. Such visits, usually constituting the culmination of the annual celebration of the birthday (*mawlid*) of a recognized Sufi saint, had probably became commonplace as early as the twelfth century.[8] Beginning with the tomb of the Prophet in Medina, the number of holy places grew until, by the thirteenth century, Islamic lands had come to be dotted with shrines great and small, where men sought to mobilize the divine favor of dead saints. A number of touristlike "guide books" to pilgrimage sites began to appear. One of the earliest known is *Kitab isharat ma'rifat az-ziyarat*, a highly detailed guide to pilgrimage sites around the Muslim world compiled by Abu al-Hasan 'Ali al-Harawi (d. 611/1215). His travels throughout the Islamic world, especially the Eastern Mediterranean, took place a few years before Ibn Jubayr's voyage.[9]

Many students would first travel to collect *hadiths* and obtain documents certifying their proficiency before joining one of the study circles teaching Islamic religious law in mosques and madrasas. Abu al-Hasan al-Andalusi (d. 541/1146), known as as-Sini (the Chinese) and a native of Valencia, set on a long journey in search of prophetic traditions at a young age, reaching as far as China. Having collected a great number of *hadiths* and braving perilous dangers during his travels, he made his permanent residence in Baghdad in order to study law with al-Ghazzali in the prestigious Nizamiyya Madrasa. He later made one other journey to Isfahan to hear traditions directly from the lips of its famous *muhaddithun*, and finally returned to Baghdad to continue his education.[10] There were also many who left the madrasa in order to carry on their scholarly pursuits and attain more credentials.

The celebrated *hadith* transmitter and jurist, Abu Tahir as-Silafi (d. 575/1179), left his hometown of Isfahan at a young age, directing his steps to Baghdad to study with al-Kiya al-Harrasi, who at that time was the *mudarris* in the Nizamiyya Madrasa. Shortly after, he moved on, wandering throughout the Islamic lands (*tafa al-bilad wa-jaba al-afaq*). In 511/1117 he reached Alexandria and settled there.[11] Abu Bakr al-Hamadhani (d. 584/1188), known as Zain ad-Din, first studied the Koran and heard traditions in his hometown of Hamadhan; later he proceeded to Baghdad to study Islamic law under Abu al-Qasim b. Hibat Allah, a professor in the Nizamiyya, while hearing *hadiths* dictated by celebrated native-born and visiting *muhaddithun* as well. After several years, however, he left the city in order to collect additional orally transmitted traditions on his own (*talaba binafsihi*). His wanderings took him to Syria, Mosul, Fars, and Hamadhan, as well as to most of the towns of Azerbaijan. Having written down traditions under the direction of nearly all the *shaykhs* of those places he visited, he finally returned to Baghdad.[12] The long chains of authorities mentioned in al-Hamadhani's biography and those of a handful of other "seekers of knowledge," testify not only to the survival of the old system of gathering of knowledge, but also the tremendous efforts made by compilers of biographical dictionaries to preserve and reassert this tradition.

Perhaps the epitome of the "traveling" scholar was Abu Zakariyya Yahya at-Tabrizi (d. 502/1109, or 512/1118), a celebrated teacher of the Arabic grammar, philology, and literature. He studied *adab* (belles-lettres) in Damascus, then traveled to Baghdad where he taught the sciences of language (grammar, syntax, lexicography) in the Nizamiyya Madrasa. Shortly thereafter, he left the Nizamiyya and went to Cairo, where he attached himself to various scholarly circles. Eventually he returned to Baghdad, where he lived and taught a circle of students in the privacy of his house until his death. To illustrate his adherence to the *rihla*, his biographer writes that while still a young boy, Abu Zakariyya set out on a journey from his hometown in the Taurus range (in southeast Anatolia) to Maragha (in the province of Azerbaijan) merely to verify the accuracy of a copy of a book by the famous tenth-century philologist Abu Mansur al-Azhari. He carried the volumes in a bag on his back from Tabriz to Maragha, not having the means to hire a beast of burden to ride. The sweat from his back penetrated the books, leaving a water mark. The biographer describes the condition of the books: "dedicated as *waqf* and preserved in a library in Baghdad, as appearing to have actually remained under water for some time."[13]

The conviction deeply embedded in Islamic tradition that a "true scholar" is one who travels in search of knowledge was adopted by political figures as well. This admiration for the "traveling" scholar comes through clearly in Nizam al-Mulk's manual, *Siyasat-Nameh*, which advises Seljuk princes how to conduct affairs of empire. Urging the princes to consult the learned, the vizier distinguishes the "traveling" scholar from other men of learning:

> Having consultation on affairs [of the state] is a sign of sound judgement, high intelligence and foresight . . . a man who had traveled widely and seen the world and experienced heat and cold and been in the midst of affairs is not to be compared with the one who is untraveled and inexperienced. Thus it has been said that one ought to take counsel with the wise, the old, and the experienced.[14]

If we accept that the pattern in twelfth-century Baghdad was true for other centers of learning, then the highly idealized descriptions of the traveling scholar betray the fact that by the time most the biographies were written, the practice of the *rihla* had become less common. Still, while the student of the period in which madrasas became widespread was probably less traveled than his predecessor, it is also true that traveling in search of learning persisted, at least as a model.[15] Moreover, rather than weakening cross-cultural ties, the appearance of the madrasa may actually have helped to strengthen them. During classical ʿAbbasid times, these ties were maintained by the travels of the ʿulamaʾ, with their chains of transmission from teacher to pupil across the generations.

As madrasas spread throughout the Muslim world from the late twelfth century, they assured the perpetuation of worldwide cultural connections in a more strongly institutionalized form. The fairly uniform pattern of the new schools, as well as the long periods during which scholars taught or studied, and sometimes resided, in the madrasas, could blur the distinctions between scholars of different intellectual traditions and geographical origins. The rise of the madrasa in Baghdad thus brought about a change in how these worldwide cultural ties were maintained, without ever changing their essence. Those who came to Baghdad to study or teach maintained deep ties to both the study circle that gathered around the *mudarris* and the local scholarly community as a whole, ties they retained long after they had left for other places. Insight into such ties is found in an anecdote concerning Muhyi ad-Din ash-Shahrazuri (d. 586/1190), a member of the famous Shahrazuri Shafi'i family of *qadis* and professors of the law, who came to Baghdad from Mosul as a youth to study in the Nizamiyya Madrasa. Upon completing his studies, he returned to his hometown and assumed the *qadi*ship of the city, as well as the professorship in a madrasa founded by his father, Kamal ad-Din. Tracing his professional life "from cradle to grave," his biographer tells that he used to send large amounts of money to Baghdad to be distributed as alms among the 'ulama' (*ahl al-'ilm*) of the city, the poets, and the destitute for many years afterwards.[16]

In addition to making a significant contribution to the expansion of Baghdad's scholarly community, the advent of the madrasa heightened the influence of a stable and prosperous cosmopolitan, cultural elite. Like their predecessors, the 'ulama' of the first century of madrasa in Baghdad played prominent roles in the networks transmitting Islamic learning and tradition which tied Islamic lands together. Over a third of the 'ulama' who taught or studied in the caliphal city's madrasas in the late eleventh and twelfth centuries were transients, drawn to the city from cities and towns throughout the Muslim world, and who eventually returned to their places of origin, or settled in other locales were they could be most rewarded.[17]

Among these transients was Abu al-Faraj al-Basri (d. 499/1105), a native of Basra who came to Baghdad to study under Abu Ishaq ash-Shirazi, the leader of the Shafi'i school and the first *mudarris* in the Nizamiyya Madrasa, as well as grammar under some of the famous grammarians of the city. Upon his return to his hometown, he was appointed to the post of *qadi*, dictated *hadiths*, and taught the legal doctrine of his *madhhab* in a magnificent madrasa founded especially for him.[18]

Abu Ishaq b. Nasr, known as Zahir ad-Din (d. 610/1213), was another aspiring student who studied in the prestigious Nizamiyya Madrasa. Born in Mosul, he studied the law first under the Shafi'i doctors in his hometown. After traveling to Baghdad, he continued his studies of the law in the Nizamiyya, returning eventually to his native town. As his prestige increased, he assumed the *qadi*ship of Sallamiyya, a town in the dependency of Mosul. In addition, he became a professor of grammar at Irbil, teaching the works of Abu Barakat al-Anbari, the famous grammarian of Baghdad (d. 577/1183), under whom he had studied during his stay in the city.[19] Other students were drawn to Syria and Egypt, which became during the Ayyubid period an attractive place for men of religious learning.

We may assume that ʿulamaʾ who taught or studied in the madrasas of Baghdad, in particular the Nizamiyya, were favored candidates for high religious office in Syria and Egypt, as well as in other regions, though explicit references about the madrasa are rare. However, what we do know about those clearly associated with the madrasas of Baghdad, reveals their importance as a source of recruitment of highly proficient graduates who played a major role in the intellectual and social life of urban centers throughout the Muslim world.

Inspired by *hadith* literature, authors of biographical dictionaries emphasized the position and reliability of their subjects in the chain of transmission of Islamic learning, tracing each one's professional life from cradle to grave. However, descriptions of places frequented by the ʿulamaʾ in their search for knowledge had other purposes and significance as well. Whether fact or fiction, stories about the "cosmopolitan" scholar, a man whose sense of belonging to the wider scholarly community surpassed local allegiances, illustrated for their readers and listeners the unity of the Islamic community, the *umma*, and heightened a universal sense of "being Muslim."[20] For the people of Baghdad, affected more than any other Islamic city by the disintegration of the universal ʿAbbasid caliphate, these illustrations must have had a special meaning. Accounts and anecdotes about scholars from around the Muslim world visiting the city or settling in it could help maintain Baghdad's image as the intellectual capital of the Muslim world and the "center of the universe," even if its central role was eroded.

Descriptions of the scholarly pursuits of ʿulamaʾ who came to Baghdad to teach or study, enhanced the city's image as a magnet for aspiring students. In a statement attributed to the renowned *muhaddith* Abu Nasr b. Makula (d. 475/1082–83), who immigrated to Baghdad from ʿUkbara (in northern Iraq), ʿulamaʾ are encouraged to leave their hometowns and seek better opportunities for recognition and reputation elsewhere: "Strike your tent and leave the land where your art is despised, avoid humiliation . . . Depart from the land where your merit is not acknowledged [for] the aloe-wood is employed for common use in its native land."[21] A somewhat similar concept is conveyed by the famous Hanbali historian, Ibn al-Jawzi, a native of Baghdad who criticized the people of Iraq for welcoming and favoring foreigners of great repute while holding their own people in contempt. "There are people in Iraq from whom I feel no friendship," says Ibn al-Jawzi, "They listen with admiration to the words of a stranger, but those of their townsmen attract no attention. If a neighbor profited by the water which falls from the roof of their houses, they would turn the spout in another direction, and when reproached, their excuse is that the voice of the songstress has no charm for the tribe to which she belongs."[22]

Through their travels and activities, religious scholars helped extend the sense of the unity among Islamic societies, preserving and nourishing the various contacts Muslims maintained with one another. However, while, in its broadest definition, travel for the sake of study was a process emphasizing universal traits common to all Muslims, they simultaneously encouraged an appreciation of one's home, inspiring a sense of local identity. Thus the traveler became more closely linked to the idea of the Muslim community as a whole through the *rihla*, but at the same time learned what is specific to his own people and culture.[23] Imbued with the values of their native lands, many scholars would return home upon completing their travels. Abu Ishaq al-Isfara'ini, a Shafi'i jurisconsult, is said to have chosen to return to his native town despite the esteem and favor shown him by the 'ulama' of Iraq who tried to persuade him to settle there.[24] The biographers of Abu al-Fath ar-Razi, another noted Shafi'i scholar who left the town of Rayy for Baghdad, write that his father came from Rayy to beg his son, who at the time was teaching the legal doctrine of his *madhhab* in al-Mubarak Mosque (in al-Karkh quarter), to return to his hometown. "Instead of teaching the youth of Baghdad," said the father, "return to your town, and I will gather the youth around you so that you will teach them."[25] His request, though rejected, reflects expectations of local allegiances.

Local allegiances were expressed in other ways as well. Scholars from the same region tended to study in the same study circles, and probably lived in the same residential quarters. According to Ya'qubi, as early as the late ninth century the entire road (*darb*) in the area surrounding Bab ash-Sham (one of the four equidistant gates of the "round city") was inhabited by people from Balkh, Marv, and Buk-hara.[26] Quarters in west Baghdad, such as at-Tustariyyin (people from Tustar), and al-Anbariyyin (people from al-Anbar), are also good examples of areas named after people of common geographical origins. In a later period, the sources indicate names in east Baghdad, such as Darb al-Kuffiyyin, Darb al-Khwarizmiyya, and Darb al-Furs, all within Bab at-Taq quarter. It is difficult, however, to determine which of these names merely reflect a past heritage, and those which reflect contemporary reality.[27]

Indeed, Muslims in the Middle Ages were proud of the distinctive heritage of their cities. Originating in the special qualities or merits attributed to Mecca and Medina in the Koran and the prophetic tra-ditions, pride in the distinctive heritage of Islamic communities, among them newly constituted communities, was widely imitated, giving birth to local histories and a literary genre called *fada'il*, or *manaqib* (the special merits, or outstanding traits).[28] Baghdad, of course, lacked a privileged pre-Islamic status and central place in Islamic tradition, unlike Mecca, Medina, or Jerusalem. But historians living in the city during the eleventh and twelfth centuries were as proud of their city as were their contemporaries in other urban Islamic communities: Al-Khatib al-Baghdadi composed the famous *Ta'rikh baghdad*, while the Hanbali historian Ibn al-Jawzi wrote the *Manaqib al-baghdad.* Yet despite their importance in creating a sense of local identity, the many descriptions of the city and the hun-dreds of scholars who settled or passed through it were primarily intended to demonstrate the centrality of Baghdad as a major center of Islamic piety and learning.

Criteria of inclusion in biographical dictionaries may also shed some light on the relation between one's attachment to the place of origin and to the wider Islamic realm. Many biographical diction-aries whose authors were natives of eleventh- and twelfth-century Baghdad, were devoted to members of the legal schools, regardless of their geographical origins—the *Tabaqat ash-shafi'iyya* of Abu Ishaq ash-Shirazi, and those of Ibn Abi Ya'la and his son Ibn Rajab on the 'ulama' of the Hanbali school, come to mind.[29] Encompassing biog-raphies of 'ulama' from different towns and villages, these diction-aries draw a picture of scholarly groupings bound together by common adherence to a prominent *shaykh* within a certain *madhhab*, not by a common locality.

The character of Baghdad as a magnet for aspiring scholars, its position and image as a center of learning, serves to explain why the transition of the city's 'ulama' from universality to localism was never completed. Their vacillation between the pull of universality and that of local allegiances was not only reflected in the overall composition of their groupings, it also influenced the set of social relations they concluded with other segments of society, and their perception of their own place and role in the society—an issue to which we shall return.

Patterns and Frameworks of Study

The idea of hearing Islamic teaching directly from a reliable *shaykh* and, through him, becoming a part of an unbroken *isnad*, survived long after the appearance of madrasas.[30] Probably influenced by the Sufi perception of the essence of training or guidance, the personal contact between master and disciple was not only intended to ensure accurate transmission of the "knowledge" contained in a certain text, or to convey personal authority with regard to that text, but to also disseminate ideals and codes of proper Islamic behavior. An essential component of this tradition was the deeply entrenched belief that the moral rectitude of the transmitter is a prime criterion for determining the validity and quality of the knowledge transmitted.

Consider, for example, the following description of the journey made by the famous *muhaddith* and historian, as-Sam'ani (d. 562/1167), to Islamic centers of learning in Baghdad, Damascus, and Khurasan: "He met there men of learning (*ahl al-'ilm*), received from them information, obtained *hadith*, and took their virtuous deeds and praiseworthy conduct as a model.[31]

Written texts undoubtedly played a significant role in Islamic learning and the transmission of all other branches of knowledge throughout the period under consideration.[32] Beginning in the late ninth century, a homogenous corpus of authoritative or fixed texts was in the process of formation, constituting an alternative to the old method of gathering and transmitting knowledge. The student in the so-called manuscript age would normally hear a professor read loud one of the accepted books of sound traditions or compilations of the legal schools' "founding fathers," or he could simply read a text silently to himself in mosques and madrasas libraries. But for all the use and accessibility of written texts, the old practices and rituals of oral transmission (recitation, dictation, oralized reading) remained intact, demonstrated by many examples of a negative attitude toward students who read to themselves. The fact that the codex (be it the manuscript or the printed book) imitated the very form of oral transmission with its *isnad* formula, is in itself an indication of the oral transmission of written culture: the author has "heard from" or "taken from" this or that authority, and is now "handing it down for him" (*rawa 'anhu*).

The book, therefore, represented a continuing and unbroken oral communication, transmitted even further by the author.[33] The *ijaza*, of course, retained its traditional character: a personal certificate conferred by the teacher to his disciple, entitling him to teach a certain text only. It never developed into an institutionalized degree, such as the *licentia docendi* granted by the European universities with the consent of church authorities, nor did its issuance involve any formal procedures.[34] This particular characteristic of the *ijaza* might also explain cases in which *ijaza*s were obtained outside specific educational frameworks, and were mingled with other pursuits. One such example is the *ijaza* granted by the Hanbali scholar and historian, Ibn al-Banna' (d. 471/1078), to one of his students who set out with a caravan to Khurasan. In his autograph diary, Ibn al-Banna' relates:

> I gave him a document, one slip (of paper), which contained matters pertaining to commerce, upon which he recorded his *sama'* (hearing) and received the *ijaza* with my signature. I hope that God would render it useful for him and for all the Muslims![35]

Because obtaining an *ijaza* depended on personal contact between teacher and disciple, studying in some capacity with a particularly prominent scholar was the goal of those seeking knowledge, rather than studying in a specific educational framework. One young student, Abu Sa'd al-Isfahani (d. 540/1145), suffered bitter disappointment when, after hearing prophetic traditions in his hometown, he set out on a long journey to Baghdad to study law under Abu Nasr az-Zainabi, a member of the famous Hanafi scholarly family. When still en route, the news of Abu Nasr's death reached him, he began to weep, lamenting the death and wondering whom he would have as a master.[36]

In any event, individual scholars imparted less an abstract body of knowledge embodied in particular texts, than a personal authority over those texts. This transmission of knowledge, imprinted with the teacher's religious outlook and etiquette, must have occurred successfully wherever the *shaykh* sat. The mosque, which up to the advent

of the madrasa, had been the main seat of religious learning, preserved its function as a center of instruction in the religious and legal
sciences. Baghdad, in the middle of the eleventh century, had only
six *jami's*—congregational or Friday mosques—but had hundreds of
masjids, or ordinary everyday, mosques.[37] In addition to teaching the
various legal and religious sciences, the *halqa*s in the *jami'* filled
other roles, for issuing legal opinions (*li'l-fatwa, li'l-ifta'*), for regular
sessions of disputation (*li'l-nazar, li'l-munazara*), for delivering sermons (*li'l-wa'z*), and for both disputation and sermons.[38]

Among the mosques frequently mentioned as meeting places for
instruction and other scholarly pursuits in the eleventh and early
twelfth centuries are the Friday mosques of al-Mansur and al-Qasr,
and the small mosques of Da'laj and al-Mubarak. Situated in the
heart of the "round city," in the quarter of Bab al-Basra, the stronghold of the Hanbalis, and housing many permanent *halqa*s, the
Mosque of al-Mansur (or Mosque of al-Madina, as it was sometimes
called) retained its status as the most important educational center
in the city. Its prestigious standing among the educational forums of
Baghdad is testified to by examples of scholars from different legal
schools who lived far away and who normally taught in other
mosques, but tried to dictate *hadith* in Jami' al-Mansur at least once
in their lives.[39]

Many members of the Hanafi and Shafi'i schools reportedly held
permanent classes in the Friday mosque of al-Qasr, as well as in the
two small mosques of al-Da'laj and al-Mubarak. Both these smaller
mosques seem to have preserved their function as central educational forums during the first century of the madrasa's appearance
in Baghdad. Even scholars who taught in one of the city's madrasas
held classes in mosques at the same time. Abu al-Qasim ad-Dabbusi
(d. 482/1089), for example, left his hometown of Dabbusiyya (in
Transoxania) for Baghdad, where he was appointed teacher of the
law at the Nizamiyya. While teaching in the madrasa, he also
dictated *hadith* and taught *fiqh* in several *majlises* in the city's
mosques. So great was the crowd attending his lectures that the
mosques of Baghdad were filled with his disciples.[40] Abu Bakr al-
Khujandi (d. 552/1157), another teacher at the Nizamiyya Madrasa
praised for his ability to memorize a great number of prophetic
traditions, reciting them accurately for dictation while standing on
the pulpit (*minbar*) of Jami' al-Qasr, where he had a permanent *halqa*
for *hadith*.[41]

In addition to study groups and circles in the mosques, religious
scholars of this period continued to meet in the private homes of the

shaykhs. The *hadith* scholar, Abu al-Qasim al-Jurjani (d. 477/1084), is reported to have held a study circle for both *hadith* and *fiqh* in the privacy of his home (*wa-kana baytuhu jami'an li'l-'ilm al-hadith wa-'l-fiqh*: "His place was a gathering for the study of *hadith* and law").[42] While most of the classes held in private homes were not regular, in some cases these assemblies gained the character and reputation of permanent forums. Among them was the *majlis an-nazar* of Qadi as-Simnani (d. 444/1052), which, according to al-Khatib al-Baghdadi, became one of the famous discussion groups of eleventh-century Baghdad.[43] Al-Khatib also provides us with information about the section of the house in which classes were held. The houses of the well-to-do Baghdadis were divided into a family portion, called the *haram*, and a sitting area, or "guest room." Located next to the entrance and adjoining a corridor, this sitting area was utilized as a study, as well as a gathering place for discussions and instruction.[44]

Powerful patrons of learning also continued to host men of learning in their homes. The vizier Abu al-Qasim az-Zainabi (d. 538/1143)—a member of the famous Hanafi Zainabi family of *qadi*s, viziers, and *naqib*s (heads of the descendants of the Prophet)—held a study circle in his home. The famous as-Sam'ani writes that during his visit to Baghdad, he heard *hadith*s recited in the home of the vizier by some of the most celebrated *muhaddithun* of the city, among them Abu as-Sa'adat Hibat Allah (d. 542/1148), one of the renowned *hadith* scholars and grammarians of Baghdad. Besides transmitting *hadith*s, Abu al-Qasim taught the content of his treatises on Arabic philology in several of the city's mosques to a great number of students who crowded his doorway, while scholars passing through Baghdad on their way to the *hajj* used to visit him.[45] The Hanbali vizier, Ibn Hubayra, an enthusiastic patron of religious learning, turned his house into a gathering place for the poor, or commoners (*fuqara'*) and the 'ulama'. Ibn al-Jawzi says he used to frequent the study circle held in the vizier's house, where attendance was free to anyone seeking religious learning. The *fuqara'* engaged in the recitation of the Koran, and the 'ulama' debated points of law.[46]

Despite the growing rapprochement of Sufis and legal scholars, there were still Sufis who oscillated between scripturalist Islam and the mystical understanding of religion. Some would hold *halqa*s for the teaching of the religious sciences in the great mosques of Baghdad, in their private homes, and occasionally in the *ribat*s. By the twelfth century they were developing into centers of both religious instruction and of public preaching and worship. The Sufi-Ashʿari scholar, Abu al-Muʾayyad al-Ghaznawi al-Waʿiz ("the preacher," d. 500/1106), while settling in the *ribat* of Abu Saʿd as-Sufi, had a *majlis* for the instruction of the Arabic language and grammar in al-Qasr Mosque. Many people, probably among his visitors in the *ribat*, are said to have repented (been "reborn" in Christian terms) under his influence.⁴⁷ In most cases Sufis who inclined to Ashʿarism were forced to leave the Shafiʿi madrasas, usually in wake of the objections raised by the Hanbalis. Viewing the madrasa as the representative of formal knowledge, book learning, and worldliness, others left the new schools of their own free will. The Sufi-Ashʿari, Ardashir b. Mansur al-ʿAbbadi (d. 495/1101), settled in the Nizamiyya Madrasa where he held his *majlis al-waʿz*, attended by al-Ghazzali as well as by large crowds which filled the madrasa's yard, chambers, and roofs. But he soon left the madrasa, settled in the *ribat* of Abu Saʿd as-Sufi, and took to preaching in one of the prayer grounds outside the city.⁴⁸ Abu al-Barakat al-Anbari (d. 577/1183), an eminent philologist of this period, was another scholar who sought an alternative to religious fulfillment and devotion in Sufism. He studied Shafiʿi law in the Nizamiyya Madrasa and philology with both Abu Saʿadat ash-Shajari and Abu Mansur al-Jawaliqi, two of the most distinguished masters of the field, and his own lessons on philology are said to have been attended by a great number of students. Toward the end of his life, however, he abstained from teaching and isolated himself in his home, leading a life of contemplation and solitary retreat.⁴⁹

For many others, however, studies in the madrasa and mystical training in the Sufi *ribat* were regarded as two complementary educational streams, rather than divergent paths to knowledge. Rulers, along with members of their entourage, founded madrasas and *ribat*s at the same time, and a number of madrasas, among them the first Hanbali madrasas founded in Baghdad, were also utilized as Sufi hostels or surrounded by *ribat*s.⁵⁰ The students, who in any event addressed themselves to study with a certain *shaykh*, rather than in a specific establishment, could attach themselves both to legal scholars and to Sufi guides, or to a single *shaykh* whose teaching combined the two.

This combination of the two streams of Islamic learning—the formal, legalistic and the mystical—reoccurs throughout the life of al-Ghazzali, first as a student and later as a teacher. The first period of his studies in Nishapur was the most important part of his education. Together with studying *fiqh* and Ashʿari *kalam* under Imam al-

Haramain, who held the post of *mudarris* in the Nizamiyya Madrasa in Nishapur, he acquired mastery in philosophy and Sufism. His interest in legal studies continued even during his period of "retreat," and toward the end of his life he returned to Khurasan and assumed the chair of *mudarris* in the madrasas of Nishapur and Tus, leading the life of a Sufi and serving as spiritual guide to those seeking the Sufi "way."[51]

Abu Najib as-Suhrawardi (d. 563/1168), the author of *Adab al-muridin* ("The manners of the adepts"), one of the most widely read handbooks of mystical training, was another "orthodox" Sufi who sought to combine advanced theoretical scholarship of the type provided in madrasas with the Sufi training and way of life. His course of education, journeys in search of God, and teaching, all remarkably resemble those of his near contemporary and spiritual guide, al-Ghazzali. He came to Baghdad from Suhraward, a town in Azerbaijan, and found shelter in some ruins on the eastern bank of the Euphrates. As his fame as an experienced mystic spread, he attracted a large crowd seeking spiritual guidance. As-Suhrawardi's scope of learning ranged from *hadith* and law to Sufi training; he heard traditions in Baghdad from several authorities, and studied law and jurisprudence (*ʿilm usul al-fiqh*) in the Nizamiyya Madrasa until he became proficient (*darasa hatta baraʿa*). Having displayed great ability in his knowledge of *hadith* and law, he began to issue legal opinions and to transmit traditions. In 545/1150 as-Suhrawardi was invited to teach in the Nizamiyya Madrasa, but after several years gave up his position as a *mudarris*. He then turned his ruins into a *ribat* and erected a madrasa next to it: the Madrasa an-Najibiyya, named after its founder. His *ribat* and madrasa became a home for his followers as well as a place of refuge for those who feared the political rulers. Continuing his travels, he set out on a journey to Jerusalem in A.H. 557, the year the war with the crusaders was launched, but reached only as far as Damascus.[52]

With students building their careers on the reputation of celebrated *shaykhs*, and with the rigorous instruction of the Islamic traditional and legal sciences still taking place in a host of forums, the madrasas had not yet monopolized or even dominated religious learning in eleventh- and twelfth-century Baghdad. Hence, it was not around the madrasas that the scholarly networks, which constituted the core of the Baghdadi legal schools, were formed and orbited. Moreover, an examination of the construction of cultural and social ties which bound the Baghdadi scholarly networks together shows that, whether taking place in madrasas or outside these new schools, the transmission of common legal doctrines did not constitute the prime ingredient in the crystallization process of the *madhahib*.

CHAPTER 4

❦

FORMS
OF SOCIAL AFFILIATION

The Prophet said: "Whomever Allah intends to do good, He gives right understanding of religion . . . knowledge is maintained only through teaching."

al-Bukhari, *Sahih*: Book of Knowledge (*Kitab al-'ilm*), 10

Scholars have long noted the informal, personal nature of Muslim education—one which rested entirely on the teacher-disciple relationship.[1] Yet neither the complexity of this major characteristic of scholarly association, nor its social significance, have been fully examined. Moreover, the a priori assumption of most research is that regardless of their amorphous and elusive character, the legal schools and the madrasas founded for the teaching of their doctrines were the primary frameworks within which the 'ulama' identified themselves and through which they tried to act.[2] This assumption has led several social historians to focus on the institutions related to the preservation and transmission of the Islamic religious law, rather on the behavior and thoughts of the individuals associated with them.

By unveiling the world of learning which lies beyond its organizational structures, we can explain how the Baghdadi 'ulama' constructed their social bonds and identities. Such an inquiry, though set in one specific historical context, may advance our understanding of the social uses of the system of transmission of Islamic lore and the inner mechanisms which assured the coherence and perpetuation of 'ulama' groupings, both as chains of transmitters and as social networks.

75

The *Halqa*

Sociologists who study groups as social networks, or the set of linkages among people, suggest four distinct patterns of networks ranging from an intimate circle of friends to a large collective mass in general agreement on a given issue. Group relations and communication within these four types of networks vary considerably, and affect the way their members feel and act. The first is the *completely connected* network, or a tightly knit clique, in which each member has constant contact with all other members. The second is the *radial* network, which orbits around one key person. The third is the *chain* network in which each member must rely on the other links in order to reach the first member. Finally, there is the *rim* network in which each member may be reached by any other member in two or more links, while no one member has a leadership position.[3]

If we are to apply the models offered by sociologists to the study of scholarly groupings as social networks, we might describe them as radial networks. Unlike the completely connected network in which all members are in direct contact with each other, each student was connected to the master, or *shaykh*, as the central link. It was around the master that the study circle, or *halqa* (literally: circle, or ring), was formed and orbited. Upon his death, the original study circle would normally dissolve, and his students would either attach themselves to other masters or form their own study circles. Once dissolved, however, the original network of master and disciples would not completely disappear. The shared experience of studying together with the same master created ties of friendship and mutual concern among its members, which sometimes extended beyond the completion of their course of studies. Especially close were the ties maintained among members of the Hanbali school, many of whom had studied together with Qadi Abu Yaʿla. However, as will be demonstrated below, even within the Hanbali school the students often saw themselves linked not so much horizontally, common members of a religious school, but as linked vertically through their *shaykh* to an unbroken chain of teachers and transmitters.

Thus, two models of scholarly affiliation coexisted: the vertical chain, in which the scholars were linked together as common descendants of teachers and transmitters; and the radial network, in which they were linked together, at a particular time, as common disciples of a certain teacher. As the core element in the culture of the learned, and as their most characteristic image of institutionalization, the construction of the links in the chain of transmitters determined the character of the scholarly network and the set of relationships within it.

Nothing better illustrates the radial network than the seating arrangement in the *halqa*: the teacher sitting on a cushion or a chair leaning against a wall or pillar, the students sitting cross-legged in a semicircle around him. Emphasizing the centrality and authority of the teacher, this classroom arrangement also signified the relative position of the disciples in the study circle, which was decided primarily by competence; the greater one's knowledge of the subject, the closer his proximity to the teacher. The significance of seating students in proximity to the teacher was exemplified by the phrase one often reads in biographical notices: (the teacher) "brought the student close to him" (*qarrabahu ilaihi*). Because both the master and the members of the *halqa* considered sitting next to the teacher a sign of recognition of their educational qualifications, students would boast of being brought close to their master. Abu Bakr ad-Dinawari (d. 535/1141), the favorite disciple of Abu al-Khattab al-Kalwadhani, who on his teacher's death succeeded to his chair in al-Mansur Mosque, related the following anecdote of his student days:

> When I began to study the law I sat at the end of the study circle. . . . One day a discussion took place between myself and a student who sat close to the teacher. . . . On the following day I took my place as usual at the end of the study circle. The man in question came and sat beside me, and when asked by the teacher why he had relinquished his place, he replied: "I am not in the same grade as this student. I shall sit with him so that I can benefit thereby." By God! It was not long before I advanced in the field of law, and became strong in the knowledge of it, so that I began to sit next to the teacher with two students between the man and myself.[4]

In this case, the student who sat next to the teacher relinquished his place of honor of his own accord. It was more common, however, for the teacher himself to move the brightest student closer to him.

A master might have appointed his closest disciples to inherit his chair on his death, or employ him as a deputy professor (*na'ib mudarris*) to teach in his name, in those instances in which he held more than one professorship in more than one mosque.[5] However, so closely was the *halqa* associated with its master that he would seldom nominate one of his disciples to succeed him before his death, because, in their view, no one could take his place. The Hanbali *hadith* expert and jurisconsult, Abu ʿAbd Allah b. Hamid, made one of these rare nominations before he left Baghdad for Mecca to perform the *hajj*. While preparing for the journey, the disciples of his *halqa* (in a mosque in Bab ash-Shaʿir), fearing to be left without a master to guide them asked: "Now that you leave, under whose direction shall we study?" "Under the direction of this young man," replied Ibn Hamid pointing to his closest disciple, Ibn Yaʿla.[6]

So deeply was the radial type of study circle entrenched in the culture of the religiously learned, that it remained alive long after the appearance of the madrasa. A remarkable testimony to the effect of the traditional patterns of learning—one that emphasized both the centrality of the teacher and the informality of the study circle— is the preservation of the seating arrangement in the madrasa study group, or *halqa*. The madrasa, it may be argued, was but a glorified *halqa*, and as such, differed remarkably from its counterpart, the Babylonian *yeshiva* with its rigid hierarchical system symbolized in the seating pattern: some seventy scholars, arrayed in seventy rows, sitting facing the *Gaon* and his immediate associates, while an additional four hundred scholars standing at the rear of the lecture hall.[7] Nor did the madrasa have a hierarchical organization similar to that of the European university, with its faculties, deans, rectors, chancellors, or presidents. There were, of course, several teachers present in the madrasa. Still, the madrasa was essentially a "one-man institution" in the sense that it provided for only one titular professor for each system of law, while the remainder of the teaching staff, holding positions subordinate to that of the titular professor, was composed of substitute professors, lecturers responsible for teaching related subjects, and repetitors.[8]

Since theoretically only one titular professor could be elected at a time, a problem arose when, in 483/1090, two professors, both with orders from Nizam al-Mulk to occupy the chair of law at the Nizamiyya Madrasa, arrived in Baghdad. This embarrassing situation was resolved by a special arrangement in which the two professors taught on alternate days. Significantly, the two professors, Abu ʿAbd Allah at-Tabari (d. 495/1102) and Abu Muhammad al-Fami ash-Shirazi (d. 500/1107), were both immigrants from western Iran whose reputation had been established before their arrival in the city. Contemporary historians describe this lone case of a divided professorship as a peculiar practice.[9]

More important than the stipulations in the deeds of the *waqf* is that, from the perspective of the ʿulamaʾ themselves, the madrasas were established not so much for a certain *madhhab*, than for a certain teacher, and were closely associated with him. The preference shown for the teacher as opposed to the establishment, and the great degree of authority given to the former, are clearly reflected in the description of events on the inaugural day of the Nizamiyya Madrasa in A.H. 459, the most glorious institution of its kind in Baghdad. Abu Ishaq ash-Shirazi, one of the greatest jurists in Baghdad and the leader of the Shafiʿi school in the city, was appointed to the post of the *mudarris*. On his way from his home to the madrasa, he was informed that the land which had been set aside for the madrasa had been illegally expropriated from its owner; he then refused to take up his position. Only after much pleading on the part of his students and a formal declaration by Nizam al-Mulk that the madrasa had been established only for his sake, did he agree to accept the appointment.[10] When ash-Shirazi died in A.H. 476, the gates of the madrasa were closed and his students went into mourning. The madrasa remained closed by order of the vizier for almost an entire year. When its gates were reopened and Abu Saʿd al-Mutawalli was appointed the new teacher, the students disapproved of his sitting in the place formally occupied by their previous master.[11]

The centrality of the teacher was expressed in other ways as well. Wherever the *halqa* was convened—be it the floor of a mosque, a private living room, a shop, a riverbank, or a chamber of the madrasa—it was apparently the teacher who determined the acceptance of students to his study group, the frequency of its assembly (*majlis*), as well as the sequence and method of all instruction. The biographies provide many illustrations of the informal nature of admission into the study circle, decided solely by the master according to educational qualifications and performance of those who gathered around him and seldom marked by any formal observance. Abu Saʿd al-Mutawalli told his students the following anecdote from his students days:

> I came from beyond the Oxus, and entered [the mosque where] Abu al-Harith b. Abi al-Fadl as-Sarakhsi was lecturing, in garments much used and not much worn by men of learning. I attended the class of as-Sarakhsi, and sat among his disciples who were seated at the end of his class. A question was brought up for disputation, and I spoke and raised objections. When my turn was over, Abu al-Harith ordered me to move up closer, and so I did. And when my turn had come up again for disputation, he brought me closer still and continued to do so until my seat was next to him.

Thereafter, he saw to all my needs and took me as one of his
followers. On this occasion I was over powered with joy.[12]

Mutawalli considered his experience with as-Sarakhsi as one of the
most pleasant incidents in his academic career. Not only was he
allowed to attend as-Sarakhsi's study circle, despite his being a new
scholar in town and despite his shabby clothes, but was invited to sit
next to him, a privilege reserved for the master's most competent
and closest disciples.

The concept of unrestricted participation in lectures held in the
halqa, and the absence of any formal admission procedures, is also
supported by the following anecdote, which tells how Abu al-Fath
ar-Razi, who came to Baghdad as a young man for the purpose of
studying philology, joined al-Isfara'ini's study circle at the mosque
of al-Mubarak. According to his account, one day he went to the
house of his philology teacher and was told that he was at the public baths. Ar-Razi started for the baths, but passing the mosque
where al-Isfara'ini was teaching, he entered and sat among the
scholars. "Pleased with what I heard," he relates, "I took notes on
the lecture [on the laws of fasting] on a blank leaf of a book I had
with me, and on returning to the house where I dwelt, I repeated
the lesson to my fellow lodgers. In order to hear the book of fasting
explained to the end and to note it down, I went assiduously to
Isfara'ini's lessons until I completed the task."[13]

In common with the accounts of the *rihla*, this, and similar anecdotes, reflect more than the customary patterns of scholarly communication and association. Indicating the openness of the *halqa* to
newcomers, these accounts were probably designed by their authors
to nourish and reassert the premise that religious education and
leadership among the ʿulamaʾ were open to talent regardless of background—a point to which we shall return.

Although enrollment in the madrasa must have been limited by
the stipulations in the deed of endowment, the selection of those
admitted appears to have been left to the teachers in the madrasa,
rather than to the founders or directors. This might partly explain
the several occasions on which a study circle in the madrasa—
consisting of a teacher, his followers (*ashab*) and other disciples—
can be traced back to the mosques. Some of ash-Shirazi's students in
the Nizamiyya Madrasa appear to have commenced studying under
him in a mosque in Bab al-Maratib. Among them was Abu ʿAli al-
Fariqi (d. 528/1134). He began his studies of law in his hometown of
Mayyafariqin in the Jazira, came to Baghdad upon the death of his

teacher, and attached himself to ash-Shirazi. He attended his new master's course in law in the *masjid*, and took up his residence in the nearby *khan*, which housed as few as ten, or as many as twenty, of ash-Shirazi's out-of-town students.[14] Abu al-Barakat al-Anbari, another out-of-town student, studied law in the Nizamiyya Madrasa while living with his master of philology, Abu Sa'adat b. al-Shajari, as his private pupil.[15] Conversely, the madrasa would occasionally host scholars of other pursuits, such as the poet Abu Ishaq al-Kalbi from Damascus who, residing in the Nizamiyya Madrasa for many years, composed panegyrics and elegies about its *mudarrisun*.[16]

With a variety of educational forums, and with masters and students teaching and studying in several *halqas*, scholarly networks naturally overlapped. But no matter how many contacts a scholar might have, it was naturally the set of linkages between a *shaykh* and those students who devoted themselves to intense study under his tutelage that surpassed all other linkages in terms of attachment and loyalty. To use the language of the sources: those students benefited or sought the benefit (*intafa'a* or *istafada*) of the *shaykh*, sat in his company (*jalasa ash-shaykh*), and worked (*ishtaghala*) with him.

Authors of biographical dictionaries frequently use the word *suhba*—"companionship" or "discipleship"—to describe the relationship between the *shaykh* and his closest students. The term described a pattern of a personal relationship which permeated medieval Muslim societies: between a scholar and the ruler who became his patron; between the rich merchant and his apprentice; or between a senior official and a junior official under him. In the context of education, *suhba* implied an extremely close personal and intellectual relationship between teacher and student, one fostered over the course of many years. Originally associated with the companions of the Prophet who carried on his teaching after him, *suhba* and its synonyms (especially *mulazama*) came to be applied principally in the fields of *hadith* and *fiqh*, but could, in fact, characterize a master-disciple relationship in any subject of instruction.[17]

The profound emphasis placed on the personal relationships between a master and his disciple, and the use of the term *suhba* to describe these relationships, is not surprising. The belief that the closer the relationship between a master and a disciple, the more the latter was considered a reliable source for future generations, lay at the foundations of the transmitting process from the days of the Prophet and his *sahaba* or Companions. In Shi'i Islam, this association between intimacy and authority had special meaning. The famous Shi'i *hadith*, which told how Muhammad dictated every

Koranic verse immediately upon its revelation to 'Ali, how he taught him everything God revealed to him, portraying him as the defender of the Prophet, his closest, most trusted companion, was meant to legitimize the Shi'is' claim that 'Ali possessed divine religious authority, equal to that of Muhammad.[18]

An entire theory was thereafter developed to show how each of the twelve Shi'i *imams* received his superior knowledge (thereby becoming a divine authority); and how, upon its transfer to the living *imam*, this superior knowledge was transmitted in reverse to all the previous *imams* back to Muhammad.[19] The Sunni 'ulama' are, of course, mere interpreters of the Sunna of the Prophet (his words and deeds eventually established as legally binding precedents). But their claim to exclusive knowledge of the Koran and the Sunna, establishing themselves as the "heirs of the Prophets,"[20] rested on the construction of personal bonds between master and disciple, links in unbroken chains of transmitters, handing down the Prophet' words over the generations.

The disciple could become a part of the chain of transmitters by hearing directly from the teacher and receiving *ijaza* from him, but in order to assure the perpetuation of the master's teaching, it had to be put into writing. However, most teachers considered their own opinions less important than their mere inclusion in the chain of transmitters. Moreover, many did not dare to make their opinions public. Hence, teachers had their disciples carry out the task of writing. The teacher would read the text aloud so that the students could check their versions against his and make the necessary corrections. The students would write their masters's commentaries on a given text in its margins, between the lines, or even between the words and later produce the lecture course with the commentaries. To assure the accuracy of the reproduced text, the students would then read it aloud to the teacher. If the teacher was the author of a book, he would normally publish it through dictation (*imla'*), given either from a written copy or from memory.[21] The combination of oral and written transmission allowed a constant dialogue with the text and between the transmitters themselves, leaving enough room for disputation, even for originality and creativity, controlling innovations and variations at the same time. This system of transmission, which stressed the personal element both in granting authority for the texts transmitted and in guaranteeing the perpetuation of the chain as a whole, was enhanced by the personal bonds between teacher and disciple.

Authors of biographical dictionaries provide us ample anecdotes illustrating the teacherís devotion to his students' religious and ethical education, as well as to all their other needs. Some teachers taught for no monetary return (*ihtisaban*), a practice ascribed by authors of biographical dictionaries to the most pious and ascetic among the 'ulama'. More interesting still are stories about the practice of some teachers supporting their students financially to help them through their long years of study. The Hanbali scholar Abu Mansur al-Khayyat (d. 499/1106) was the *imam* (prayer leader) of Ibn Jarada Mosque in *Dar al-khilafa*, where he lived and taught the Koran. He refused any payment for his work, teaching only for the sake of heavenly reward, but would beg for money and food for his disciples.[22] Abu al-Hamid al-Isfara'ini, the *ra'is* (leader) of the Shafi'i school in Baghdad, received large sums of money sent from various parts of the Muslim world to distribute among his followers (*ashab*). On one occasion he distributed one hundred sixty dinars to his poor disciples who attended his lectures on law in al-Mubarak Mosque.[23] Some went as far as to support their students from their own pockets. Al-Khatib al-Baghdadi, for example, is reported to have given one of his students five gold dinars on two occasions for writing paper (*kaghid*).[24] On his deathbed, he left instructions to the *hadith* scholar, Ibn Khayrun, to donate his books as *waqf* for the benefit of men of religious learning. He also left all his riches as alms (*tasadaka*) to aid *hadith* students in general.[25] Large amounts of money do not appear to have been involved; nevertheless, such aid could reinforce the bonds between a master, his *ashab*, and other disciples.

The very language and images employed in biographical dictionaries reflect patterns of a master-student relationship built on deep attachment. Abu al-Fath ar-Razi, who is said to have been extremely fond of his disciples, used to sit in their company as if he was a teacher of children (*wa-kana shafiqan bi'l talaba, yajlisu baynahim hatta yazunnu zanna annahu mu'addib as-sabyan*).[26] Frequently the relationship between teacher and student is described by the metaphor of father and son. Ibn Rajab tells us that Abu Muhammad al-Hinna'i (d. 493/1099) was so close to his master Abu Ya'la, whom he served as assistant in the instruction of *hadith* (*mustamli*) in al-Mansur Mosque, that he was regarded as one of his sons.[27] Some masters married their daughters to their disciples. Abu Nasr al-Ibari (d. 506/1112), for example, married his daughter Shuhda al-Katiba, herself a renowned *hadith* transmitter, to his domestic servant and close *hadith* disciple, Abu al-Hasan al-Anbari.[28]

Communication and assistance between a master and his disciples flowed in both directions. Owing their training, promotion, and financial assistance to their masters, disciples were expected to show their gratitude to their benefactors. The verbs *sahiba, lazima* (to keep company, to be closely associated), and *ʿaliqa* (to cling), are used to describe the attachment of the *sahib* to his master. A *sahib* would often serve his master of law in the capacity of repetitor (*muʿid*). Sitting at the master's side, the *muʿid* would repeat his words to the students and explain difficult points.[29] The Hanbali jurisconsult ash-Sharif Abu Jaʿfar (d. 470/1077), for example, began his studies of law under the direction of Abu Yaʿla in A.H. 428 and continued to attend his class until A.H. 451. During this period, he assisted his professor in lecturing and copied his *taʿliqa*, a work on *usul al-fiqh* based on the notes a student took from the master's lectures or books.[30]

The writing of commentaries, abridgements, and sequels to masters' compilations was thus not merely a method applied in the process of transmission, but a way in which devoted students expressed respect for their masters' achievements and commitment to the dissemination of their teachings. Abu Nasr b. Muhammad, known as al-Aqtaʾ (d. 474/1081), studied *fiqh* with the Hanafi jurisconsult al-Quduri. After leaving Baghdad, he taught law in Ramhurmuz and wrote a commentary on the celebrated *Mukhtasar* ("compendium") of his master.[31] The Shafiʿi jurisconsult, ash-Shashi, studied *fiqh* under ash-Shirazi and read the *Shamil* with its author as-Sabbagh. He later attached himself to ash-Shirazi (*sahibahu*), serving him in the capacity of *muʿid*, and accompanied him on his journey to Nishapur. At the same time he showed his admiration for his teacher and his commitment to passing on his teaching by writing both a commentary and an abridgement of his famous treatise on *fiqh*. The deep affection and admiration he felt toward his two masters is revealed by his grief for their deaths, repeating the following phrase: "The dwelling is empty, and I am now the leader of the school (*imam*),"[32] stressing his belief that they were superior to him.

The close bonds between a master and a disciple were sometimes extended to the second generation. Many ʿulamaʾ are said to have become the teachers of their masters' children, whom they might have known since childhood. For example, Ibn Abi Yaʿla (d. 526/1131), the compiler of *Tabaqat al-hanabila* and son of the renowned Hanbali *qadi* Abu Yaʿla, commenced his studies of *hadith* and law under his father, and on the latter's death became the *sahib* of ash-Sharif Abu Jaʿfar, who had been Abu Yaʿla's close disciple.

The young Ibn Abi Ya'la followed his master in the struggle against Ash'arism, and his great respect for him is manifested in the long biographical notice he dedicated to him in his biographical dictionary.[33] There were also cases in which the bonds between a master and a disciple extended to a third generation. Abu Muhammad at-Tamimi (d. 488/1095), for instance, was the most celebrated disciple of the Hanbali scholar al-Qadi Abu 'Ali al-Hashimi (d. 428/1037), who had been among the students of his paternal grandfather, Abu Hasan at-Tamimi (d. 371/981).[34]

The fact that the madrasa is scarcely mentioned in the literature of the period, as opposed to the many testimonies of study circles either outside the madrasa or overlapping it, and the centrality of the teacher-disciple relationship in the transmission process both testify to the marginality of the madrasa, indeed of any form of organization, in the culture and society of the learned. Teachers came to the madrasa in order to obtain an official post and its accompanying salary, students in order to receive stipends and living quarters. This is not to imply that madrasas were not educational frameworks, but that the world of learning took place both inside and outside the new "law colleges," according to its customary forms.[35] Created as a means of safeguarding "true" religion and guaranteeing financial support to the religiously learned, the madrasa was, in other words, merely a new and more institutionalized form of organization into which the essential cultural and social practices were poured.

Orbiting around celebrated Baghdadi 'ulama', throughout the period under consideration the *halqa* remained the central scholarly association in the culture and society of the learned. No matter how loose or unstructured the *halqa* may appear to modern historians and sociologists, it represented the 'ulama''s own perception of hierarchy, authority, and mutual commitments, and, as such, could take over the role of formal and stable institutions.

The *Madhhab*

Some historians, seeking to explain the consolidation of the *madhahib* during the Sunni revival, tend to attribute a false aura of the madrasa's centrality in this process. United hitherto by the worldwide system of scholarly connections, with the advent of the madrasas, the law schools found a new center for the teaching of their legal methods, religious propaganda, and political action. The identification of a madrasa with a particular school of law thus lent the *madhahib* a greater unity and identity, sharpening the differences between the law schools, adding barriers and heightening the competition between them.[36] This interpretation of the social significance of the "institution" overlooks the character and image of the madrasa as portrayed by contemporary observers. If we bear in mind that madrasas were associated with a single teacher who ordained his disciples to transmit only that "knowledge" which he imparted to them, and that he could teach anywhere his *halqa* could meet, then we must reassess the accepted historical narrative which ascribes to madrasas a major role in the consolidation of the *madhahib* and their evolution into religious factions.

Certainly, the ʿulamaʾ, from time to time, would rally round their madrasas, thereby stressing their *madhhab* affiliation. However, they did so only in the face of great threat or danger, such as the battle waged by the Hanbalis against the Shafiʿis a result of the latter's attempts to preach Ashʿarism in the Nizamiyya Madrasa via the *waʿz* or popular "academy" sermon.[37] One of the most serious incidents of this kind occurred when the famous Ashʿari theologian and preacher, Abu Nasr al-Qushairi an-Nishapuri, arrived in Baghdad while on *hajj* in 469/1067. He preached in the Nizamiyya Madrasa, mixing theological remarks with his sermon. Mobilizing the masses, a group of Hanbalis, led by Ash-Sharif Abu Jaʿfar, mercilessly attacked the Shafiʿis, accusing them of leaning toward Ashʿarism. The riots were so violent that they are described in the sources as *fitna* (lit. "civil strife" or "rebellion"). One poet, a witness to these events, wrote to Nizam al-Mulk and pleaded with him to put an end to the *fitna*: "Order and security in the city have crumbled . . . the soldiers fight one another . . . and the people of Baghdad are oppressed and their honor has been trampled."[38] As the *fitna* intensified and a member of the Shafiʿi school was killed, the Shafiʿis fled to the Nizamiyya and closed its gates. In a letter to the caliph's vizier Fahr ad-Dawla, ash-Shirazi, the leader of the Shafiʿi school, appealed to the caliph for support, explaining the fears of the small Shafiʿi community in Baghdad in light of the increased number of Hanbalis and the wide public support they enjoyed. The Shafiʿis, ash-Shirazi complained, suffered from the lack of sufficient followers and governmental support, and hence had rallied round their madrasa, which was erected to serve their small community as a home (*dar*) and a place of refuge (*maljaʾ*) in good times and in bad.[39]

However, the ties of social solidarity among the various law schools' adherents were based primarily on shared theological and moral postures, rather than, as one might have expected, on legal interpretation per se.[40] This explains why the Hanbali school achieved greater coherence. Not only was the *hanabila* both a theological and legal school, but its scholars attributed more importance to principles of creed (*'aqida*) and righteous Islamic conduct than to legal matters.[41] While debate still raged between the "rationalists" or *ashab al-ra'y* ("masters of free opinion"), and "traditionalists" or *ahl al-hadith* ("the people of *hadith*") within the Hanafi and Shafi'i schools, the Hanbalis formulated a rather uniform position in matters of theology, dogma, and morality. Consequently, Hanbali preachers and theologians succeeded in becoming the dominant force in the Sunni restoration movement beginning in the late tenth century. The Hanbalis, it is also important to remember, were the last to adopt the madrasa as an educational framework, and even when they did, most of their teaching and preaching activities continued to take place in mosques and private homes.

Avoiding the patronage of the ruling elite, the Hanbalis still depended on personal support among the school's adherents to finance their scholarly activities and help the needy. *Shaykhs* with private means and wealthy patrons and supporters of the school founded mosques and madrasas and provided financial support to teachers and students. Among the most generous benefactors of the Hanbali school were the caliph's vizier Ibn Hubayra and the wealthy merchant family of Shaykh al-Ajjal Abu Mansur b. Yusuf (d. 460/ 1067). In addition to founding a madrasa to sustain groups of scholars, Ibn Hubayra supported individuals directly. The Hanbali historian Ibn al-Jawzi, who was among Ibn Hubayra's close associates (*ashab*) and beneficiaries, recalls that Ibn Hubayra had offered him a teaching position in a mosque which had an endowed plot of land adjacent to it yielding one thousand *ratl* to provide for his needs.[42] Shaykh al-Ajjal founded a mosque for the teaching of the Hanbali *madhhab*, as well as a girls school, where he selected the teachers. In his diary, Ibn al-Banna' relates that he taught courses at the mosque assigned to him by Shaykh al-Ajjal. The post of teacher in the girls school was assigned to Abu Talib al-'Ukbari, whom Ibn al-Banna' describes as a follower of the Koran and the Sunna, and as one of the *ashab* of the school.[43]

Begun in a general commitment to upholding the religious community and used, in turn, as a means of disseminating the teaching of the *madhhab* and enlarging its circle of followers, ties of patronage reinforced the social identity and unity of the Baghdadi *hanabila*.[44] But even the Hanbalis, who seem to have formed a unified scholarly group around which a community of followers coalesced, and which was able to mobilize supporters for its activities—even they built their social relationships on the personal and individual base of teacher and disciple. The devotion, in other words, was to the teacher, rather than to the *madhhab* as a scholarly establishment or a formal entity.

Testimony with regard to the centrality of the *shaykh* is reflected in the manner by which the Hanbali biographees are presented: the scholars are identified as the disciples and followers of a certain teacher, rather than members of a certain *madhhab*. The terms *shaykhuna* (our *shaykh*) and *imamuna* (our *imam*), which appear in their biographies over and over, further attest to the personal attachment of the disciples to their teacher. Modeled after biographical dictionaries of early generations of teachers and transmitters, and inspired by the transmission of *hadith*, the biographical dictionaries devoted to the Hanbali *madhhab* also emphasize teacher-disciple ties. They are divided into *tabaqat*, or layers of transmitters, each of which includes biographies of the disciples (*ashab*) of one of the famous *shaykhs* of the *madhhab*. For example, the sixth *tabaqa* in *Tabaqat al-hanabila* of Ibn Abi Ya'la is begins: "and they are *ashab* al-Walid [Qadi Abu Ya'la] may God be pleased with them all." Their biographies appear in chronological order according to the dates of their deaths; each mentions one of the prominent disciples of its subject with the recurring phrase: "so and so became one of the companions of the community of followers of our *imam*" (*wa sahiba min ashab imamuna jama'a minhum*).[45] While linked directly to only a single teacher, the subjects of each *tabaqa* are tied together vertically as common descendants of the teachers and transmitters of the preceding layer, back to the generation of Ibn Hanbal and his followers.

The compilers of the Hanbali *tabaqat*—themselves members of the *madhhab*—frequently depart from the biographical formula (who, when, where, scholarly achievements, reputation) to provide their readers and listeners with detailed descriptions of master and disciple relationships. Many disciples of the Hanbali school are said to have clung to their *shaykh*, attending his study circle for an extended period of time, sometimes until his death, in order to serve as his *mu'ids* and publish the legal texts they had studied with him, together with his commentaries. Ash-Sharif Abu Ja'far, who led the fight against Mu'tazili and Ash'ari scholars in eleventh-century Baghdad, studied with Qadi Abu Ya'la for more than seventy years, serving as his *mu'id* in his lectures on the *furu'* (the doctrine of the branches—that is, the applied law) and jurisprudence (*'ilm usul al-fiqh*). As he excelled in his knowledge of the *madhhab*'s doctrine, he began teaching and issuing legal decisions during the lifetime of his *shaykh*. Compiling a book on *masaʾil*, or disputed legal questions, in which he explicated matters concerning prayer and purification according to the *madhhab*, Abu Jaʿfar followed Abu Yaʿla's method (*tariqa*). But Abu Jaʿfar's devotion to his *shaykh* extended beyond the adoption of his methods in dealing with legal questions to include an extensive religious outlook and perception of ethical conduct. Thus, in his piety, his modesty, his adherence to the path of righteousness, as well as in his rejection of the "innovators" (*ahl al-bidaʿ*), he is said to have followed the "way" of his master (*salika nahj* al-Walid as-saʾid).[46]

Indeed, biographers pay as much attention to the acquisition of codes of upright behavior in the transmitting process as to the body of "knowledge" imparted. The belief that the *shaykh* passed on his virtues (*manaqib*) and morals (*akhlaq*), or even the divine blessing (*baraka*) with which he was believed to be endowed—all the attributes that made him indispensable—was most likely adopted from Sufism, just as orthodox Sufis borrowed the idea that education under a *shaykh* should not be divorced from his writings from the ʿulamaʾ.[47] Thus, in addition to teaching the law and transmitting traditions to his disciple, Abu Bakr al-ʿAlathi, Abu Yaʿla bestowed his *baraka* upon him, whereby he became pious and ascetic (*fawada barakatahu ʿalayhi fasara zahidan ʿabidan*).[48] A collection of anecdotes about the moral attitudes and personal habits of celebrated teachers constitutes a series of role models. Included in the pages of biographical dictionaries—the Hanbali *tabaqat* in particular—are countless individuals known for their piety (*ʿibada*) and asceticism (*zuhd*), more than for their intellectual abilities and scholarly achievements. Sufi values and practices of altruism, austerity, self discipline, and self control, without the *tasawwuf*—the quest for mystical reunification with God through the annulment of the self (*fanaʾ*)—were the attributes of those who were considered role models.

Similarly, their attraction to asceticism infers a critique of materialism and worldliness without a complete renouncement of the world. Thus, these moderate ascetics, representatives of an old and continuous socio-religious current in Islam—though renouncing the patronage of men of wealth and power, and abstaining from self-indulgence—would be active participants in religious public life, as well as in learned circles, and even work for their living.[49] Abu al-ʿAbbas ash-Shami, a disciple of Abu Yaʿla who became an ascetic (*tazahada*), resigned the position of *shahid*, or witness notary, which he held for a short time only, and shut himself up in his home, though he always attended the Friday prayers in one of the great mosques of Baghdad.[50]

A more telling anecdote is that which describes the personal habits of self-control and austerity of Abu ʿAbd Allah b. al-Baghdadi, another Hanbali legal scholar who was among the most prominent *hadith* teachers of the *madhhab*. He never slept unless sleep overcame him, and as he fell asleep holding an inkwell or a drinking bowl, there were always stains on his body and face. A detailed description of his austerity and modesty follows: he never entered the public bath (*hammam*); never shaved his head, but cut his hair with shears when too long; he washed his clothes with a small amount of cold water, and ate only poor quality barley bread. When asked about this choice of diet, he replied: "Barley and wheat bread are all the same to me."[51]

The sources do not provide us with any indication of an organized community (*jamaʿa*) of *zuhad* and Sufis in Baghdad during the period covered by this study. Nor has present scholarship inquired into the internal divergences and nuances of Islamic asceticism and their social meanings. What we do know, however, shows that shared ideals and forms of proper conduct could bring scholars together, as much as an intensive study of the law within a certain *madhhab* could do.[52] Abu al-Wafaʾ Tahir al-Baghdadi, for example, attached himself to the *zuhad* (*sahiba az-zuhad*) while studying law according the *madhhab* of Ibn Hanbal.[53] Abu Ismaʿil al-Harawi al-Ansari, a Hanbali scholar who excelled in all the Islamic sciences and who was the leader of "the people of the Sunna" (*ahl as-sunna*) in his hometown of Herat (in eastern Iran), adopted the Sufi way of life or behavior (*sira at-tasawwuf*). He was never preoccupied with earnings, remaining satisfied with the same few things that pleased the Sufis. He never took a thing from the sultans or the elite of the regime (*arbab ad-dawla*), nor paid them a visit. The money he received from his disciples in his *majlis* was spent on bread and meat only. He not only adopted Sufi values, but was also closely associated with them. At the end of each day of teaching, he joined the Sufis in their *ribat*, praying and eating with them, as one among equals.[54]

As a path embraced by many men of religious learning, *ʿibada* and *zuhd*, both as perceptions of proper conduct and as actual practices, transcended the alleged lines of division between the ʿulamaʾ and the Sufis. No wonder then that many legal scholars living in eleventh-century Baghdad—Hanbalis in particular—bear the appellations *ʿabid*, *zahid*, and *Sufi*. ʿUlamaʾ and Sufis taught or studied together in mosques, *ribats*, and even in madrasas, grouping themselves around the same *shaykh* who combined the role of jurist or *hadith* transmitter with that of the Sufi guide.[55]

However, it was still the knowledge of the prophetic traditions, that above anything else, tied members of different schools of law and thought together. Representing the Islamic heritage common to all Muslims, and involving the entire learned society as well as a very large number of Muslims in general, the study and transmission of *hadith* blurred the boundaries between the ʿulamaʾ and the Sufis, and created overlapping scholarly networks which cut across affiliation to the legal schools. Members of the various schools of eleventh-century Baghdad routinely sat side by side in the same *halqa*s for the transmission of *hadith*, and a member of one school could be proud of having studied under a member of the other. Consequently, a celebrated teacher's student, even his closest disciple, was not necessarily of his legal school. The Hanbali *shaykh*, Abu ʿAli al-Hashimi (d. 428/1037), known for his several works on Hanbalism, among them *al-Irshad* and *Sarkh al-Khiraqi* (one of the many commentaries written on the *Mukhtasar* by the celebrated tenth-century *muhaddith* al-Khiraqi), led a study circle in al-Mansur Mosque. Both ash-Shirazi and al-Khatib al-Baghdadi, two of the most renowned scholars of the Shafiʿi school in Baghdad, studied *hadith* under al-Hashimi and speak very highly of him in their biographical dictionaries.[56] Abu Tahir b. al-Ghubairi (d. 432/1040) is another Hanbali scholar to whom ash-Shirazi dedicated a long biographical note in his *tabaqat*, describing him as one of his close associates and taking pride in his friendship.[57] The Hanbali school in Baghdad was self-contained: the entire education of its ʿulamaʾ was usually acquired within their own *madhhab*. At least in one case, however, Hanbalis were attracted to a noted Shafiʿi scholar, the *faqih* and *hadith*-transmitter, Abu ʿAbd Allah an-Nawqani, known as Fakhr ad-Din (d. 592/1195). Described by his biographer as one of the leading Shafiʿi scholars of his time, as well as a pious man (*ʿabid*), he came to Baghdad from Nawqan in Azerbaijan and attracted a large group of students. Several of the students who gathered around him (*ijtamaʿa ʿalayhi*) were affiliated with the Hanbali school.[58] These disciples most likely continued attending one of his *halqa*s after he assumed the professorship in al-Qaysariyya Madrasa erected for the Shafiʿis, and where enrollment was restricted to members of the *madhhab*.

Patronage of one law school by members of another through control over posts was another source of overlapping scholarly networks. Students of both the Hanafi and Hanbali schools were obliged to study *fiqh* under the Damaghani family of chief judges in order to obtain their "law degrees," or to become *shuhud*, witness notaries.

During the thirty years he served as *qadi al-qudat*, Abu ʿAbd Allah ad-Damaghani, head of the family, "graduated" a great number of people, some of whom he appointed to key positions and who became his most fervent followers (*ashab*). Among members of the Hanbali school whom he accepted as *shuhud* were the Sharif Abu Jaʿfar, leader of the Hanbali faction, and Ibn ʿAqil, the famous Hanbali jurist and theologian.[59]

Studying with a *shaykh* of another legal school sometimes resulted in a change of affiliation from one school to another. Abu al-Fath al-Barhan, for example, was originally affiliated with the Hanbali school, while reading the collection of sound *hadiths* of al-Bukhari with the Hanafi scholar Abu Talib az-Zainabi. At a certain point he attached himself to the leading scholars of the Shafiʿi *madhhab*, and was eventually nominated to the position of *mudarris* at the prestigious Nizamiyya, where he was a tremendously popular teacher.[60] If, however, the change from one school to another was clearly in quest of material benefits, the scholar was subject to criticism. A good example of this is Abu Bakr al-Mubarak (d. 612/1215). Born in Wasit, he moved to Baghdad in his early youth and attached himself to some of its Hanbali jurists and grammarians. Some time later he abandoned the Hanbali school, applying himself instead to the Hanafi system of jurisprudence. But when the position of teacher of the Arabic language in the Nizamiyya Madrasa became vacant, he moved to the Shafiʿi school in order to obtain the post. As a result, one of the poets of Baghdad addressed the following verses to him: "Say to him: you did so because you had nothing to eat. It was not for devotion that you adopted the doctrines of ash-Shafiʿi, but because you desired to obtain a profitable result. You will soon go over to the school of Malik; mark what I say!"[61]

These are but a few examples of ʿulama' of different schools engaged in common scholarly pursuits, bound by shared ideals of proper behavior and by ties of patronage, even changing affiliation from one *madhhab* to another, long before (as well as long after) the appearance of the madrasa. This is not surprising at all if we bear in mind that theological-doctrinal perspectives, rather than legal interpretation, constituted the source of animosity between the religiously defined factions, turning the *madhahib* into solidarity groups. The Hanbalis mobilized their followers against those Hanafis and Shafiʿis whom they suspected of having rationalist tendencies; Shafiʿis and Hanafis protested against the attempts of Hanbali theologians and preachers to impose their rigid orthodoxy,[62] and accused them of holding the false doctrine of anthropomorphism (*tashbih, tajsim*).[63]

During the last decades of the eleventh century, however, though still constituting a source of religious factionalism, the struggle against rationalism seems to have lost the vigor it had early in that century. In their unpredictable and unstable milieu, ʿulamaʾ of the different schools sought to furnish a set of concepts based on correct Islamic communal and general behavior. To this end they set aside doctrinal differences and acted as a unified group. One of the most telling accounts of action for a common cause is that describing how ash-Sharif Abu Jaʿfar, the head of the Hanbalis, and Abu Ishaq ash-Shirazi, the leader of the Shafiʿis, fought together against the spread of immorality, regarded as the cause for the great flood of the year A.H. 464. Mobilized by their *shaykhs*, the Hanbalis gathered in al-Qasr Mosque and called ash-Shirazi and his followers to join them in their struggle against prostitution, the charging of interest, and the drinking of wine. The two *shaykhs* demanded that the caliph, al-Qaʾim, destroy the brothels and uproot the other malicious iniquities of the local population. At the same time, a letter was sent to the Seljuk Sultan informing him of this demand.[64]

By the time the multisystem Mustansiriyya Madrasa was founded in Baghdad (in 631/1233), the debates over proper Islamic creed and behavior between the factions, named after the schools and led by their *shaykhs*, had faded away. Consequently, affiliation with the *madhahib* of Baghdad had become increasingly formal, having meaning in the legal context only. There were still some differences on matters of principles of interpretation of the law, but most of them were of minor importance. Moreover, even after the process of the law schools' consolidation was complete (around the end of the thirteenth century), there was still room for diverse opinions, and moving from one school to another, even remaining unaffiliated, was common.

If, the madrasas were not centers around which ʿulamaʾ groupings were formed and crystallized; if the school of law for which they were founded was not the prime collectivity with which the ʿulamaʾ identified themselves, and through which they acted, then what social effect did the establishment of madrasas have? The following chapter seeks the answer to this question in the biographies of the ʿulamaʾ who taught or studied in the madrasas of Baghdad—the career options open to them, the career paths they followed, and the ways they themselves regarded the new educational frameworks and profited from them.

CHAPTER 5

༄

MECHANISMS OF
INCLUSION AND EXCLUSION

Abu Mas'ud related that he had heard the Messenger of Allah
saying: "The man who knows most of the Book of Allah shall act as
imam of a people; and if there are people equal in their knowledge
of the Koran, then he who has greater knowledge of the *sunna*
(*hadith*), then he is first in *hijra*; and if they are equal in *hijra*, then
he who is older in years."

Muslim, *Sahih*: Book of Prayer (*Kitab az-zakat*)

In the eleventh century a religious establishment, composed of
men profoundly learned in Islamic religious law and regularly employed to carry on their scholarly activities, had not yet been consolidated. The educational system, as we have seen, stressed the
importance of *hadith* as a central ingredient of *'ilm*; hence anyone
devoted to the study and the transmission of the prophetic traditions
was likely to be considered an *'alim*. This included a large number of
partially educated individuals from widely different walks of life.[1]

The idea that all those versed in the words of the Prophet
Muhammad might be considered 'ulama' was raised in a legal decision (*fatwa*) attributed to the celebrated eleventh-century Shafi'i
scholar al-Kiya al-Harrasi. At the same time, this *fatwa* reflects concerns over the openness of the intellectual elite. In answer to the
question whether *hadith* transmitters could be included in a testa-
ment (*wasiyya*) supporting the 'ulama' and *fuqaha'*, he responded:
"Of course, why not?," basing his *fatwa* on the *hadith*: "Those who
learn by heart forty *hadith*s concerning the religious matters of my

95

community (*umma*), God will restore to life among the 'ulama' on the Day of Judgment."[2] The fact that famous Muslim scholars of the high medieval period—the example of Abu al-Fadl al-'Askalani (d. 852/ 1449) comes to mind—devoted their dictionaries to *hadith* transmitters further indicates that knowledge of *hadith* was still perceived, at least by some 'ulama', as a primary characteristic of their group.[3]

This chapter seeks to explain how the 'ulama' of Baghdad emerged as a more exclusive and structured group beginning in the late eleventh century, though never constituting an institutionalized class such as the clerical elite in the medieval West. In particular, we will explain how a small elite of legal experts utilized the system of transmission and the newly founded madrasas to reinforce its own coherence and self-perpetuation.

Membership

Little information is available regarding the socio-economic background of medieval scholars at any given time, except in the few cases in which their professional *nisba*s are indicated. Authors of biographical dictionaries probably did not consider information about the scholar's profession relevant. Compiling their works for scholarly purposes, they considered the extent to which the transmitter was considered reliable far more important than his social status. Moreover, even in cases in which the scholar's professional *nisba* is indicated, it is not clear whether he himself, or his family, belonged to one or another of the social and professional classes (*asnaf*), or whether these individuals were primarily religious scholars who engaged in secular professions, or vice versa.[4]

For all the difficulty in determining the scholars' socio-economic background, a glance at the professional *nisba*s of individual 'ulama' (listed in figure 5.1, below) might support the idea of unrestricted inclusion in their ranks in terms of profession and family background. Nearly one-half of those whose names appear in biographical dictionaries during this period, for whom we have professional *nisba*s, were merchants (*tujjar*) or came from merchant families. It was not uncommon for merchants to send their sons to be educated by religious scholars in order to acquire a knowledge of the Koran and the *hadith*, as well as of law. One of these was Abu Mansur al-Baghdadi (d. 429/1037–38), who studied law with the Shafi'i scholar al-Isfara'ini and later rose to the professorship of Shafi'i law in one of the teaching mosques in Nishapur, to which he emigrated. Born to a wealthy

Figure 5.1
The Secular Professions and Family Background of
5th/11th–Century 'Ulama' of Baghdad

	MUHADDITH	QARI'	FAQIH	ZAHID, 'ABID, SUFI	TOTAL
GOVERNMENT AND QUASI-GOVERNMENT OFFICIALS:					
AMIR army commander	1 (1)				
KATIB clerk	8 (2)		(2)		16
NASIKH copyist	1		1		
GREAT MERCHANTS:					
BAZZAZ cloth merchant	13 (2)	1	1 (1)	1	
DAQQAQ flour merchant	3 (4)	(1)			
FAWALI bean merchant	1				
KHASHAB lumber dealer	1				44
QAZZAZ silk merchant	2	1			
RAZZAZ rice dealer	3		(1)		
SAWWAF wool merchant			(1)		
TAJIR merchant	4		3		
VENDORS:					
BAQQAL grocer	6	1	(1)		
HINNA'I henna plant vendor	2				

Figure 5.1 (continued)

	MUHADDITH	QARI'	FAQIH	ZAHID, 'ABID, SUFI	TOTAL
KAYYAL corn vendor	1				13
QADURI cooking pot vendor			(1)		
TABBAN straw vendor		(1)			
BANNA' builder	1		(1)		
DABBAGH tanner	1				
GHAZZAL yarn spinner	4				
HADDAD blacksmith	2	(1)		(1)	
KHAYYAT tailor		(1)	3	(1)	
NAJJAR carpenter	1	(1)			29
SARRAJ saddler		1	(1)		
SABBAGH cloth dyer	4	(1)		(1)	
SAFFAR brass & coppersmith			2		
SA'IGH goldsmith		(1)			
DALLAL FI AL-AMLAK real estate dealer		(1)			
HARRATH plowman			1		
JANNAN gardener		(1)			
KHADDAM domestic servant	1				8
SAWWAQ animal driver			2		

Figure 5.1 (continued)

	MUHADDITH	QARI'	FAQIH	ZAHID, 'ABID, SUFI	TOTAL
SARAFI money changer		1			
TAHHAN miller	1				
	61 (16)	13 (3)	5 (9)	1 (2)	80+(30)=110

Notes:
1. The data are derived from all indications of the professional *nisbas* of individual 'ulama'.
2. Parentheses indicate that the secular profession relates to the scholar's family background, rather than to the scholar himself.
3. Not included are the 'ulama' of the madrasa.

Baghdadi merchant family (*wa-kana min arbab al-amwal al-kathir*), "he possessed such great riches that he never had to rely on his teaching as a source of livelihood."[5]

While some of those from the different *asnaf* that overlapped the 'ulama' acquired legal learning, the majority were *hadith* transmitters. Among them were the civil officials (*kuttab*), or the "men of the pen" (*arbab al-qalam*). Perhaps more than any other professional class, the *kuttab* emerged as a definable coherent group. To begin with, under the early 'Abbasids (from the mid-eighth to the tenth century) this peculiar class was composed primarily of non-Muslims of Iranian origins. Those who converted to Islam continued to admire the pre-Islamic models of the secretarial culture inherited from their forefathers. Although it was not necessary to be a son of a *katib* to practice this profession, families of *kuttab* began to arise at a rather early stage of the 'Abbasid era—the famous Barmakis come to mind. In a society sufficiently fluid and mobile to permit appointments to public office, regardless of family background, sons of merchants and landowners also held top-level positions in the 'Abbasid central administration, even as viziers. Conversely, there were *kuttab* who engaged in trade and owned estates. Together, members of the early 'Abbasid bureaucratic "class" formed a recognizable social group, proud of its cultural style and authority.[6] The *kuttab* derived the necessary linguistic and literary background for their work from "stylistic guide books," in addition to other works on the training of secretaries composed by the *kuttab* themselves. They contained all the knowledge required by the "cultured and educated man," the *adib*.[7] Although many of the *kuttab* had become Muslims by the end of the third Muslim century, their pride in their earlier traditions, their professions, and the spirit in which their work was carried out created a spiritual and social antagonism between themselves and religious scholars. In a well-known treatise, al-Jahiz, the famous ninth-century Arab essayist, renounced the arrogance of secretaries and their sympathies toward Iranian traditions. Indeed, he accused them of manifesting only lukewarm support for the Islamic cause, neglecting the Islamic sciences, and even the Koran, preferring instead the outlandish of Sassanian worthies.[8]

During the Buyid and Seljuk periods, though still following a somewhat different educational path which emphasized mastery in the official styles of handwriting and composition, some *kuttab* demonstrated a keen interest in religious education, primarily in *hadith*. Abu Hasan b. Hilal (d. 423/1032) the son of a courtier, was a celebrated *katib* skilled in the art of writing. He heard prophetic traditions which had passed through a chain of transmitters extending back to the Hanbali *muhaddith* an-Najjad (d. 347/954), and was himself considered a trustworthy transmitter.[9] Abu al-Mansur al-Katib (d. 465/1072), one of the scribes in the service of Nizam al-Mulk, is praised by his biographer for his thorough knowledge of the Koran and the *hadith*;[10] so is Nizam al-Mulk' son, Abu al-Hasan Ahmad, who succeeded him in the office of the vizier. He heard a great number of prophetic traditions, as well as acquiring a thorough knowledge of the Arabic language and grammar. His biographer describes him as a man of high aspirations, highly qualified, attributing his promotion to the office of the Sultan's vizier to his broad learning.[11]

Military officers are also included in the lists of *hadith* scholars. Abu 'Abd Allah an-Niqash, for example, the commander of the pilgrimage caravan to Mecca (*amir al-hajj*), heard prophetic traditions from a chain going back to the Hanbali *shaykh* az-Zaghuni. Later, after qualifying to transmit *hadith*s on his own, he would dictate them on the way to the *hajj*.[12] The study of the prophetic traditions during the period under discussion was so widely accessible that even domestic servants are mentioned in the biographical dictionaries as students of *hadith*. Playing a formative role in the shaping of Islamic society, the oral transmission of *hadith* was never exclusively for a learned elite, but rather involved a great number of people who might become 'ulama'.

Entry to the Ranks of the 'Ulama'

Authors of biographical dictionaries describe a particular course of study which young people seeking religious learning were expected to pass. Education usually began at a very young age among the child's relatives. In addition to members of the child's family, private tutors, and neighborhood Koran schools (the *maktab* or the *kuttab*) provided the foundations of education, which included recitation of the Koran, basic literacy, and elementary knowledge of arithmetic.[13] Those proceeding to a more advanced level of religious education would normally begin by attending the recitation of *hadith*.

The selection of a teacher was of critical importance for a number of reasons. By studying with a respected and accomplished teacher, one could learn a greater number of traditions, as well as benefit from his authority for the sake of one's own reputation as a *muhaddith*. Moreover, by selecting an older teacher a young student could increase his chances of eventually becoming the sole surviving *muhaddith* in a particular location to transmit *hadith* on the direct authority of that teacher. The biographical dictionaries frequently mention boys who were later to become famous scholars, being introduced to *hadith* at extraordinarily young ages by their fathers or other close relatives who would also occasionally provide their sons with a basic education in religious law. Other students, not born to 'ulama' families, were sent to study with famous scholars of their native towns. Then, usually as a young man, the typical student of religion would begin to travel from one place to another in order to collect prophetic traditions, study texts with renowned scholars, and obtain *ijaza*s certifying his proficiency and inserting him into a chain of teachers and transmitters.

Notwithstanding the stages aspiring students were expected to pass, neither rules nor institutions seem to have interfered with their search for learning. The best available evidence suggests that admission into the study circle, the *halqa*, wherever it was convened, was unrestricted in terms of age, origin, or previous educational path. Formal procedures of admission, gradation, and authorization were similarly absent. Nor does there seem to have been any limitation on the size of the audience. Students were free to attend any study circle they wished, presumably with the permission of the teacher, and many lectures appear to have taken place with open doors.

By the twelfth century the number of institutions teaching law—the madrasas and ordinary mosques (*masjids*)—increased steadily. Still, as has already been shown, the transmission of religious lore in this society was never limited to a particular institution. Rather, it took place wherever the *shaykh* sat down, often as part of acts of worship, public sermonizing, and popular religious celebration.[14] At the same time, there appears to be no real distinction between formal (exclusive) and informal (public, inclusive) forums of instruction. This blurring of distinctions was nowhere revealed more clearly than in the sessions intended for the transmission of *hadith*, where, in addition to students, large segments of society would gather to display their piety and demonstrate their interest in this field of Islamic learning.

Despite the apparent informality and openness of this system of transmission, hierarchies or barriers developed which limited access to knowledge, or at least barred participation in the transmission of legal learning, thereby setting apart a learned elite. At the heart of this process lay the social uses of the ideals and methods of transmission of knowledge formulated by earlier generations of Muslim jurists and thinkers to guarantee their control over the preservation and dissemination of religious lore. In other words, rather than limiting the ability of the 'ulama' to control admission into their groupings, this system served as a mechanism of inclusion and exclusion in the society of the learned.

True knowledge derives only from a learned person, not from books, insisted Badr ad-Din b. Jama'a, an early fourteenth-century Shafi'i jurist. Those who attempt to rest their education on the written word are guilty of "one of the most scandalous of acts," for "taking books [alone] leads to spelling errors and mispronunciation."[15] But the insistence on the absolute necessity of learning from individuals and not from books alone stemmed from reasons other than accurate reading and transmission of the texts which constituted the body of Islamic religious and legal sciences. Self-education by books might have posed a challenge to leading scholars within the various schools of law and theology. Only they could impart true knowledge and grant authority to the very texts transmitted from one generation of scholars to the next. Moreover, there probably also existed the threat that individual, private, or silent reading could lead to misinterpretation, or perhaps even introduce innovations.

By the time of Ibn Jama'a, earlier patterns of oral transmission had long faded away. Still, for all the existence of educational institutions and the availability of written texts, an individual could be recognized as a scholar only by receiving an *ijaza* from the author of an authoritative text, or from a chain of transmitters extending back to the author. In the case of religious law, an aspiring student had to do more than collect *ijazas* from as many as distinguished jurists as possible. He also had to become an adherent of a leading *shaykh* within one or the other schools of law, devoting himself to intense study under the master, following his "path." As demonstrated above, included in this "path" was not only the master's legal method, but also his religious outlook and ethical posture. These modes of transmission, and the social practices that grew up around them, might explain how, though theoretically religious knowledge and education was available to all, the specialized study of the law was in fact a privilege. Given the determination of Muslim jurists and thinkers during the Sunni revival to define the parameters of legitimate knowledge and transmit that knowledge to later generations of Muslim scholars, it is not surprising that the old system of gathering and preserving the texts constituting the body of Islamic religious and legal sciences persisted, at least as a model.

To the cultural and social practices used by the ʿulamaʾ of eleventh-century Baghdad as a means to guarantee the distinctiveness and perpetuation of their group, were added the new madrasas, sponsored by the Seljuks later in that century to support their educational and legal activities. As has already been argued, it was not around madrasas that scholarly groupings were formed, acquiring their cultural distinction and useful identities. Nor did the rise of the madrasa change the highly personal process by which individuals were recognized as scholars, gaining prominence among the ʿulamaʾ "class." Indeed, some of the noted Baghdadi ʿulamaʾ of the late eleventh and twelfth centuries taught outside the institution. Nonetheless, blessed with large endowments given in perpetuity for the instruction of the Islamic sciences, the rise and proliferation of madrasas in Baghdad served to consolidate a small local elite of legal experts whose members utilized the new schools for their own needs.

In evaluating the social significance of the appearance and proliferation of madrasas in Baghdad, the following discussion focuses primarily on the biographies of teachers and student ʿulamaʾ clearly associated with these new schools during of the late eleventh and first half of the twelfth centuries. This period covers four to five scholastic generations, which corresponds to approximately three genealogical generations. The nature and development of the various scholarly professions, career options, and career patterns of the group under review, and the interplay of patronage, scholarly qualifications and family background in determining accession to academic positions, are the major themes around which this discussion revolves.

Founding a School: Career Options

Some of the finest historians of the period have noted that the foundation of madrasas played a significant role in the formation of a body of 'ulama' entirely devoted to the transmission and application of the legal and religious sciences, relying on educational or legal activities for its livelihood.[16] In Baghdad—the cradle of the madrasa in its mature form—this trend toward the so-called professionalization of the 'ulama' occurred as early as the first century of the madrasa's appearance. Thus, in contrast with the large number of part-time semiprofessional 'ulama' living in the city before the introduction of the madrasa, and those outside the institution (primarily scholars of the Koran and the *hadith*), the 'ulama' clearly associated with the madrasa appear to be full-time scholars of religion. An examination of their professional *nisba*s may indicate that this change in the ratio of part-time 'ulama' occurred over a period of several generations of fathers and their descendants (figure 5.2). In the first instance, this transition meant the procurement of salaried positions (*manasib*, sing. *mansab*).

Information about the scholarly and bureaucratic positions held by the 'ulama' for whom we have clear association with the madrasa (figure 5.3, below) provides an insight into the variety of career options open to the group under review. The data are arranged in four professional categories, each subdivided into several types of positions: a. academic professions in the endowed madrasa (Category I—the group under review); b. legal professions (Category II); c. religious functionaries (Category III); d. bureaucratic professions (Category IV). The columns show the several types of positions within the first category and the number of individuals holding them. The rows show the distribution of positions held by members of the first category in each of the remaining three groups, thus indicating a crossing of career lines.

As indicated above, there are no deeds of *waqf* for the madrasas founded in Baghdad during the late eleventh and twelfth centuries, with the exception of a budget for the Nizamiyya Madrasa and its beneficiaries. Nor are there any treatises on education that might shed light on the functioning of the madrasas. The authors of these

Figure 5.2
The Geographical Origins and Family Background of
5th/11th–Century 'Ulama' of the Madrasas of Baghdad
(549/1067–610/1213)

FAMILY BACKGROUND	NATIVE-BORN	NATIVE-BORN DESCENDANT OF IMMIGRANTS	IMMIGRANT	TRANSIENT	TOTAL
'Ulama'	8	7	4	8	27
Merchants	1 (1)	(1)	1		4
Landowners	(1)				1
Craftsmen	(4)			(1)	5
Clerks			(1)	(1)	2
Soldiers	1				1
Commoners (Poor)				1	1
Unknown Background	14	2	30	18	64
TOTAL:	30	10	36	29	105

Notes:
1. Included are only 'ulama' for whom we have a clear association with the madrasas of Baghdad, and whose places of birth and death are indicated.
2. Parentheses indicate that the secular profession relates to the scholar's family background rather than to the scholar himself.

invaluable sources, such as Ibn Jama'a, Muhammad b. al-Hajj, and Taj ad-Din as-Subki, lived in the fourteenth century and were from cities other than Baghdad. Taken together, however, single areas of documentation, such as biographical dictionaries and contemporary observations, give the impression that the size of the endowments guaranteed the perpetuity of these new establishments and provided ample means of support for those who assumed various salaried positions within them. The staff of the madrasa probably depended on its size and the wishes of the founder. In addition to the *mudarris* and occasionally his deputy (*na'ib-mudarris*), there were a number of teachers of Koran recitation, the teacher of *hadith* and of Arabic grammar (*shaykh al-qira'a, shaykh al-hadith, shaykh an-nahw*), as well as a number of assistants in the various fields of study. There could also be a librarian (*khazin dar*) and a preacher of the "academic"

Figure 5.3

The Professional Positions Held by the 'Ulama' of the Madrasas (459/1067–610/1213)

	MUDARRIS	NAʾIB-MUDARRIS	MUʾID	MUʾID/MUDARRIS*	MUFID	SHAYKH AL-QIRAʾA	SHAYKH AL-HADITH	NAHWI	WAʾIZ	MUʾID WAʾIZ	KHAZIN AL-KUTUB	MUʾID KHAZIN AL-KUTUB	FUQAHA**	
	28	1	5	9	3	2	1	3	4	1	1	1	6	58
Category II														
QADI	5		2										6	13
NAʾIB-QADI (deputy-judge)	1		1											2
NAʾIB-QADI, MUFTI	1									1				2
QADI AL-QUDAT (chief-judge)	1													1
SHAHID (witness-notary)	1													11
SHAHID, QADI, MUFTI	1													1
SHAHID, MUFTI			1									1		7
MUFTI***	4			2										1
MUHTASIB (market inspector)	1												1	1
ʿADIL (jurist adjunct assigned to a judge)														
Category III														
IMAM (prayer leader)							1							1
khatib (preacher of the Friday sermon)	1		1											13

												TOTAL
Category IV												
NAZIR AWQAF (waqf contoller)	2							1				1	5
AMIN (trust officer)		1											1
WAKIL (financial agent)	1												1
Katib (secretary)	1												1
NAZIR DAWLA (financial bureaus controller)												1	1
Categories II & IV													
Qadi Al-Qudat, Na'ib-Vizier	1												1
Mufti, Nazir	1												1
TOTAL	50	2	11	11	3	2	2	4	4	2	1	10	103

Notes:

   * Refers to students in the madrasa who first served as muʿids and then assumed the professorship.

   ** Considered are only fuqahaʾ who obtained professional positions.

   *** Every *faqih* was both a lawyer and a jurisconsult, one who knows the law and issues legal opinions. listed are *fuqahaʾ* who became renown *muftis*.

sermon (*wa'iz*). Three positions frequently referred to in the sources have been selected for the purpose of this discussion: the *mudarris* and his two assistants, the repetitor (*mu'id*) and the docent of law (*mufid*).

A *mudarris* in the endowed college was a salaried official, his appointment often marked by an inaugural lecture, noted by the historians for many years after the foundation of the madrasa. Their accounts may attest that, while far from developing into a defined occupational type in terms of salary arrangement, teaching in the madrasa was considered to be a rewarding "craft" (*sina'a*). The first clear definition of the professor's functions and duties appears in a critique by Taj ad-Din as-Subki the *mudarris* in *Mu'id an-ni'am wa-mubid al-niqam* ("The repetitor of blessings and the destroyer of misfortunes")—a work devoted to defining the proper behavior of those employed in a variety of teaching, religious, and administrative tasks. Upset with professors who lacked sufficient qualifications for their posts, as-Subki says:

> One of the most reprehensible deeds is that of a *mudarris* who memorizes two or three lines from a book, takes his seat, delivers them, then rises and leaves the classroom. Such a person, if incapable of anything but this amount, is not fit to teach law. . . . If, however, the professor of law is capable of more than that amount, but lightens the burden of study (*yusahhil*) and makes excuses for the students, that is also shameful. . . . On the other hand, if learned men were to safeguard learning, and the professor of law among them were to give the teaching of law its full due, by taking his seat, delivering a fair amount of learning, expounding upon it as a master scholar by posing and receiving questions, by objecting and responding, speaking at length and speaking well in such a manner that when there is a layman in attendance, or a student . . . such a person would know himself to be incapable of accomplishing as much. . . . This being the case, the unqualified person would not covet such a level, and laymen would not aspire to take the posts of learned men.[17]

A professor, according to Subki's description, was to be an expert in Islamic religious law and its ancillaries, devoted to instruction in holy knowledge, and adhering to the ideals of proper transmission. Ideally, he was to do more than memorize the texts he transmitted and hand them down accurately. He would also encourage disputation (*munazara*) on controversial questions in order to teach his students how to derive the law from its sources.

During the Seljuk period, the sources at our disposal suggest no clear definition of the *mudarris'* functions and responsibilities in the transmission of the law to his students. Similarly, the teachers of law in the madrasas are not described in terms different from their contemporaries outside the institution, or designated by distinctive titles and honorifics. On occasion, however, biographers provide us with a glimpse into the qualifications expected of those chosen as the schools' professors. Their accounts may attest that, in their hopes of ensuring the quality of teaching talent in their institutions, founders shared the same concerns as the ʿulamaʾ. Abu Muhammad al-Fami ash-Shirazi, who, for one year shared the professorship in the Nizamiyya Madrasa with at-Tabari, was eventually removed from his chair in the madrasa. Although his biographer does not specify the reason for his removal, he states elsewhere that ash-Shirazi (whom he describes as one of the prominent Shafiʿi scholars of his age) failed to correctly cite the traditions he transmitted, and therefore was accused of falsifying *hadith*s.[18] Criteria for appointment to the endowed chair range from competence in teaching the law and its foundations to the professor's personal merit and esteem. Abu al-Qasim Yahya al-Baghdadi, known as Jalal ad-Din (d. 595/1199), was nominated to the post of professor at Madrasa Darb Dhahab. The leader, or *raʾis*, of the Shafiʿis in Iraq, he is described by his biographers as an outstanding legal scholar versed in the *khilaf* (divergence of the law) and *jadal* (dialectic), possessing the traits of leadership (*riyasa*) and prestige.[19]

As in the *halqa*s in the mosques, many students became their *shaykh's* assistants, either as repetitors, *muʿid*s, or assistants-at-large, *mufid*s ("one who benefits [another]"), "a sort of walking encyclopedia" for students in need of extra help and guidance."[20] Existing well before the advent of the madrasa, the function of the *muʿid* was peculiar to the field of law itself, rather than to particular educational institutions; the term *mufid* is used also in the fields of *hadith* and Koranic studies. As-Subki deals with the two functions in *Muʿid al-niʿam*, and outlines the responsibilities of the *mufid* in the transmission of knowledge to students after that of the *muʿid*. The *muʿid*, according to as-Subki, should explain the lesson to the students, be of use to them, and perform the function required by the term *iʿada*—that is, repeating and explaining the lessons dictated by the professor until the students under his charge have mastered them.

As for the *mufid*, his duty is to pursue the study of the law beyond that of most students to such a level which would enable him to benefit them.[21] Our sources do not clearly differentiate between the responsibilities of the *mu'id* and the *mufid* in the transmission of knowledge to students. Yet despite the similarity in their basic function as teaching assistants, there appears to be a practical distinction between the two positions. For while the biographical dictionaries refer to the *i'ada* as a paid position for which the endowments of particular schools made provisions, the *ifada* ("to benefit") in many cases does not appear to be an endowed position.[22]

Aside from the chance of obtaining employment in the madrasa, an education in the new law schools provided access to a host of traditional employment opportunities, including that of the *qadi*, the *shahid*, the *mufti*, the *khatib*, and the *imams* who led the prayers in the hundreds of mosques throughout the city. Nearly a third of the total number of 103 madrasa scholars surveyed assumed positions in the administration of the law (*qada'*), primarily as *qadi*s (figure 5.3). It was not uncommon for scholars to hold the posts of the *qadi*, *na'ib-qadi* (deputy judge), and *shahid* simultaneously with a professorship of law in a madrasa. The Hanafi jurist Abu al-Husain al-Yazdi (d. 571/1175), for example, was a *mudarris* at the Sultan Mahmud Madrasa as well as in the great Hanafi madrasa of Abu Hanifa, and at the same time held the post of *na'ib-qadi*. Upon moving to Mosul, he taught Hanafi law in one of the city's madrasas and continued to serve as a *na'ib-qadi*.[23] We also find the chief *qadi* Abu al-Qasim b. Abu Talib az-Zainabi (d. 543/1148) teaching the law in the great Hanafi madrasa. Unable to serve in both capacities at the same time, he nominated one of his followers as a *na'ib-mudarris* to teach in his stead.[24]

The origins and development of the various scholarly professional positions are not within the scope of the present study. Attention should be paid, nevertheless, to the nature of the top-level legal professions available to the learned elite in the period under discussion— the *qadi*ship and the *mufti*ship.

The upholder of Islamic religious law in Islamic societies ever since the classical age, the *qadi*, has been the subject of voluminous study.[25] Since the *shari'a* covers every aspect of life, the religious courts, headed by the *qadi*, theoretically regulated all aspects of public and private life, and could have no rival. There was, however, one other jurisdiction originating in earlier times: the civil court, or *mazalim*, essentially a criminal court exercising what amounted to residual jurisdiction. During the Seljuk period the administration of justice in the *mazalim* court was exercised by the sultan himself or by his agents on the basis of custom, equity, and governmental regulations, whereas the *qadi* applied the *shari'a* according to certain formal rules of evidence and procedure in his own court. This court sat in the mosque, in the *qadi*'s residence, or in some other duly appointed place. It was concerned primarily with the settlement of litigation, the execution of testaments, and matters of inheritance, escheat, the transfer of property, and the administration of the affairs of orphans, widows, and others legally incapacitated.[26]

The prevailing custom was to refuse the post of the *qadi* because it meant association with political rulers, thus hindering adjudication in accordance with the principles of the *shari'a*. But since the office involved salary and allowances, and carried moral authority and prestige, some scholars sought it eagerly. For example, when the Hanafi chief *qadi* Abu 'Abd Allah ad-Damaghani died (in 478/1085), his son sought to succeed him and, to this end, offered great sums to the caliph. This is understandable, given that large amounts of money were often sent to the chief *qadi* from outside Baghdad. The caliph, in his wish to avert suspicion that the post was for sale, offered it to the Shafi'i Abu Bakr ash-Shami who was known for his righteousness.[27]

The *qadi* had *shahid*s, a clerk, an archivist, and other salaried officials attached to his court. He also appointed deputies who had their own attendants. Since the field of *shahada* involved the composition of formal legal documents, and the *shahid*'s attestation was important in many legal matters, he had to be a man learned in religious law as well as a good calligrapher. Usually, though not invariably, the chief *qadi* under the Seljuks was also entrusted with the "general supervision" (*nazar 'amm*) of the pious endowments (*waqf*), in particular the mosques and the estates of orphans and other persons, as well as the supervision of officials in the legal administration, notably the *muhtasib* (market inspector) in the area to which he was appointed.[28] His supervision of the mosques sometimes included the power to nominate the *khatib* and the *imam*, though in Baghdad the *khatib*ship was often secured for the Hashimis, descendants of the clan of Muhammad.[29] With regard to the administration and supervision of the endowments supporting institutions of learning, there were a variety of practices during the Seljuk period. If the founder had not appointed a controller supervisor of the endowment (*nazir*), the chief *qadi* administered the *waqf* directly; if, however, as occurred in Seljuk Baghdad, each of these endowments had its private controller, the chief judge merely exercised general supervision over the administration of the *awqaf*.

Teaching law and its relation to its sources (*usul al-fiqh*), as well as the science of jurisprudence in deriving the law from its sources in higher stages of madrasa education, the madrasas produced accomplished jurisconsults known as *mufti*s. The rank of the *mufti* was considered the highest achievement in the legal sciences. He was the legal specialist sufficiently qualified to give an authoritative opinion on points of doctrine. Advisory legal opinions (*fatwa*s) were frequently sought from the *mufti*s, but these were the personal opinions of the men issuing them, rather than actual judgments rendered by the *qadi*. On the other hand, the doctrinal development of Islamic religious law owes much to the activity of the *mufti*, who acted independently of all outside power, especially governmental power. From the outset, the function of the *mufti* was essentially private. His authority was based on his reputation as a learned and pious man. His opinion had no official sanction, and a layman might resort to any scholar he knew in whom he had confidence. The individual soliciting the *mufti* for his legal opinion remunerated him; but many *mufti*s performed the service without charging a fee, especially when they had other means of support.[30] During the late thirteenth century the political rulers created a salaried post for the *mufti* and placed it in their pay. Only under the Ottomans, however, did a rigorous system emerge in which only official scholars were entitled to give authoritative opinions in court.[31] Hence, we cannot properly speak of a career as a *mufti* in the same sense that we can of a career as a *mudarris* or a *qadi*.

The ʿulamaʾ who taught in the madrasas could also enter the state bureaucracy as chancery and fiscal officials. For example, Abu al-Waudud, the son of the celebrated Shafiʿi scholar al-Mujir al-Baghdadi (d. 592/1195), taught law in a madrasa founded for him in the vicinity of Bab al-Azaj, and simultaneously held the office of the commissioner or financial agent of the government (*wakil*).[32] In addition, there were *mudarrisun* who were entrusted with administering the endowments of one or several madrasas in the city. For example, Abu al-Mahasin al-Wasiti (d. 605/1208), who taught in Madrasa Abu Hanifa, was also charged with the administration and supervision (*nazr*) of the *awqaf* of all the Hanafi madrasas in the city. The verb used to denote his nomination was *wulliyya*: to be entrusted, charged with the administration; to be appointed to the post with complete authority.[33]

Several studies have suggested that the instruction provided in the newly founded madrasas was regarded as the proper qualification for a career as secretary in the higher administration of the Seljuk state. Their underlying assumption here is that the madrasas were intended by their founders both to create and employ scholars of religion and to train loyal bureaucrats for the Seljuk administration.[34] Consequently, madrasas had an established curriculum which, in addition to Islamic religious law, could include belles-lettres (*adab*), Arabic grammar, and sometimes arithmetic and algebra.[35]

Even if studies in the madrasas of Baghdad were not restricted to Muslim law, there is nothing to attest to the existence of any program for the training of potential bureaucrats. In fact, as has already been argued, there is no evidence that madrasas had a curriculum or preferred format of learning per se. Rather, the teacher would teach the texts he himself compiled, or those passed on to him in a chain of authorities. This teaching was neither limited to a certain institution, nor does it appear to have been framed in an established curriculum.[36] The admission of men who had acquired profound learning (either from teachers in madrasas or elsewhere) into the civil administration was probably a by-product of the decline of the class of secretaries, the *kuttab*—a legacy of the Persian tradition—who had staffed the bureaucracy under the early ʿAbbasids on the one hand, and the favoring of the ʿulamaʾ as candidates for office on the other.[37]

The following description, preserved in the *History of the Seljuks of Iraq* by ʿImad ad-Din al-Isfahani, though making no mention of the madrasa, is evidence of the entry of the ʿulamaʾ into the government bureaucracies in place of the old bureaucracy:

> In his day [during the rule of Nizam al-Mulk], new groups of talented secretaries arose, joined the ranks of the civil administration and held office. His court became a permanent place of assembly for scholars and a home for religious scholars. . . . He ensured that the most honest and talented of them would be promoted to high positions in accordance with their qualifications. Whenever he heard of a religious scholar who was renowned for his scholarship, he fulfilled all his material needs and gave him many presents.[38]

The patronage of the ʿulamaʾ during the Seljuk period and their preferential treatment as candidates for office might have motivated men born to families of *kuttab* to pursue the career of an *ʿalim*, which now offered a better chance for employment and standing in society. The biography of ʿImad ad-Din himself comes to mind. Born in Isfahan to a family whose members included several secretaries and holders of high administrative positions, ʿImad ad-Din's family left Isfahan temporarily during a conflict between members of the ruling elite. ʿImad ad-Din and his brother were taken to Quchan, in the province of Khurasan, where they studied in the Koranic school (*maktab*), and frequented the Mujidiyya Madrasa. Later, ʿImad al-Din traveled with his father to Baghdad where he studied both law and *adab* at the Nizamiyya Madrasa. In A.H. 552, Ibn Hubayra, the ʿAbbasid caliph's vizier, made him his representative, first in Basra and then in Wasit. Losing his position upon Ibn Hubayra's death (in A.H. 560), ʿImad ad-Din moved to Damascus, where he was soon appointed secretary by the Ayyubid sultan Nur ad-Din, and later assumed the professorship in the Nuriyya Madrasa, afterwards called al-ʿImadiyya in his honor. His status under Nur ad-Din rose until he became the head of *diwan al-insha*ʾ (the government office for the composition of official letters and decrees), and was entrusted with governmental affairs. When Nur ad-Din died, ʿImad ad-Din was forced to leave Syria, returning only when it was invaded by Saladin.[39] Ibn Khallikan states that the high favor enjoyed by him under Saladin "placed him on a level with the most eminent men at the court, enabled him to assume the state of a vizier and to engage in the career."[40] Abu Nasr ʿUthman (d. 561/1165), grandson of Nizam al-Mulk, was another descendent of a family of *kuttab* who rose to high position after having acquired an advanced legal education. He studied law in the Nizamiyya of Baghdad, founded by his grandfather, and on his professor's death assumed the professorship in the madrasa. He later moved to Damascus and was appointed professor of al-Ghazaliyya Madrasa, as well as administrator of its *awqaf*. His biographer tells us that the military governor of the city assigned generous provisions to him.[41]

The madrasas no doubt presented the ʿulamaʾ with a rich array of career options, but the attainment of high-ranking offices was not reserved for scholars who taught or studied in them. Hence, it is not unusual to find the holders of important office, such as the *qadi* and *khatib* in the great mosques of Baghdad, to be men who had not studied or taught in one or several madrasas. Moreover, our sources give little evidence showing that study in the madrasa and the holding of endowed chairs were important ingredients in the scholar's reputation and prestige. On the contrary, many ʿulamaʾ prided themselves, and were praised by others, for refusing to benefit from the *awqaf* of the madrasa.[42] Yet while not considered essential for sons of well-established, local ʿulamaʾ families, it may well be that study in the madrasas of Baghdad, especially the prestigious Nizamiyya Madrasa, benefited members of other professional groups, as well as immigrants who sought to establish their position in the city, and transients who

eventually returned to their hometowns or pursued their careers elsewhere (figure 5.2., above).[43] The madrasa, in other words, served these
particular groups as an apparatus through which they were included
among the ranks of the 'ulama' of Baghdad and those of other Muslim
cities, even if they were held to be relatively inferior to those born to
local 'ulama' families.[44] Attracting individuals of different geographical origins and educational traditions, it may thus be suggested that
the social significance of madrasas in Baghdad lay both in tightening
and facilitating the worldwide scholarly connections, and in crystal-
izing a more coherent learned elite within the city.

Career Patterns

The biographies are replete with anecdotes illustrating scholarly
piety and learning. They recount the teachers with whom each
scholar studied and whose study circle he attended, as well as his
own disciples in the various fields of learning. Yet while listing the
positions the scholar held in the course of his lifetime, biographical
notices give little guidance as to precisely what career paths might
be followed by a young man aspiring to a scholarly career in the
eleventh and twelfth centuries. If biographical literature is, on the
whole, relatively vague about the stages of the scholar's career course,
it is probably because the inclusion and position of that scholar in
the chain of transmitters was considered much more important than
the positions he held. It is, however, also noteworthy that during the
period under consideration, there had not yet developed a highly
organized, scholarly career course which would lead to qualification
for high-ranking positions in a religious establishment. Only toward
the end of the fifteenth century, under the Ottomans, were the basic
principles of what might properly be called a learned hierarchy
formulated.[45] As the hierarchy of scholarly professions developed and
became more rigid, the terms by which the 'ulama' judged themselves, and by which they were judged by others, gradually changed.
Thus, while in the earlier period a scholar's prime concern—and the
standard by which he was measured—was to achieve excellence in
'ilm, importance and success among the 'ulama' in later periods
increasingly became associated with the attainment of high office,
power, salary, and the prerequisites that went with them.[46]

The formulation of provisions regarding a scholarly profession
under the Ottomans was an integral part of the development of the
three separate hierarchies, more or less confined to men of a particular

family background and training: slaves of the Palace School, the ʿulamaʾ, and men in the bureaucratic professions (*kalemiye*). These provisions also included the establishment of a standardized system of advancement through the ranks of the separate hierarchies. Prior to this, a member of the various professional groups and, of course, one of the ʿulamaʾ "class," aspiring to a scholarly career could attain lucrative scholarly positions (such as a judge or a professor in one of the madrasas), without having to plow his way through a succession of religious offices. Similarly, it was possible for a man educated in the religious sciences to reach a high ranking bureaucratic position, including that of vizier, even though he had not proceeded step by step through the subordinate bureaucratic positions and ranks. In light of this background, it would be impossible to discern an entirely typical scholarly career during the period covered by this study. Rather, a glance at the sequence of occupations pursued by some high ranking scholars, whose educational careers fall in the late eleventh and twelfth centuries, may illustrate the existence of a variety and career lines characteristic of this period.

In a biographical note on Abu al-Hasan ʿAli al-Fariqi (d. 602/ 1206), Ibn as-Saʿi provides us with some details of the career path taken by this professor of law. Born in Mayyafariqin, he studied *hadith* and law in Tabriz, and later moved to Baghdad where he became a close disciple, or *sahib*, of the Sufi Abu Najib as-Suhrawardi. He studied law in the Nizamiyya Madrasa, and was made a *muʿid*. Later he assumed the posts of *naʾib-qadi* and *shahid* in the court of the Hanafi *qadi* Abu Talib ʿAli al-Bukhari. In A.H. 583, however, he resigned these posts, confining himself to the repetitorship of the Nizamiyya. He became deputy professor there upon the death of its professor, the Shaykh Abu Talib al-Mubarak al-Karkhi (in A.H. 585), until he was appointed to the professorship of law in a madrasa founded for the Shafiʿis by Zumrad Khatun, mother of the caliph an-Nasir li-Din Allah.[47] His contemporary, the celebrated al-Mujir al-Baghdadi (d. 592/1195)—who according to adh-Dhahabi, surpassed all other scholars of his time in his knowledge of the different scientific disciplines (*funun*) including medicine—proceeded along different career lines despite a similarity in education. Born in Wasit, he moved to Baghdad in his early youth where he studied the law in the Nizamiyya Madrasa under its professor Abu Mansur b. al-Razzaz and others, and later served Abu Najib as-Suhrawardi as his *muʿid*. He then went first to Damascus and then to Shiraz, where a madrasa was founded for him by the Seljuk sultan. Eventually he returned to Baghdad and assumed the chair of the *mudarris* in the Nizamiyya

Madrasa. Highly estimated by the political rulers, he was sent as an envoy to Isfahan, and died on his journey.[48]

The career of an earlier scholar, Abu ʿAli an-Naharawani al-Isfahani (d. 525/1130), proceeded along the following lines. His family moved from Naharawan to Isfahan, where he was born. His father was a man of letters (*adib*), and was in charge of the education of Nizam al-Mulk's sons, but he himself pursued a career of an *ʿalim*, studying law with Abu Bakr al-Khujandi and other Shafiʿi legal scholars in Isfahan. Upon completion of his course of studies he assumed the *qadi*ship in one of the towns of Khuzistan, and then came to Baghdad where he was appointed to the chair of *mudarris* in the Nizamiyya Madrasa.[49] We thus find religious scholars establishing their reputation and obtaining top level positions in the legal administration well before they would assume the endowed chair in the madrasa.

The absence of separate hierarchies might explain the widespread phenomenon of overlapping educational paths and crossing career lines characteristic of this period. To give two examples, one might first cite the career of ʿImad al-Din al-Isbahani described above. The second example is that of caliph's vizier, Abu Shujaʿ ar-Rudhrawari, known as Zahir al-Din ("champion of religion"), another *katib* well versed in all desirable knowledge. He studied law according to the school of ash-Shafiʿi under Abu Ishaq al-Shirazi (the *raʾis* of the Shafiʿi school in Baghdad and the first *mudarris* in the Nizamiyya Madrasa) and cultivated the literary arts. Having acquired a perfect command of the language, and trained in the art of writing of official documents, he was appointed vizier to the caliph al-Muqtadi, a position he held for fifteen years.[50]

The educational qualifications expected of a public official during the Seljuk period are well illustrated in the biography of the famous Hanbali scholar Ibn Hubayra—vizier of the caliphs Muqtafi and Mustanjid. Born in A.H. 499 in a village in the Tigris district, his father, a village farmer or laborer, would take him to Baghdad to watch the councils and assemblies of the prominent men in the city, urging him to acquire a proper education and to obtain useful knowledge so that a good career would be open to him. He went to Baghdad as a young man, studied Hanbali *fiqh*, read *adab* literature, and learned *hadith* with several masters. He also acquired a good knowledge of grammar, philology, and metrics (prosody), and is said to have composed works in all these branches of learning. In addition, he taught traditions, some of which he learned from the caliph al-Muqtafi, and composed a commentary of several volumes on the two canonical *hadith* collections of Bukhari and Muslim. Under the caliphate of al-Muqtafi, Ibn Hubayra entered government service and gradually worked his way up to be this caliph's vizier.[51] The Hanbali school flourished under his ministry and patronage, and its educational forums continued to multiply, a trend which began before his arrival and might have eased his accession to power.

By not being locked into a rigid hierarchical structure, both teaching and bureaucratic positions remained open to men of widely different scholarly backgrounds. But it was this flexibility that, in the long run, enabled the most reputable and powerful scholars of Baghdad to transfer their scholarly positions to their closest disciples, sons, and relatives.

Accession to Teaching Positions

It has already been noted that, unlike other educational frameworks founded on the law of *waqf*, the madrasas were supposed to remain under the control of their founders and their descendants, in perpetuity if so desired. The control of the endowment could mean that in addition to authority over the building and its financial affairs, the power of appointment to teaching positions was the first and foremost prerogative of the founders, often Seljuk sultans and their viziers, or the controllers appointed by them or succeeding to their prerogatives after their death. Considering, however, the uncertainty of the literature of the law of *waqf* as it pertains to institutions of learning, and the incomplete information of the deeds of *waqf* dating from the early madrasa period, there is, in fact, no definite answer to the question of whether founders were actually privileged to make appointments in the madrasas.[52]

The question of the power of appointment is rendered even more difficult in light of the character of the literary record pertaining to the period under discussion. Biographical dictionaries and chronicles frequently report that the founder appointed a scholar professor in a particular madrasa. However, rarely are there any official acts of appointments in the form of a "government" document or an authorization (*tawqiʿ*, pl. *tawaqiʿ*) appointing professors, indicated in their accounts. Rather, there are many occasions in which biographers simply state that a certain professor assumed the professorship in a particular madrasa, replacing his predecessor (*jalasa yudarrisu* or *jalasa liʾt-tadris*) without a deliberate act of appointment or the name of the founder being mentioned. Only at the end of the Ayyubid period were authorizations appointing professors to academic positions issued.[53] For the Mamluk period we have al-Qalqashandi's administrative handbook, *Subh al-aʿsha*, which supplies examples of documents of appointment to teaching positions drafted by secretaries in the Mamluk royal chancellery. Many of these "royal" appointments may have been purely formal, making the naming of the chosen candidate official.[54]

To be sure, wealthy patrons of learning in Seljuk Baghdad do at first seem to retain the power of appointment in the schools they founded. Occasionally we are told that a certain scholar obtained the professorship at a particular madrasa from its founder on the day of its inauguration. Furthermore, we find benefactors making appointments to the madrasas they had founded well after the inauguration of a new school, especially when the endowment involved great sums of money and the schools came to be of great importance and high prestige. The Nizamiyya Madrasa, which, no doubt, was the most important madrasa in medieval Baghdad, at least until the establishment of the Mustansiriyya, is a good example of a school subject to continuous intervention in the appointment process by its famous founder.

In the view of several historians, with the foundation of madrasas more direct patronage ties were established between members of the ruling elite and the ʿulamaʾ. The ʿulamaʾ depended not only on the central government for protection against external enemies, but also on gifts and endowments supplied by the military elite, who controlled and manipulated the main sources in society. In return for state support and sponsorship, the ʿulamaʾ were expected to legitimize regime policy and ensure the obedience of the local population.[55] However, the pattern of appointment to teaching positions, if there was any definite pattern, seems to preserve its old informal character, depending more on personal ties between an individual patron and a particular scholar than on ties of patronage binding the ʿulamaʾ as a group to the political rulers.

Because the Great Seljuks could not establish their right and ability to rule on religiously based claims and bureaucratic forms of administration, they built their administration from the beginning on a network of personal relationships. Personal loyalty rendered by officials and local notables in return for protection and generosity took the place of formal machinery. Indeed, our sources suggest that Seljuk sultans and viziers founded madrasas not so much for members of a certain school, as for a particular scholar with whom they were probably closely associated. The close association between

Nizam al-Mulk and the celebrated al-Ghazzali is a well-known example. After the death of al-Imam al-Haramain in A.H. 478, al-Ghazzali came to Nizam al-Mulk's court at Isfahan and was sent by him to Baghdad to occupy the chair of law in the Nizamiyya Madrasa. Not only was Nizam al-Mulk an enthusiastic Shafiʻi-Ashʻari himself, but, like al-Ghazzali, was born and raised in the small village of ar-Radhakan.

Abu Bakr al-Khujandi, later al-Isbahani (d. 552/1157), another Shafiʻi scholar who assumed the professorship in the Nizamiyya of Baghdad also seems to have developed close relationships with the political rulers well before he was appointed to the chair of *mudarris*. So closely was he associated with the ruling elite that, according to his biographer, "in the respect he gained he was more like a vizier than like an ʻalim." When he walked in the streets people would remove their swords from their sheaths as a token of honor.[56] Such personal patronage sometimes extended to succeeding generations, as in the case of al-Khujandi's descendants. His grandson, Muhammad (d. 592/1195), became leader (*raʼis*) of the Shafiʻi school in Isfahan upon his father's death. Having moved to Baghdad, the caliph bestowed honors upon him in an unprecedented manner. He entrusted him with the supervision of the Nizamiyya Madrasa, as well as the oversight of all matters concerning the *fuqaha*ʼ (*nazr an-Nizamiyya waʼn-nazr fi ahwal al-fuqahaʼ*).[57]

Although at first glance they seemed entirely dependent on the decision of the founders, able to raise men to prestigious teaching positions and strip them of these honors according to their wishes, a careful examination of the actual process of appointment reveals a far more complex picture. To begin with, a distinction must be made between appointments to teaching positions in madrasas founded for the benefit of members of the Shafiʻi and Hanafi legal schools. There is, in fact, no evidence of any involvement of the founders in the appointment process in madrasas founded for members of the Hanafi school, nor are founders reported to have built and endowed schools for a particular Hanafi scholar. Rather, the choice of *mudarrisun* in the Hanafi madrasas seems to have been left to the decision of the leading scholars within the school, who would select their closest disciples to succeed them as *mudarrisun*, *qadi*s, or both. Abu Tahir ad-Dailami (d. 461/1069) was the disciple of Abu ʻAbd Allah as-Saimari and Abu ʻAbd Allah ad-Damaghani. Having returned to Baghdad from Wasit, he taught the legal doctrine of his school in the great mosque of al-Mansur, as well as in a small mosque where his master, as-Saimari, held his *halqa*. Apart from succeeding his master in the mosque, he assumed the *qadi*ship in al-Karkh quarter, a post as-Saimari had held for several years. In A.H. 467, when the first madrasa for adherents of the Hanafi school was established, ad-Dailami assumed the endowed chair.[58]

The fact that his other master, Abu 'Abd Allah ad-Damaghani, himself an immigrant of humble origin, had succeeded in laying the foundations of a strong line of judges and chief judges in Baghdad, no doubt reduced the dependence of Hanafi scholars on patronage and recognition by their sponsors. In addition to controlling the appointments to positions in the legal administration, the Damaghani Hanafi family seems to have made nominations to scholarly positions in the Hanafi madrasas, thus managing to secure another valuable source of patronage.

The influence of high-ranking 'ulama' upon the appointment process was, however, not peculiar to nominations in the Hanafi madrasas. In order to ensure the excellence of their foundations, the founder had to go by the reputation of the man he chose. These appointments, in other words, confirmed an existing leadership, rather than creating a new one. The scholars who taught in the Shafi'i madrasas of Baghdad during the first century of the new schools' foundation had already required renown. These included those who arrived in the city from other towns and villages. Hence, it may well be that, in practice, appointments were subject to the decision of the masters themselves, who would naturally recommend their most qualified and closest disciples, just as they did in their study circles elsewhere. Whether or not professors actually nominated their own successors, our sources attest that many students who were closely associated with their masters, and who served them as *mu'id*s, did eventually succeed them in their teaching positions, or assumed the professorship in one or several other madrasas.

Abu Bakr ash-Shashi, for example, the famous disciple of ash-Shirazi and his *mu'id* in the Nizamiyya Madrasa, taught first in his own madrasa; then, when Taj al-Mulk founded the Tajiyya Madrasa, he was appointed its professor. In A.H. 504, however, after the death of al-Kiya al-Harrasi, he succeeded him in the chair of professor in the Nizamiyya Madrasa, a post he held until his death in A.H. 507.[59] Abu Mansur b. al-Razzaz (d. 539/1144) studied *hadith* with several scholars, including the Hanbali Abu Muhammad at-Tamimi, and Shafi'i law under al-Mutawalli, ash-Shashi, al-Ghazzali, and al-Kiya al-Harrasi—all teachers in the Nizamiyya Madrasa. Upon the death of al-Harrasi, he was nominated to the endowed chair in the same madrasa, a post which he later resigned. In addition to his teaching position, he was nominated *shahid* by the Hanafi chief judge, Abu al-Qasim az-Zainabi. Even more important than his official position was the high esteem he enjoyed in society. He was considered the leader, or *imam*, of the Shafiʿis in Baghdad following the death of ash-Shashi, whose respected standing extended beyond his own legal school, as indicated by the large attendance at his funeral wake.[60]

Yet the involvement of the ʿulamaʾ in the appointment process could go beyond mere suggestions regarding which of their disciples was appropriate for a teaching position. In their endeavor to further extend their control over such an important source of patronage, the most reputable and powerful scholars took advantage of the ambiguity of rules concerning the right of appointment in order to pass their positions on to their own sons and relatives. Abu Muhammad ash-Shashi (d. 528/1133), for example, studied law under his father, Abu Bakr, and succeeded to his position in the Tajiyya Madrasa.[61] Later, his own son, Abu Nasr (d. 576/1180), assumed the professorship in at-Tutushiyya Madrasa.[62] Abu ʿAbd Allah b. Yahya al-Baghdadi (d. 631/1233) was the son of Abu al-Qasim, the professor of Madrasa Dar Dhahab and the *shaykh* of the Shafiʿi school of Iraq. He received his early education from his father. After a journey to Khurasan, he assumed the endowed chair of the *mudarris* in the Nizamiyya Madrasa, later becoming the chief judge. He was removed from the chief judgeship afterwards, but appointed the first Shafiʿi professor in the newly established Mustansiriyya Madrasa.[63]

Biographies of scholars coming to Baghdad during the eleventh and twelfth centuries play down their family background, stressing instead their knowledge and personal merits. From the late eleventh century, however, the privilege of attaining teaching positions in mosques and madrasas, and, more importantly, the gaining of religious leadership (*riyasa*), seems to have depended at least as much on family background and connections as on scholarly qualifications.[64] Biographies of noted *shaykhs* and *mudarrisun* belonging to local families with established traditions of learning often contain the phrases: *wa-kana min bait al-hadith waʾl-ʿilm waʾt-tadris* ("so and so belonged to a house of religious knowledge and learning"), or *wa-kana min bait al-hadith waʾl-ʿadala* ("so and so belonged to a house of men known for their knowledge of *hadith* and for their proper conduct"), designating their scholarly descent. ʿUlamaʾ born to such families often studied with their fathers and in some cases succeeded them in their positions. The description of their career paths testifies to the importance of ancestry and inherited merit (*nasab-hasab*) for inclusion in the ranks of the ʿulamaʾ, and the choice of masters among them.[65]

The phenomenon of inherited teaching positions, already discernible in the late eleventh century, became more visible in the course of the subsequent century, the period which witnessed the decline of the Seljuk empire. Members of the ruling elite continued to build and endow madrasas and to assign religious scholars to teach in them. Still, as the ties of patronage between the political rulers and the ʿulamaʾ loosened, Baghdadi ʿulamaʾ came to enjoy a greater freedom in the choice of their successors. Thus, many of the Shafiʿi professors in Nizamiyya and Mustansiriyya madrasas during the late twelfth and thirteenth centuries were descendants of professors in one of the madrasas of the city. In addition to teaching positions, these ʿulamaʾ held high-ranking offices in the legal establishment, including that of the chief *qadi*.[66] As the phenomenon of inherited high-ranking posts intensified—in particular the holder of the endowed chair in the madrasa and the *qadi*—a number of ʿulamaʾ families combining wealth, prestige, and scholarship, rose in Baghdad.[67]

However, compared with eleventh-century Nishapur and Damascus in the Seljuk and Ayyubid periods, the phenomenon of ʿulamaʾ households (*buyut*) was limited, both in its scope and in the depth of ʿulamaʾ dynasties, so that, in the beginning of the thirteenth century it did not exceed four generations.[68] Renowned ʿulamaʾ throughout the Seljuk period might still arrive in the city from the provinces and be offered a variety of options for employment, as the number of immigrant scholars holding prestigious positions testifies.[69] In the mosques of Baghdad, where study of the various Islamic sciences took place long after the rise of the madrasa, *majlis*es were convened for out-of-town scholars. As-Suyuti tells us that when the celebrated *hadith* scholar Abu Zakariyya b. Manda (d. 511/1117), a native of Isfahan, arrived in Baghdad on his way to the *hajj*, the news of his arrival spread rapidly among the *shaykh*s of the city. A *majlis* was convened for him in the Mosque of Mansur, the stronghold of the Hanbalis and a major center of *hadith* studies. There he dictated *hadith*s to an audience of Baghdadi *shaykh*s who took notes on his commentaries on the prophetic traditions.[70]

The involvement of the ruling elite in making nominations to high-ranking positions, in a city which constituted a center of government, ever-changing patronage ties, as well as constant migration and a turnover of elites—explain why only a few dynasties of ʿulamaʾ monopolizing prestige and honor within the continuity emerged in Baghdad during the eleventh and twelfth centuries. This study argues that despite the lack of familial continuity, there evolved in

Baghdad no less an exclusive and structured local elite of ʿulamaʾ as did in some other Islamic cities during the course of the Sunni revival.[71] Not only did Baghdadi ʿulamaʾ of this period manage to exploit their "knowledge" in order to assure their self-perpetuation, but they also enjoyed an autonomous role vis-à-vis their patrons in the frameworks related to the application and transmission of the *shariʿa*, and the city's public sphere in general.

CHAPTER 6

ॐ

PLACE AND ROLE
IN THE PUBLIC SPHERE

Allah will raise to high rank those of you who believe and are
granted knowledge.

Koran 58:11

Only by looking at how the ʿulamaʾ lived and worked as members of an entire society, can we comprehend why and how the commitments and activities which defined them as a coherent group were significant to other members of society.[1]

The Sunni population of eleventh-century Baghdad—a community ruled by an alien military elite and subject to constant political upheaval—had a special need for communal patrons and leaders who could maintain social order and lend society a common identity and measure of stability. Did the ʿulamaʾ assume this role? If so, did they enjoy an autonomous position vis-à-vis the political rulers, both in the administration of the *shariʿa* institutions and in the shaping and organizaion of communal life? What were the frameworks in which the Baghdadi ʿulamaʾ of this period carried out their social roles and the forms their communal leadership took? Such an inquiry should involve an examination of both the actual functions performed by the ʿulamaʾ in society at this time, and the manner in which they themselves perceived their roles and duties.

125

The Religious Elite and the Ruling Authorities

Historians of medieval Islamic societies have long noted that with the emergence of the Seljuks as the new ruling elite in the central lands of Islam, patronage and sponsorship of Sunni religious institutions, and the 'ulama' reached unprecedented heights. This policy, which was nowhere more clearly revealed than in the foundation of madrasas on substantial endowments and the employment of their graduates, increased the dependence of the 'ulama' on the ruling elite, who controlled and manipulated the main sources of wealth in society. This dependence of the upper sectors on the political rulers, somewhat weak and vague at first, became stronger and more definite during the Ottoman period. The establishment of a hierarchical system of madrasas, which appointed their scholarly population to increasingly higher positions at the head of a religious establishment deeply involved in the official sphere.

In eleventh-century Baghdad, however, the 'ulama' still enjoyed an autonomous role in the public sphere, as did similar groups in some other Muslim cities. Given their inherent status in Islamic societies and the nature of the ruling elite during this period, this is not surprising. Deriving their moral authority and their standing from the *shari'a*, they were the sole civilian elite capable of bridging the gap between the alien Turkish military elite and the indigenous population. Moreover, the 'ulama' could legitimize the Seljuk regime by enjoining obedience on the local population, as well as by performing a host of tangible and intangible services for the government. The heterogeneous character of their socio-economic background and networks further enabled the 'ulama' to assume a variety of socio-political roles in Seljuk Baghdad, that of intermediaries between the rulers and their subjects in particular. For the Baghdadi 'ulama' came from, or had representatives in, all segments of society, including members of the ruling elite.[2]

In theory, it was the rulers—Seljuk sultans and their viziers—who appointed scholars to religious posts (that of the *qadi* and that of the *mudarris*), paid their salaries, and dismissed them at will. However, as discussed earlier, the appointments of *mudarrisun* confirmed an existing leadership rather than creating a new one. Furthermore, once a jurist was appointed to the post of teacher of the law in the madrasa, he seemed to enjoy complete freedom in the admission of students, the sequence and method of all instruction, as well as the choice of treatises. Although the madrasa was founded for the teaching of the traditional religious and legal sciences (to the exclusion of the so-called ancient rational sciences), what a professor taught was not closely regulated; he would teach what he knew. Nor are there any examples of a trustee (*mutawalli, nazir*), the administrator of the *waqf* on which the madrasa was founded, complaining about the study content, or reprimanding or dismissing a *mudarris* because he taught the "wrong books" or in the "wrong way." Concerned with public order, political rulers tried to influence the curricula of the madrasa only when the preaching of Ash'ari theology through the popular or "academic" sermon (*wa'z*) led to strong objections of the Hanbalis, who headed the movement of the "people of *hadith*."[3]

Although more dependent (than the *mudarris*) upon the rulers for his employment and status, the *qadi* enjoyed no less autonomy in the administration of the *shari'i* court and the judicial procedures than did the *mudarris* in the instruction of the law in the *madrasa*. The *qadi* was guided by the *shari'a*, not the government. The political rulers, it should be stressed, did not intervene in the *qadi*'s court except in matters relating to public order—namely, penal law. The maintenance of public order was maintained by the civil court (*mazalim*), which was essentially a criminal court. Under the Great Seljuks there was a general trend of extending the *mazalim*'s jurisdiction at the expense of the *shari'i* courts, and a wide range of officials other than *qadi*s were involved in matters related to the administration of justice, especially public order. In Baghdad there was, to some extent, a conflict of jurisdiction. The people tended to refer to the caliph, who was always accessible to them, even though he could do little but refer back to the sultan and his representatives. At times, the caliph's vizier held a *mazalim* court, but in theory this was the prerogative of the sultan.[4]

Data on those holding lucrative posts—*qadi*s in the main courts, teachers in the great schools, preachers in the principal mosques, as well as civil officials (figure 6.1 below)—suggest that each of the law schools controlled particular positions.[5] There were numerous *qadi*s among the 'ulama' during this period. The judicial class was divided into four schools of law: the Hanafis, who were the first to accept governmental positions and dominated Baghdad's judiciary for a long time; the Hanbalis, whose prominence within the judiciary began at the end of the Buyid period and continued throughout the Seljuk period; the Shafi'is, whose backing came mainly from outside the city, and who gained power under the vizierate and the auspices of Nizam al-Mulk; and finally, the Malikis, who were a small minority in Baghdad.[6] Our data shows that fifteen of the thirty-six

Figure 6.1
The Composition of the Group of Religious and Civil Officials according to School Affiliation and Geographical Origin (409/1018–549/1154)

	SHAFI'I			HANAFI			HANBALI			MALIKI			TOTAL
	immigrant	transient	native	immigrant	transient	native	immigrant	transient	native	immigrant	transient	native	
RELIGIOUS OFFICES													
QADI	3		2	2		5			3		1		16
KHATIB	1								2				3
QADI, KHATIB							1		2				3
MUDARRIS (MOSQUE)	3	3		1		4	5		30			1	47
QADI, MUDARRIS (MOSQUE)	2			1			2		4				9
MUDARRIS (MADRASA)	10	5	7	1		1							24
QADI, MUDARRIS (MADRASA)			2			2							4
CIVIL OFFICES:													
VIZIER	1								1				2
AMIL (tax official)						1							1
AMIN (trust officer)									1				1
WAKIL (financial agent)									1				1
QADI, DEPUTY-VIZIER				1		1							2
RELIGIOUS & CIVIL OFFICES:													
QADI. MUDARRIS (MADRASA), DEPUTY VIZIER						1							1

MUDARRIS (MADRASA) NAZIR	2				2
QADI, HAJIB (chamberlain)		1			1
NAQIB AN-NUQABA', VIZIER		1			1
	42	24	53	2	121

*qadi*s for whom we have school affiliation were Hanafis, thirteen were Hanbalis, seven were Shafiʿis, and only one was Maliki.

Information about the school affiliation of madrasa professors shows that Shafiʿis predominated in this office. Of a total of forty-two Shafiʿis holding religious or civil offices, twenty-four were *mudarrisun*, comprising approximately 80 percent of the thirty-one professors in the madrasas of Baghdad. Most of these *mudarrisun* taught in the Nizamiyya Madrasa. After the death of Nizam al-Mulk in 1092, Seljuk policy oscillated between patronizing the Shafiʿis and patronizing the Hanafis through the foundation of madrasas. Until the middle of the twelfth century, the Hanafis were the most favored, but in the second half of that century the Shafiʿis recovered and were endowed with new schools.

The preference of the Shafiʿis as benefactors for governmental patronage was not designed to establish the Ashʿari "middle–road" orthodoxy, as has been asserted.[7] Nor did it reflect an attempt to strengthen the position of the central government by spurring competition between the religiously defined factions. In contrast with several ʿAbbasid caliphs before them, Seljuk sultans and their viziers rarely participated in religious life in general. They knew very little about theological and legal controversies, and did not strive to define Sunnism according to a centrally espoused dogma. After all, as an alien political elite, the Seljuks could not raise similar religiously-based claims to authority in religious matters. Indeed, except for one effort to exert religious control during the vizierate of Amid al-Mulk al-Kunduri, who in 543/1048 charged all proponents of Ashʿari theology in Nishapur with being heretical innovators, the Seljuks refrained from taking an unequivocal stand in matters of local religious authority.[8] The main objective of Nizam al-Mulk and other members of the ruling elite was to put an end to, or at least reduce, the turmoil caused by battles over proper creed and behavior.[9] Hence, only when the internal rivalries of the ʿulamaʾ involved large segments of society and seemed to pose a threat to public order, did they step in to end riots and restore peace and order. On such occasions, they usually acted in favor of the religious faction which had already gained the largest local following. This may explain why, while founding madrasas for Shafiʿi scholars, Nizam al-Mulk took the side of the Hanbalis, the Shafiʿis' rivals in Baghdad, yielding to their demand to frustrate any attempt to preach Ashʿarism in the city's madrasas and mosques.

If not through the establishment of madrasas and appointments of professors and judges, was it through the incorporation of the ʿulamaʾ into the governmental apparatus that the ruling authorities tried to create and dominate a religious establishment? The trend of combining religious and administrative functions, which culminated in the use of the *qadi* in some instances as a purely governmental official by the Ottomans, is already apparent in the Seljuk period. There are examples of the chief judge in Baghdad and other officials acting as vizier or deputy vizier for the caliph. Abu al-Hasan ad-Damaghani served in the capacity of deputy vizier for both al-Mustazhir and al-Mustarshid.[10] His father, Abu 'Abd Allah, who was the chief judge before him, had also served as deputy vizier on two occasions during the reigns of al-Qa'im and al-Muqtafi.[11] *Qadi al-qudat* 'Ali b. Abi Talib—a member of the Zainabi family of *qadi*s and *naqib*s—was deputy vizier of the caliph al-Mustarshid and later of al-Muqtafi, who was installed as caliph by the Seljuk sultan at az-Zainabi's suggestion.

The fate of the Zainabis in the political arena demonstrates how dependent upon the personal patronage of the rulers (including that of the caliph) leading 'ulama' incorporated into the administrative apparatus might have become, even though they belonged to influential families with a strong local base. The objective of this particular story was probably to warn other 'ulama' of any involvement in the official sphere, to teach them a lesson. The biographer of 'Ali b. Tirad (*naqib an-nuqaba'* and the caliph's vizier) relates that an estrangement (*'ajiba*) occurred between the caliph al-Muqtafi and his vizier. The caliph turned away from him altogether (*taghayyara 'alayhi wa-a'rada 'anhu bi'l-kullya*), appointing his cousin, the chief judge 'Ali b. Abi Talib, as deputy vizier, and 'Ali b. Tirad sought refuge with Sultan Mas'ud in *Dar as-saltana*.[12] No explanation of the sudden change in the caliph's attitude toward his vizier is provided by our sources. In a letter to the newly appointed *naqib an-nuqaba'*, 'Ali b. Abi Talib complained about the harm caused by al-Muqtafi to both him and his cousin, claiming his cousin was kept under close watch in *Dar as-saltana* and deprived of his position and authority.[13] Several years later, following the death of 'Ali b. Abi Talib, the Zainabis lost the position of chief judge and the Damaghanis were reinstated in the post.[14]

However, apart from 'ulama' assuming offices in the *qadi*ship—a special category between religious scholarship and governmental service—the number of religious scholars who entered the state bureaucracy was relatively few (see figure 6.1). The 'ulama' were by no means the only group performing public functions. To begin with, many offices were entirely within the sphere of the military elite, particularly those dealing with taxation, the minting of coins, and the postal system. Given the fundamental military nature of the Seljuk empire, it is hardly surprising that members of the military "class," or "men of the sword" as they are also called (primarily military commanders of Turkish origin), almost exclusively staffed the category of the executive and military professions. Many members of the standing army—composed primarily of Turkish slaves—were trained for war and for government, and had the opportunity to rise through the ranks at court and in the provinces.[15]

As mentioned earlier, it was not impossible for the ʿulamaʾ to fill purely bureaucratic positions such as chancery and fiscal officials, nor was there any insuperable barrier keeping a secretary or men from *kuttab* families from pursuing the career of an ʿalim. In spite of the gradual emergence of a new bureaucratic class educated in the religious sciences, some of the most effective viziers and functionaries in Baghdad at this time were those who had received private tutoring or specialized training for a particular office in addition to, and more frequently in place of, the general madrasa type of education. Thus, although there were exceptions, for the most part viziers and other highly placed individuals, including those who had been trained in the religious sciences, were still recruited from the personnel of the central or provincial bureau who, by training or family tradition, belonged to the *sinf* of the *kuttab*.[16]

Even more important than the offices the ʿulamaʾ came to hold are the functions they were expected to perform, and their own perception of their place and duties in society. While reading the sources, we often get the impression that the initiative for absorbing the ʿulamaʾ into the governmental apparatus, and their involvement in political affairs, came from the government rather than from the ʿulamaʾ themselves. At the same time, our sources suggest a certain ambiguity concerning the duties and the type of involvement in political affairs members of the ruling elite expected from leading ʿulamaʾ in return for their patronage.

This ambiguity is implied in an account of the involvement of the chief *qadi* Abu ʿAbd Allah ad-Damaghani in the contraction of a marriage alliance between the houses of the sultan and the caliph. In 453/1061 Tughil Beg sent the *qadi* of Rayy to Baghdad to ask for the hand of al-Qaʾim's daughter in marriage. The demand angered the caliph, and led to a disagreement between himself and Tughil Beg. After a series of threats and counterthreats, the caliph agreed to the marriage. However, when the sultan's vizier came to Baghdad to claim the bride, he was told that the object of the marriage had been honor, not union.[17] In a letter sent by the sultan to the chief judge he reminded him of his main duty, teaching and implementing the law, charging him with responsibility for the dispute, yet asking him to intercede at the same time.[18]

How the 'ulama' themselves felt about assuming functions outside their traditional scope is implied in an account of a *qadi* from the Damaghani family who resigned his office and accepted the position of court chamberlain (*hajib al-bab*) of the caliph, a post normally reserved for military officials. His biographer tells us that his resignation was a cause of embarrassment to his brother, the chief judge at the time.[19] Not only were there 'ulama' during this period who were reluctant to enter government service, some even refused to accept paid positions altogether, including that of the *qadi*.

The concept of a pious man refusing to serve as a *qadi* appeared early in Islamic history. Consider, for example, the following story of Saliman b. 'Attar (served as *qadi* in Egypt from A.D. 660 to 680), told by Kindi (d. 350/961) in his treatise *Kitab al-wulah wa-kitab al-qudah* ("The book of governors and the book of judges"). Ibn 'Attar's friend, 'Abd Allah Ibn 'Umar b. 'As, came to him and said: "When you were a *qas* (a "story teller," one who provides religious education to the community) angels stood on either side of you, advising you and guiding you along the straight [path]. Now that you have become a *qadi*, your companions are two devils who mislead you and distance you from the truth."[20] In the same vein, a famous *hadith* says: "He who is appointed *qadi* is truly sacrificed without a knife."[21] Another warns those who might be tempted to serve that on the day of judgment when all believers are resurrected, the judges will join the sultans and the *muftis* will join the prophets.

The refusal to serve as *qadis* stemmed from a deep fear of pious men of being torn between their devotion to the religious law and their loyalties to the ruler who had appointed them. But fear of corruption, the loss of their primary values, must have also played a role in their decisions. Hence, even those who accepted the office refused to accept any payments, or distanced themselves from court life so as not to be identified with political rulers. Ibn Abi Ya'la tells us that his father, Qadi Abu Ya'la, agreed to serve as the *qadi* of *Dar al-khilafa* only after the caliph accepted a series of conditions, among them that he would neither be obliged to be present in ceremonial processions, nor attend the sultan's residence.[22] Abu Bakr ash-Shami's first refusal to serve was also followed by his reluctant acceptance. Recommended to the office by the caliph's vizier, Ibn Shuja' ar-Rudhrawari, he posed the following conditions: he would not receive any remuneration for judicial rulings; there would be no intervention in the favor of the disputants; and he would not be obliged to alter his dress. His biographers then state that, notwithstanding his high position, he maintained a pious life style for the remainder of his life.[23]

If there are stories in the biographies of pious *qadi*s about their disassociation with men of the regime, we find even more in biographies of pious ʿulamaʾ who held purely bureaucratic positions. One particularly relevant anecdote concerns the Hanbali vizier Ibn Hubayra who "never wore silk garments and turned back the precious gifts sent to him by the caliph. When the caliph's servant returned with the gifts, the caliph declared that Ibn Hubayra surpassed all other viziers of the ʿAbbasid family in his modesty and righteous conduct."[24]

The need to abstain from any connections with officials in the regime was explained in detail by the famous al-Ghazzali, who himself served as a personal example when he resigned the prestigious appointment of *mudarris* in the Nizamiyya Madrasa of Baghdad. In a section of *Kitab al-ʿilm* ("The book of knowledge"), al-Ghazzali states that one of the characteristics of the learned man is that he maintains a distance from the magistrates, avoiding their company, despite their efforts to seek him out, as association with them would necessarily involve seeking their approval even though they are unjust and unrighteous.[25] Al-Ghazzali goes on to warn the learned man against believing he might have a positive influence on the ruler, or be able to induce him to observe the dictates of the law.[26] He had earlier criticized those ʿulamaʾ who accepted even judicial posts, in "The book of knowledge."

The inclusion of jurists in government, he explains, began when the caliphate passed from the first four "righteous caliphs" to the Ummayads, who were not versed in legal decisions and who were compelled to seek the aid of jurists. Consequently, "These contemporaries [those sought by the political rulers] turned their efforts toward the knowledge they hoped to acquire in order to attain power and glory through the solicitation of governors. They bent themselves to governors from whom they sought offices and reward. . . . After having once been sought, [they] have now become the job seeker; after having once been indifferent to sultans, they have now become obsequious by waiting upon them."[27]

For all the rise in their status and the autonomous role they enjoyed, leadership among the ʿulamaʾ, and in society as a whole, was not reserved for scholars in paid positions. On the contrary, those who did not benefit from the financial patronage of the political rulers acquired much greater reputation and prestige. Among them were teachers of *hadith* and the law who lived on individual donations and gifts, or sustained their teaching activities with other professions (notably trade), and the *muftis*, who acted independently of all outside powers, especially governmental power. Indeed, the same doubts about whether to associate with the government at all, which had characterized their predecessors under the early ʿAbbasids, continued to disturb many of the ʿulamaʾ during the Seljuk period. They probably increased as a result of the nature of the ruling elite and the growing ties of patronage between the political rulers and the ʿulamaʾ.

Accordingly, there began to appear distinctions in the sources pertaining to this period between official ʿulamaʾ and those who maintained a distance from the government. Such phrases as "to pursue worldly success" (*talab ad-dunya*), "to meddle in worldly matters" (*dahkhl fi ashghal ad-dunya*), or "to mingle with the people of the world" (*khalt abnaʾ ad-dunya*) convey the criticism and disrespect felt toward ʿulamaʾ associated with men of wealth and power. In contrast, refusal to accept the financial patronage of rulers, and abstention from any connection with them became a source of pride, respect, and prestige.

The ability of the ʿulamaʾ to extend whatever potential influence many had in government activity was thus limited by the distance between men of religious learning and men of the regime, a rift created by the ʿulamaʾ themselves. Criticizing all governments which claimed legitimacy, yet did not live up to religious ideals of justice, many ʿulamaʾ placed a high value on separating themselves from the moral corruption which tainted government actions. However, while insisting on refusing the benefits of material wealth resulting from association with the rulers, higher ranking ʿulamaʾ could use the salaries and gifts they received to assume the role of patrons and benefactors of the people. This point is well illustrated in the following anecdote about the piety and generosity of the Shafiʿi vizier Abu Shujaʿ ar-Rudhrawari (Zahir ad-Din), as related by Ibn Khallikan:

> He never left his house without having first read and transcribed a portion of the Koran, paid the required alms-tax on all his property, and gave generous alms anonymously. After receiving a note informing him of a widow with four needy children, he ordered one of his servants to provide them with clothing and food. He then removed his own clothes and vowed neither to dress nor warm himself until the order was carried out.[28]

Unsurprisingly our sources are replete with accounts of virtuous ʿulamaʾ wholly dedicated to community service. In an era of political upheaval, and internal disorder created by the breakdown of the ʿAbbasid caliphate and the ascendance of an unstable, alien regime, the role of the ʿulamaʾ as the sole group capable of, and willing to, sustain the community as an Islamic community, by carrying on the teachings of Islam and enforcing its morals, assumed new meanings.

The *Madhahib* as Social Solidarity Groups

The religious scholars of eleventh-century Baghdad shared an ethic of public service, providing educational, religious, and legal guidance to the Muslim community. Phrases such as "he served the people" (*afada an-nas*), "the people derived benefit from him" (*intafaʿa an-nas bihi*), and "he educated the people with *fatwas*" (*ʿarafa an-nas biʾl-fatwa*) appear frequently in the biographies of ʿulamaʾ during this period. It is difficult to determine what the term *an-nas* specifically means in this context. It might refer to notables, but it may be assumed that it refers to the broad Muslim populace, not merely a small group of students who would form the academic and judicial elite.

The sources at our disposal do not provide any indication of *shaykh*s employed to transmit religious knowledge in organized public sessions. But in a society where there were no distinct boundaries between instruction and devotion, and where learning took place in a very open world, *shaykh*s were likely to teach many besides aspiring students. Ibn al-Jawzi comments that the Hanbali *qadi* and *khatib* Abu al-Husain al-Muhtadi al-Hashimi, known as Ibn al-Ghariq (d. 465/1072) attracted people from all parts of the Muslim world (*rahala an-nas ilayhi min al-bilad*). He was the last to transmit *hadith* based on the authority of the celebrated tenth-century *hadith* expert, ad-Daraqutni, and dictated *hadith* to the people (*qaraʾ ʿala an-nas*).[29] A scholar's popularity as teacher and spiritual guide are commonly indicated by accounts of his funeral and the degree of grief occasioned by his death. Sibt b. al-Jawzi relates that Abu Fawaris (d. 499/1105), an expert on the Koran and *hadith*, taught the art of reciting the Koran for many years and to thousands of people. His funeral was attended by a large number of ʿulamaʾ accompanied by commoners (*an-nas*), and the city markets were closed for an entire week.[30]

Accounts of ʿulamaʾ deeply dedicated to public service further convey the impression of a group playing a vital role in daily community life. The Hanbali *hadith* and legal scholar, Abu ʿAbd Allah as-Salamasi, is reported to have been famous for his care and generosity to the poor (*kana mashhuran biʾl-birr wa-fiʾl-khair wa-iftiqad al-fuqaraʾ wa-kithra as-sadaqa*).[31] The Hanbali vizier Ibn Hubayra, the famous patron of the Hanbalis, is also praised for his dedication to community service, not only opening his own home to the poor (*fuqaraʾ*), but also giving them a significant portion of his income and providing them with all their needs.[32] On the day of his death, all the markets in the city were closed and great crowds gathered in the markets, on the rooftops, and along the bank of the Tigris to mourn him in recognition of his generosity and justice (*wa-kathara al-bikaʾ ʿalayhi li-ma yafʿalahu min al-birr wa-yuzhiruhu min al-ʿadl*).[33] Abu Hamid al-Isfaraʾini, leader of the Shafiʿi school in Baghdad, was another leading scholar committed to the spread of religious learning (*nashr al-ʿilm*) and other community services. Ibn al-Jawzi relates that people used to bring him their payments of the poor tax (*zakawat*) and alms (*sadaqat*) so that he could distribute the money. Besides distributing a monthly allowance to his poor followers (*ashab*), he donated money for the pilgrimage caravan.[34]

The same informal pattern of patronage ties binding the ʿulamaʾ to the political rulers connected some of the leading ʿulamaʾ to specific groups in society. They served as a substitute for the binding force of a structure of offices and institutions. Because patronage of the local population by the ʿulamaʾ was more likely to occur within a religiously defined group, it no doubt tightened the social bonds and mutual affection among men adhering to a certain law school, turning the *madhahib* into an attractive entity around which local groups or factions might crystallize.[35] The phrase "he became a leader in religious and worldly matters" (*intahat ilayhi riyasat ad-din wa-ʾd-dunya*), appears in al-Isfaraʾini's biographical notice, indicating his position both as the *raʾis* of his school and leader of the people. Our sources tell us that the two leaderships were later combined in his closest disciple Abu Ishaq ash-Shirazi ("he was *imam ad-dunya* and one of its most ascetic *shaykhs*").[36] The extent to which the legal schools in Baghdad during the period under discussion became the organized bodies in which society was structured and the focus of solidarity remains, however, obscure.

We may assume that by the twelfth century the majority of the ʿulamaʾ belonged to one or another of the legal schools. This is evidenced by an increase in the number of law school *nisbas* appearing in the biographical dictionaries. But there is as yet no way of estimating what percentage of laypersons identified themselves with a specific school, nor of assessing exactly what this affiliation meant. Did they look to the particular school's scholars for guidance in proper Islamic conduct, its witnesses to register contracts and marriages, and its judges to mediate disputes? Did they have customs, leaders, and patrons of their own?[37] Nor do we know much about the internal structure of the *madhahib*. Circles of teachers and their students, along with legal functionaries such as deputies, notaries, and clerks in the service of the *qadis*, probably made up the core of the schools. It is also possible that this core membership, the schools, led by their *shaykhs*, branched out to include a larger number of people who adhered to them on the basis of birth, or the traditional membership of their quarter. They may have prayed in the same mosque, studied in the same Koranic school or madrasa under the teachers of their respective *madhahib*, even married each other.[38] Bab al-Basra is a good example of a quarter associated with a particular school of law. Yet, as we have seen, though generally considered to be the Hanbali section of town, a least one madrasa for the members of the Hanafi school was founded in this quarter, while members of all legal schools taught or studied in the quarter's mosques as a matter of course. Only when attempts were made to preach Ash'arism in the mosque of al-Mansur—the stronghold of the Hanbali community—did it become an arena of conflict between the religiously defined factions.[39] Moreover, as discussed above, people tended to settle in quarters according to common professional pursuits and/or geographical origins. The issue of the various schools as social organizations in specific residential quarters is thus complex, and the resulting picture unclear.

In dealing with the legal schools as the focus of solidarity and the organizing cadre for the local community of eleventh-century Baghdad, however, a distinction should be made among the three legal schools dominating the institutions related to the application and transmission of the *shari'a*. The differences between members of the schools related both to their geographical origins and the kind of offices they held (figure 6.1, above), and consequently to their networks of social relations as well. Nearly a third of the Shafi'i and Hanafi scholars surveyed held paid civil and religious offices, often as professors in the madrasas founded by wealthy patrons for legal scholars of the two schools, as well as various positions in the judiciary. Shafi'i *qadis* were largely recruited from beyond the city. Immigrants and transients filled more than half of the professorships in the Shafi'i madrasas and native-born Shafi'i and Hanafi scholars shared status and position with them. In contrast, the majority of Hanbali and Hanafi *qadis* are explicitly said to have been born or raised in the city. Our data also shows that native-born Hanbalis filled the overwhelming majority of professorships as well as the *khatib*ships in the great mosques of Baghdad, positions that were not subsidized by the state.

So closely were high-ranking Hanafis and Shafi'is associated with men of wealth and power that they sometimes appeared to their contemporaries as members of the ruling elite (*khawass*).[40] In contrast, only rarely do we find any references in their biographies to their association with other social groups, such as the merchants or the commoners. Since there are few biographical dictionaries of Hanafis, it would be difficult to describe any general features of this school in Baghdad. The many Shafi'i biographies, however, convey the portrait of an exclusive, elitist group of legal scholars, immersed in intensive study and transmission of the law in their study circles, teaching mosques, and madrasas. We should also remember that the majority of Shafi'is in Baghdad came from elsewhere, primarily the provinces of eastern Iran. Some settled in Baghdad and gained a reputation in their own small scholarly groupings, others moved to other Islamic cities or returned to their hometowns. To judge from Shafi'i writers, their school remained a minority community, unable to put down roots in the caliphal city and attract a large local following.[41] The inclination of some leading 'ulama' of the school toward Ash'arism, and even more important, their financial patronage by the political rulers through the foundation of madrasas, certainly did not contribute to their popularity. It served instead as a pretext for criticism of them by the Hanbalis and their followers. As far as the Hanbalis were concerned, relations with the political rulers could not be separated from theological controversies. Ibn al-Jawzi reports that in A.H. 484, Nizam al-Mulk convened a group of Hanbalis while visiting Baghdad to inquire into the theological debate between the Shafi'i and Hanbali schools regarding the divine attributes. When accused by the Shafi'is of anthropomorphizing God, the Hanbalis declared: "Those who associate with the political rulers and seek worldly benefits (*talab ad-dunya*) have no right to fight us over theological questions."[42]

In dealing with the *madhahib* as social solidarity groups, we should also remember their amorphus and heterogeneous character. Except for the Hanbalis, who emerged as a rather cohesive school, the Baghdadi schools were liable to doctinal dissentions, as well as class or status divisions. Added to the dissentions between the "rationalists" and "traditionalists," there were in eleventh-century Baghdad rivalries within the Shafi'i and Hanafi schools over important *waqf* revenues—judicial positions, as well as teaching positions in the great mosques and madrasas—which extended to competition for governmental support. Noteworthy is the long rivalry over the chief judgeship between two Hanafi families: the Zainabis—a local family with established traditions of learning—and the "implanted" Damaghanis.[43] As for the Shafi'i camp, native and foreigner scholars, together with those who belonged to their study circles, competed over the prestigious position of the *mudarris* in the great Shafi'i madrasas.

Hanbalism—a school of law and theology—was the most localized and inclusive of the schools (see figures 2.4 and 2.5, above). Stressing the importance of the Koran and the *hadith*, and preserving the old, informal style of scholarly association, the school was open to a relatively large number of part-time scholars from various professional and social "classes," committed to the study and transmission of the prophetic traditions. From its circles of masters and disciples, Baghdadi Hanbalism reached out to include a community of followers from among the unlearned people to become a genuinely popular movement. In his account of one of the encounters between the Hanbalis and the Shafi'is, Ibn al-Banna' relates: "I sent a tailor from among us, who was neither a jurist (*faqih*) nor of any other class of learned men (*ahl al-'ilm*)."[44] In another part of the diary he tells of a marriage ceremony conducted by a group of Hanbali 'ulama' for a retail merchant whom he describes as a close associate (*sahib*).[45]

Driven primarily by religious motives, Hanbali preachers and theologians sought a remedy for the decline of the 'Abbasid caliphate and its capital by insisting upon public morality and individual action to combat religious and social innovations (*bida'*, sing. *bid'a*). But while defending the institution of the caliphate itself—commonly perceived as a symbol of legitimate government and unity among Muslims—the Hanbalis did not hesitate to act against individual caliphs, who, in the view of many Baghdadians, had failed to defend Islam and combat the spread of immorality. Ibn al-Athir relates that, during the terrible flood of A.H. 466, ash-Sharif Abu Ja'far, head of the Hanbali "traditionalist" movement, accused the caliph al-Qa'im of not having taken energetic enough action against prostitution, claiming that Allah had answered his pleas to halt the spread of immorality in the form of the flood. Led by Abu Ja'far, the people smashed the musical instruments of female singers and urged the caliph to destroy the brothels and wine shops.[46] It was probably the ability of the Hanbali ʿulamaʾ to present themselves as the defenders of "true" religion, as well as the distance many kept from the government, which enabled their movement to cultivate a large following. Abu Jaʿfar is praised for renouncing the patronage of the powerful and wealthy, and his biographer devotes long passages to describing his pious and ascetic habits and, of course, his deep commitment to "enjoin right conduct and forbid evil" (*amr biʾl-maʿruf waʾn-nahi ʿan al-munkar*), admonishing against typical "sins" such as playing musical instruments, dancing, and drinking liquor.[47] The descriptions of public demonstrations led by this Hanbali preacher give the impression of a close-knit group, bound together by common adherence to the school.

The valuable autograph diary of Ibn al-Bannaʾ offers a wealth of information about the strong ties of mutual affection and solidarity among adherents to Baghdadi Hanbalism, describing gatherings associated with funerals and weddings, visits to the sick and the provision of financial support to those in need by wealthy patrons of the school. Special attention is paid in the diary to describe the generosity of a wealthy Hanbali merchant, Shaykh al-Ajjal Abu Mansur b. Yusuf, and his support of the Hanbalis in their fight against innovation and sin. Upon his death, a group of Hanbalis went to his grave, rubbed their cheeks against it, and cried:

> O Master! Heretical innovations have gained the upper hand, and they wish to obliterate the truth. Whom do we have who will assist the Muslims after you? In whom shall we seek refuge after seeking it in God?[48]

Ibn Ridwan, the son-in-law of Shaykh al-Ajjal, followed his example. Once, while ill, Ibn al-Bannaʾ asked one of the pious *shaykh*s of the *madhhab* to pray for him during the Friday public prayer. The next day, a group of Hanbali followers traveled across the city to wish him a speedy recovery. Ibn Ridwan then gave numerous gifts to the poor, slaughtered cattle for distribution, and gave away coats and silver-coins.[49] Delivered from his illness, he went to the caliph's court preceded by the people, congratulating him and rejoicing in his recovery.[50]

Phrases such as "he guided the people" (*sada an-nas*), "the people adhered to him" (*ʿakafa an-nas ʿalayhi*) and "the Sunnis gained victory" (*intasara bihi ahl as-sunna*) are common in biographies of Hanbali *shaykh*s. There is, however, nothing in our sources to indicate that these leading men were actually successful in mobilizing the entire Sunni population to fight for their school's cause. Similarly, there is no evidence of Hanbali *shaykhs* providing places of refuge to the Sunnis of Baghdad, or even protecting the people of their own quarters. Notwithstanding the declining authority of the caliphate, many Baghdadians, including Hanbali 'ulama' and their followers, still sought refuge in *Dar al-khilafa* during periods of turmoil and upheaval. At the time of the Basasiri revolt (450/1058), for example, after an attack launched by the Shi'is of al-Karkh against the Sunni population of al-Basra Gate, many fled to *Dar al-khilafa.*[51]

Later, in 462/1069, a fight (*fitna*) broke out in al-Mansur Mosque as a result of attempts to free a woman from a Turk who had embraced her at the mosque's door. The Turkish soldiers fired arrows at the crowd praying in the mosque, killing a man and wounding a considerable number of people. Fearing the armed Turks present at the mosque, the crowd sought help at the caliph's palace, demanding that revenge be taken against the assassin and that the criminals be punished. In order to settle matters a delegation was sent to the caliph's *diwan*, or government center, comprised of jurisconsults (*fuqaha'*), noblemen (*sharaf*), merchants (*tujjar*), and notables (*amathil*). Several meetings ensued, some devoted to complete recitations of the Koran, others to fund-raising. All the while, the caliph's vizier and others were distributing garments and provisions to pacify the mass of the population.[52]

If Hanbali theologians and preachers did not emerge as popular leaders representing and protecting the people as a whole, this study suggests that it was not only because they had no means of coercion at their disposal, but because other popular movements with distinctive interests existed in society as well. As the political, economic, and cultural metropolis of the 'Abbasid caliphate, Baghdad was directly and forcefully affected by the all-embracing, radical changes produced by the disintegration of the Islamic state. This would appear to explain why most popular movements took place in Baghdad, partly as reaction to these changes. Viewed together, the three popular movements existing in medieval Baghdad between the ninth and eleventh centuries—the 'ayyarun (youth gangs or gallants), the Hanbalis, and the 'amma-led movements—can be considered variations on one great popular movement. By attacking the foreign Buyid and Seljuk regimes, all of these movements struggled to defend the caliphate and to restore its authority. The 'amma defended the caliphs and their power; the 'ayyarun opposed all foreign regimes of occupation, despite the different attitudes of the Sunni and Shi'i 'ayyarun toward the Buyids; and the Hanbalis fought against the political Shi'ism of the Buyids, as well as the Sunni Seljuk policy of patronizing Shafi'ism and strengthening the sultanate at the expense of the caliphate.

Yet, despite their common goals, each movement had its own distinctive interests. The main distinction can be seen most clearly in the socio-economic domain. 'Amma and 'ayyarun represented social movements which fought against members of the higher social strata and the ruling forces. The Hanbalis were a political-religious movement which insisted on public morality, showing little interest in socio-economic problems.[53]

Little is known about the relationship between popular groups such as the futuwa clubs (association of young men, fityan) or ayyar gangs, and the 'ulama'. What we do know, however, may support the assumption that there existed common interests or factions distinct from those of the 'ulama', even possessing their own leaders in Baghdadi society of the period under discussion. Ibn al-Jawzi tells us that in A.H. 473, the cloth merchant 'Abd al-Qadir al-Hashimi became leader of the local futuwa clubs. Having proclaimed himself chief secretary (katib) of the fityan, he tried to control membership in the organization by issuing certificates of admission to each new member, and even attempted to extend his leadership over futuwa clubs in other Muslim cities. Urged by a group of Hanbalis led by 'Abd as-Samad, the caliph vizier, 'Amid ad-Dawla, ordered the head of the police (shihna) to subdue the fityan's leader (ra'is) and his followers (ashab). Fearing the organization would become a source of factionalism and disorder, the jurists (fuqaha') then issued a legal opinion ordering the fityan to end their disturbance (fasad).[54]

This last story, so indicative of the conflicting group interests, provides us with another piece of evidence of 'ulama' of different schools collaborating to secure a degree of law and order. From the late eleventh century onward, the spirit of tolerance among members of the madhahib grew, and their popular activism began to wane. A more equal distribution of remuneration by the authorities among the madhahib also contributed to peaceful coexistence and a mutual recognition of the legitimacy of the four madhahib. It is therefore no wonder that the schools of law lost their characteristic element as social solidarity groups. Affiliation with them became thereafter purley formal, solely in the legal context.

Pious and Charismatic Leaders

Urban groups or factions named after a *madhahb* should not be confused with *madhhab* as a scholarly establishment. Yet, in dealing with the schools as social organizations, we should bear in mind the forms of social affiliation within the scholarly units which formed their cores. The students were bound together, not so much as common members of a certain school, but as common disciples of a certain *shaykh*. Just as in the small scholarly units, the devotion of the common people was to the *shaykh*, rather than to the school as a social organization. Members of the schools' extended circles, in other words, were drawn to a celebrated *shaykh*, just as the disciples themselves orbited around a leading *'alim*.

Although some *shaykh*s who attracted a public following held lucrative legal and educational positions, the commoners seem to be drawn more toward *shaykh*s who lived an ascetic and exemplary life, refusing any worldly benefits. Some combined religious learning with the special form of asceticism particular to Sufism, or, on occasion with charisma (*baraka*). Others were not particularly learned, nor were they Sufi or charismatic *shaykh*s. Significantly, authors of biographical dictionaries speak more about the outstanding *zuhd* (piety, asceticism) of these men than about their learning. They appear in our texts as teachers and models—examples of the Islamic way of life. Yet, though living an ascetic life, they served the community in a variety of ways.

Abu Muhammad at-Tamimi (d. 488/1095) is a good example of a *shaykh* whose fame rested on his piety. A member of a local Hanbali family with an established tradition of learning, and a disciple in his father's study circle on legal decisions and "academic" sermons convened in the mosque of al-Mansur, he suddenly ceased to attend the mosque and moved to *Dar al-khilafa*. He then made it his habit to visit Ibn Hanbal's grave four times annually, preaching publicly and reciting *hadiths*. Many people gathered around him to display their own piety and demonstrate their interest in prophetic traditions. He did not cater to their spiritual needs alone; though having received a great sum of money from the caliph in order to build a dome over Ibn Hanbal's grave, he refused to use it for this purpose, giving it to charity instead.[55]

The story about the Sufi-Ash'ari preacher, al-'Abbadi, whose academic sermon at the Nizamiyya Madrasa attracted a huge crowd, has already been mentioned. After he left the madrasa, he settled in the *ribat* of Abu Sa'd as-Sufi and took to public preaching in one of the prayer grounds. His biographer does not relate the exact content of his lectures to the thirty thousand men and women who followed him, yet it appears he followed the precept of "enjoin right conduct and forbid evil." The effect of his preaching on the people of Baghdad was so profound that they abandoned their work and daily occupations. Young men shaved their heads, barricaded themselves in mosques, poured barrels of wine on the ground, and smashed musical instruments. His fame as a charismatic *shaykh* soon spread among the people of Baghdad. Hoping to receive his divine blessing, or *baraka*, people used to fill bottles with water from the pond in the *ribat* where he performed his ritual ablution, until there was no water left. Bringing him gifts was another meaningful religious experience for local men and women. One story concerns a woman who begged him to accept the money she had earned from the sale of thread she had spun. Refusing to accept the money, he told the woman to buy food and bring it to the *ribat*.[56] The flow of such gifts probably increased, turning the *ribat* into a center for charity. This point is well illustrated in the following story, told by one of al-ʿAbbadi's fellow Sufis:

> He [al-ʿAbbadi] said to me: "I would like you to do something for me today." So I sold the chickens and sweets and received for them more than forty dinars. He then ordered me to summon people, and started to distribute the money to them, taking nothing for himself.[57]

Abu Bakr al-ʿAlathi (d. 504/1110) was another pious and charismatic *shaykh* totally devoted to serving others. Unlike al-ʿAbbadi, however, he was born in Baghdad and lived his entire life within the society that adored him. He did not take part in the international world of Islamic scholarship, nor was he a member of an ʿulamaʾ family. In his youth he was a plasterer and lime maker, but later quit this profession, devoting his efforts instead to intense religious learning. Upon receiving the divine blessing of his master, Qadi Abu Yaʿla, he became a pious and ascetic man, highly respected, loved, and adored by the people. Refusing to accept any worldly benefits from anyone, he sold a plot of land he had inherited from his father piece by piece, and lived on the proceeds. His biographer goes on to describe the ascetic customs of this venerated *shaykh* in detail: his supererogatory acts of worship, his frugality, austerity, and altruism. Though refusing to ask anyone's assistance, even that of his associates, he hastened to tend to the needs of the common people who adored him (*musara'an ila qada' hawa'ij al-muslimin, mukarraman 'ind an-nas*). In addition to teaching them the Koran and leading them in prayer, al-'Alathi performed many miracles for the benefit of those people who had faith in him. Among these deeds was the healing of a young man by reading to him some Koranic verses and moistening him with his own saliva.[58]

Modern scholarship has seen the veneration of the *shaykh*, who was believed to enjoy a special intimacy with God and, as a consequence, to possess unusual powers, a typical feature of religious life in rural and tribal societies far from urban centers.[59] Yet it may be argued that the need of such a pious and charismatic man to bridge the enormous gap between believers and Allah, bringing the presence of God into the community, was felt among city dwellers as well. Proof of a belief in such men in eleventh-century Baghdadi urban community is provided in lists of miracles (*karamat*) found in biographies of its pious and charismatic men. By the time these biographies were composed, the belief in *karamat* had been long recognized in learned circles as part of Muslim faith, and was even incorporated in written theological tracts.[60] However, Muslim writers had serious reservations about miracles, hence the tendency of biographical authors, who were themselves 'ulama', to play down the importance of *karamat* and stress instead the other qualities of the performers. The fame and influence of the pious and charismatic *shaykh* is commonly attributed to his outstanding piety; no less important seems to be his devotion to serving others. Obviously there existed strong links between the *shaykh*'s activities and his recognition in society. The more he provided the common people with their spiritual and nonreligious needs, the more they gathered around him; the larger his following became, the more he was admired.

Beginning in the late twelfth century, with the appearance of the Sufi fraternities, a new framework for communal services and social affiliation developed. However, until the Sufi fraternities became the central element in the public arena, religious and social life of the Baghdadi populace orbited, to a large extent, around local pious and charismatic *shaykhs*. No matter how limited the influence of these religious leaders might appear, they seem to have occupied as important a place in the public sphere of eleventh-century Baghdad as did the leading scholars of the *madhahib* at courts, mosques, and madrasas.

In the end, as the *madhahib* became rigid and elitist collectivities in function and recruitment, and their 'ulama' increasingly involved in the official sphere, they lost their significance as social organizations: a framework for religious, social, and even political life. Though leading ʿulamaʾ within one or another of the *madhahib* continued to provide a variety of religious and social services for the Baghdadi Muslim community, in the wake of the Sunni revival the schools of law were no longer the leading factor in providing social affiliation and identity, and in focusing solidarity in this urban society.

CONCLUSION

Eleventh-century Baghdad—the city in which the severe upheavals and religious fomentation of the post-ʿAbbasid era reached a climax—was a major site in which the first stages in the trend toward a greater degree of conformity and uniformity in religious and intellectual life took place. During this period of the Sunni revival, the Baghdadi ʿulamaʾ (like those of other Islamic cities) were seemingly more determined than their predecessors to define the boundaries of legitimate knowledge and transmit that knowledge to later generations of scholars. One of the main purposes of this study has been to shed light on the practices by which our subjects constructed their identities and loyalties, in order to guarantee their exclusive right to transmit "true" knowledge and secure the perpetuation of their groupings. The social significance of the advent of the madrasa and the consolidation of the Sunni schools of legal interpretation lie at the center of this inquiry.

Institutions can play an important role in generating social change. However, they can assume this role only after the process of institutionalization is completed—that is, after the organization, which forms the institution's core, becomes infused with commonly accepted values, comes to symbolize the community's aspirations and its sense of identity, and develops its own distinctive characteristics (as opposed to the characteristics of its members).[1] The madrasa is a good example; only gradually did it come to dominate religious learning and develop its distinctive tradition. Even then, it was no more than an organizational framework (as opposed to an "institution" in the usual sense of the term) where the customary cultural and social practices continued to prevail.

149

While questioning the importance of the madrasa and the *madhhab* as the principal frameworks with which the 'ulama' identified themselves and through which they acted, this study presents an alternative interpretation of the interrelationships between institutionalization and social change. By shifting the focus of our inquiry from the organizational frameworks to the cultural and social practices beyond them, from modern definitions of institutions to 'ulama''s characteristic image of structure and order, we were in a better position to understand the process of institutionalization and its social significance. At the same time, this unveiling demonstrated the dynamic of change in this society's prime characteristics.

The need to maintain the position and image of Baghdad as a major cultural center and seat of learning, during a period in which the city lost its political centrality, must have determined some of the primary characteristics of its learned society. This society was essentially a cosmopolitan, scholarly, and religious elite composed of native-born, immigrant, and transient 'ulama', who were part of a worldwide system of Islamic scholarship. Common beliefs and practices created a universal Muslim community in which a scholar, whatever his origin could take his place in the city on the basis of his established position, international reputation, and connections, irrespective of political boundaries.

The establishment and endowment of madrasas which provided financial support to teachers and students certainly contributed to a shift toward a local basis of recruitment in the course of the twelfth century. A wave of scholars from all parts of the Muslim world passed through Baghdad early in the eleventh century, but later scholars traveling to the city were more inclined to stay there. This free-floating world of scholars, however, did not disappear. The cosmopolitan character of Baghdadi learned society remained intact. Moreover, the advent and spread of madrasas in Baghdad and other Islamic cities reinforced the cultural contacts that cut across political and geographical boundaries. Nor did the old style of study, of wandering from teacher to teacher, and the highly personal, "informal" system of instruction fade away.

Various social practices grew up around the system of transmission over the course of time, strengthening it in their turn. Guaranteeing the social distinction and perpetuation of 'ulama' groupings, traditional modes of scholarly association and communication not only survived outside the madrasa, but influenced its "system" of education. An examination of these modes highlighted the centrality of the *halqa* as the core around which scholarly groupings constructed their identities and loyalties. Based on mutual commitments between a master and his disciples, this association preserved its crucial role in the world of the ʿulamaʾ, symbolizing their own perception of hierarchy, structure, and social order.

The intensive teachings of religious law, whether in madrasas and teaching mosques, or, more often, in *halqas* outside these educational forums, resulted in close bonds between a master and his disciples. But above all, it was the shared theological and moral perspectives that tied adherents to a particular *madhhab* together. This observation explains why, as the debates over proper creed and behavior between the factions, named after the legal schools and led by their *shaykhs* faded away, the *madhahib* lost their social essence. Affiliation with them became increasingly formal. Discernible as early as the first decades of the eleventh-century, a period which witnessed severe religious factionalism, overlapping scholarly networks were created, that cut across affiliation to the legal schools.

Continuous migration, as well as ever-changing patronage ties in a city which was a center of government, resulted in a turnover of religious elites. To this was added the comparative openness of this learned society to new leaders known for their religious learning and piety, beyond considerations of family background and connections. Outside the courts and madrasas, there were a large number of individuals from different walks of life who did not rely primarily on teaching or legal activities for their livelihood. After all, the knowledge of *hadith* still continued to distinguish an ʿalim in this society; its oral transmission was part and parcel of worship and devotion, thereby involving the entire Muslim community.

The perturbing question is how, despite the absence of any formal system of control and the apparent openness of the world of learning, there developed during this crucial period of the Sunni revival barriers which limited access to knowledge and barred admission to the ranks of the ʿulamaʾ. I have proposed that the root of the process lay in the manners by which a small local elite of legal experts managed to exploit the system of transmission, developed in earlier decades of the accumulation and dissemination of Islamic learning, to ensure its exclusive right to preserve and transmit "true" knowledge. The transmitting methods and the social practices which grew up around them guaranteed the coherence and perpetuation of *fuqahaʾ* grouping both as chains of transmitters and as social networks, setting these groupings apart at the same time. However, the financial patronage by the political rulers—through the foundation of madrasas, in particular—must have also played a role. This is true, in particular, of the rich array of career opportunities open to those 'ulama' who accepted the patronage of the wealthy and powerful, as well as the practice of sons inheriting the rank and office of fathers and other male relatives.

Although the phenomenon of 'ulama' families monopolizing prestige and honor within this urban community was too limited to supply the cadres of communal organization, Baghdadi 'ulama' played no less an important and autonomous role in the city's public sphere than did similar groups in some other Islamic cities. Their communal leadership took on a variety of forms, covering almost every aspect of religious and social life. Given the growing weakening of the political authorities since the late eleventh century, and the Seljuks' noninterference in the internal affairs of 'ulama', it is no wonder that their associations were developed and restructured according to their own dynamics, independently of the official sphere. During the eleventh century and immediately after, the *madhhab* was a meaningful social framework in Baghdadi urban society as a whole. At the end of the subsequent century, following the consolidation of the *madhahib* as legal bodies, Sufi fraternities began to offer a new framework for communal services and social affiliation. Their beginnings, however, were modest, as religious and social life orbited around *shaykh*s who led an ascetic and exemplary life, refusing worldly benefits.

Cosmopolitanism versus localism, inclusiveness versus exclusiveness, recognition in the necessity of the regime for defending Muslim territories against external enemies (Byzantines, crusaders) as opposed to abstention from any connections with the political rulers—these contradictions lie at the center of this study. Above all there was the paradox of an attempt to preserve the traditional methods of gathering and transmitting religious lore, and the adaptation to new organizational forms, which might have posed a threat to these methods. Never so profound as in this period of transition, these conflicting trends and ambivalences serve to explain the complex realities of the Baghdadi learned society.

For all that they are a social category difficult to define, and despite their internal differentiations, eleventh-century Baghdadi 'ulama'—those devoted to the transmission of Islamic learning and ethics—had a self-conscious identity which marked them as a distinct group. Bound by a shared tradition and common identity, they possessed a cohesion encouraged by the city's geographical, political, and intellectual significance. The highly elaborate techniques they applied in the process of the transmission of Islamic learning allowed them both to reproduce their forms over generations, and to transmit Islam's teachings and moral attitudes to other groups of society.

Even if organized patterns of the kind historians expect do not emerge, once we undertake to understand society in its own terms, we may further our ability to exploit the literary sources written by ʿulamaʾ for ʿulamaʾ. The working hypothesis of this study has been that the composition and preservation of biographical dictionaries constituted an integral element of the process of cultural and group reproduction. Not only did these texts serve as a primary means of preserving and disseminating the ideals and techniques of proper transmission of religious lore, whether true or false, the accounts and anecdotes in biographical dictionaries, together with the idealized descriptions of the biographees, nourished and reasserted the cultural and social practices which they echo. Creating a reservoir of role models, they must have also played a very important role in the process by which this, and other learned societies, defined their identities and assured their self-perpetuation.

APPENDIX A

❧

SCHOLARLY FAMILIES OF
ELEVENTH-CENTURY BAGHDAD

The families described below spanned at least three generations and supported themselves from generation to generation with paid professional positions. Local scholarly families achieved prominence on the basis of the old Baghdadi *hadith* and legal traditions, as well as on the basis of the new legal traditions and Sufi doctrines brought to the city throughout the eleventh century. The roots of certain families extended back at least a century. New families, established by native-born and immigrant scholars, combined to form a local group of ʿulamaʾ in Baghdad, which made a significant contribution to scholarly life of the city.

Families of Hanbali Legal Scholars

Eleventh-century Baghdad boasted four Hanbali scholarly families, all of which were established by native-born ʿulamaʾ: the Banu Yaʿla, the Tamimis, the Banu Musa al-Hashimi, and the Samads.

1. Banu Yaʿla

Al-Qadi Abu Yaʿla was certainly the most prominent Hanbali scholar in Baghdad during the first half of the eleventh century. Unlike his father, a Hanafi who introduced him to the Koran and the prophetic traditions, he became an adherent of the Hanbali school, apparently at a young age. He studied first with a Koranic teacher known as Ibn Mufriha, who guided his studies of the famous Hanbali

Figure A.1
Banu Ya'la

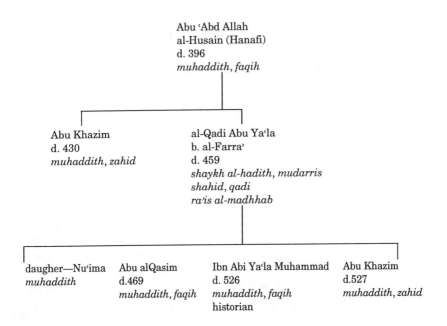

Abu 'Abd Allah
al-Husain (Hanafi)
d. 396
muhaddith, faqih

Abu Khazim
d. 430
muhaddith, zahid

al-Qadi Abu Ya'la
b. al-Farra'
d. 459
shaykh al-hadith, mudarris
shahid, qadi
ra'is al-madhhab

daugher—Nu'ima
muhaddith

Abu alQasim
d.469
muhaddith, faqih

Ibn Abi Ya'la Muhammad
d. 526
muhaddith, faqih
historian

Abu Khazim
d.527
muhaddith, zahid

treatise *Mukhtasar al-Khiraqi*—a work on which he later wrote commentaries—and then joined the study-circle of Ibn Hamid. On the death of his master, the young Abu Ya'la began his long career as *mudarris, muhaddith*, and *mufti*. A great number of people were attracted to his study circle, held in a mosque in Bab ash-Sha'ir, including members of other *madhahib*, Sufis, and scholars engaged in various fields of learning. He was nominated to the post of *shahid* by the chief qadi Abu 'Abd Allah ad-Damaghani, and later also as *qadi* of the Harim (the quarter of the caliphal palace), a post which he had previously refused.[1]

Abu Ya'la had a daughter and three sons. All began their education with their father apparently at extraordinarily young ages and are described as *muhaddithun*. The second son was the famous historian Ibn Abi Ya'la, author of *Tabaqat al-hanabila*. The youngest, Abu Khazim, is the last family member mentioned by the sources. He studied *fiqh* with Ya'kub al-Barzabini, who had been one of his father's closest disciples.[2] There is no mention of any of the sons holding religious or civil posts, and none appear to have equaled their father's reputation.

2. The Tamimis

This local Hanbali family, whose prominence in Baghdad's scholarly life can be traced to the ninth century, produced a number of renowned masters of legal scholarship and *hadith* studies. ʿAbd al-ʿAziz is the first member of the family for whom we have extant biographical material. He was the disciple of the famous Hanbali scholar Abu al-Qasim al-Khiraqi and the master in *fiqh* of al-Qadi Abu al-Hashimi.[3] In succeeding generations, ʿAbd al-ʿAziz's two sons, Abu al-Fadl ʿAbd al-Wahid and Abu al-Faraj ʿAbd al-Wahhab, as well as his grandson, Abu Muhammad, known as Rizq Allah, were among the most influential Hanbali scholars of their time.

Abu al-Fadl had a study circle in Jamiʿ al-Mansur for *waʿz*, *fatwa*, and the dictation of *hadith*. Upon his death, his younger brother Abu al-Faraj succeeded him.[4] His son Abu Muhammad, a student in *fiqh* of his grandfather's disciple Abu ʿAli al-Hashimi, played an important role both in the scholarly and political arenas of his period. In addition to succeeding his father in his circle of *waʿz* and *fatwa*, he taught *hadith* in the mosque of the caliphal palace. Unlike many Hanbalis of his generation, Abu Muhammad led the life of a courtier. He is said to have maintained close relationships with the caliphs al-Qaʾim and Muqtadi whom he served as an envoy to the Seljuk court.[5] Ibn Rajab relates that one of Abu Muhammad's sons used to wear silk clothing, a practice regarded improper by the ʿulamaʾ and especially by the Hanbalis.[6] Abu Muhammad had two sons, Abu al-Fadl and Abu al-Qasim. Both had *halqa* of *waʿz*, most likely in the tomb of Ibn al-Hanbal, but do not seem have been significant figures. Following the death of Abu al-Qasim in A.H. 493, the family faded away (*"khatama bihi baituhu"*).[7]

3. Banu Musa al-Hashimi

The tremendous respect in which the Hashimis—descendants of the clan of the Prophet Muhammad—have been held throughout Islamic history constitutes a social phenomenon of great importance. The Hashimis might be described as a blood aristocracy, a special category, which in a sense, may be considered "above" religious, social, and political distinctions. Similarly such families were likely to enjoy high esteem in eleventh-century Baghdadi society at large, and to

Figure A.2
The Tamimis

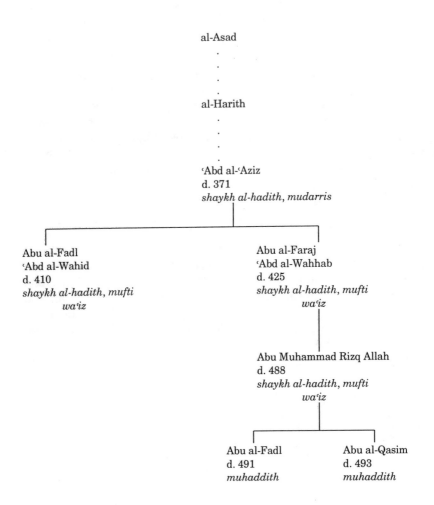

al-Asad

.

.

.

al-Harith

.

.

.

ʿAbd al-ʿAziz
d. 371
shaykh al-hadith, mudarris

Abu al-Fadl
ʿAbd al-Wahid
d. 410
shaykh al-hadith, mufti
waʿiz

Abu al-Faraj
ʿAbd al-Wahhab
d. 425
shaykh al-hadith, mufti
waʿiz

Abu Muhammad Rizq Allah
d. 488
shaykh al-hadith, mufti
waʿiz

Abu al-Fadl
d. 491
muhaddith

Abu al-Qasim
d. 493
muhaddith

acquire high positions which reflected this social status. One such family was that of Abu Musa.

The first member of the Baghdadi Hashimi family in our period for whom biographical material is extant is Abu ʿAli Muhammad. This renowned jurisconsult-*hadith* transmitter was a disciple in *fiqh* of Abu al-Hasan at-Tamimi, the paternal grandfather of his closest disciple, Abu Muhammad at-Tamimi, in his *halqa* in Jamiʿ al-Mansur.

Figure A.3
Banu Musa al-Hashimi

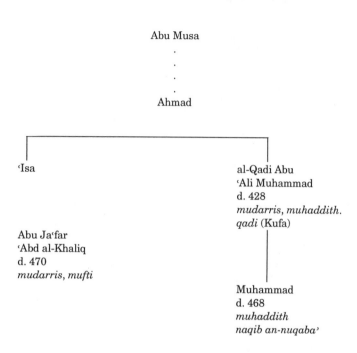

Abu Musa

Ahmad

'Isa

al-Qadi Abu
'Ali Muhammad
d. 428
mudarris, muhaddith.
qadi (Kufa)

Abu Ja'far
'Abd al-Khaliq
d. 470
mudarris, mufti

Muhammad
d. 468
muhaddith
naqib an-nuqaba'

Abu 'Ali is described as a wealthy man with landed property. We are told that at a certain point his fortune declined and he was forced to sell his property. Eventually, the caliph al-Qa'im, with whom he was closely associated, appointed him judge in Kufa so that he could regain his wealth.[8]

Abu 'Ali's son, Muhammad, held the office of *naqib al-hashimiyyin* (which signifies that a person is the chief of the Hashimis in a given locality) for a short period of time, and is described as a *muhaddith* in his own right.[9] Still, his cousin, Abu Ja'far, seems to be a more prominent figure in the history of the Hanbali school in Baghdad, being the leader of the popular movement against rationalism. Like other Hanbalis of his time, he combined the fields of law and *hadith*, studying with the famous Abu Ya'la and becoming one of the two most celebrated *fuqaha'* of the school after his death (the other being Abu Ali al-'Ukbari). He taught *fiqh* in several great mosques and issued legal opinions. Among the numerous students attending his study circles was Ibn Abi Ya'la, son of his master.[10] We thus find local Hanbali families during the period under consideration bound together in scholarly networks over the generations.

4. The Samads

The most prominent figure of this native Hanbali-Hashimi family of *khatibs* was Abu al-Husain Ahmad al-Muhtadi, known as Ibn al-Ghariq. Before assuming the *khatib*ship in two mosques, Jami' al-Mansur (succeeding his cousin) and al-Mahdi, he was only nominated *shahid* and *qadi*. The first nomination took place when he was only sixteen. Ibn al-Ghariq, famous most of all for his leading

Figure A.4
The Samads

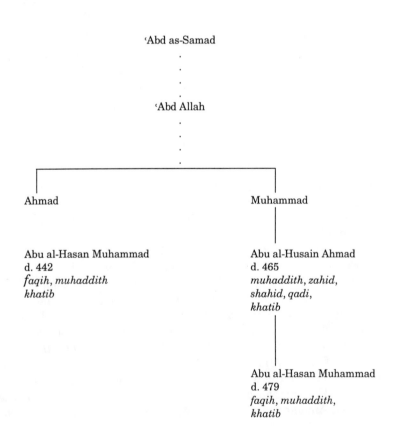

'Abd as-Samad

'Abd Allah

Ahmad

Abu al-Hasan Muhammad
d. 442
faqih, muhaddith
khatib

Muhammad

Abu al-Husain Ahmad
d. 465
muhaddith, zahid,
shahid, qadi,
khatib

Abu al-Hasan Muhammad
d. 479
faqih, muhaddith,
khatib

public demonstrations against Muʿtazilis and Ashʿaris, is described by Ibn al-Jawzi as a pious man and renowned *muhaddith*. His son Abu al-Hasan, also considered a trustworthy *muhaddith*, succeeded him in his chair in Jamiʿ al-Mansur.[11] The family disappears from the historical record upon his death in A.H. 479.

Families of Hanafi Legal Scholars

More than any other legal school during the period under review in Baghdad, the Hanafi school succeeded in establishing a strong family system of ʿulamaʾ notables. Members of two Hanafi families whose prominence spanned more than five generations acquired paid professional offices and passed them on to their sons and other male relatives in succeeding generations.

1. The Damaghanis

We have already discussed the life and career of Abu ʿAbd Allah ad-Damaghani, founder of the dynasty and the first to leave Damaghan in the province of Jibal. Following the death of the Shafiʿi chief *qadi* Ibn Makula in A.H. 447, Abu ʿAbd Allah succeeded him in the office, laying the foundations for a strong line of judges and chief judges that was to flourish for two centuries. There were periods when the Damaghanis were temporarily out of office, but they always managed to be reinstated. Once a member of the family became chief judge, he proceeded to appoint his brothers, sons, and nephews to important judicial posts. Thus, the Damaghanis supplied more judges than any other scholarly family during this period. In addition, their control over the judgeship enabled the Damaghanis to build up a clientele of *shuhud*, deputies, clerks, and other attendants attached to their courts. The Damaghanis were connected by marriage to the Simnamis, a small local Shafiʿi family which originally came from Simnan in the province of Jibal.[12]

2. The Zainabis

In early ʿAbbasid times, as well as the Buyid and Seljuk periods, members of the Zainabi-Hashimi family (descendants of the imam-martyr Ibrahim and his son-in-law Zainab) held the office of *naqib an-nuqabaʾ* or *naqib al-hashimiyin* in succeeding generations. The Zainabis also took over the chief judgeship in Baghdad in A.H. 513 upon the death of Abu al-Hasan ad-Damaghani, along with the

Figure A.5
The Damaghanis

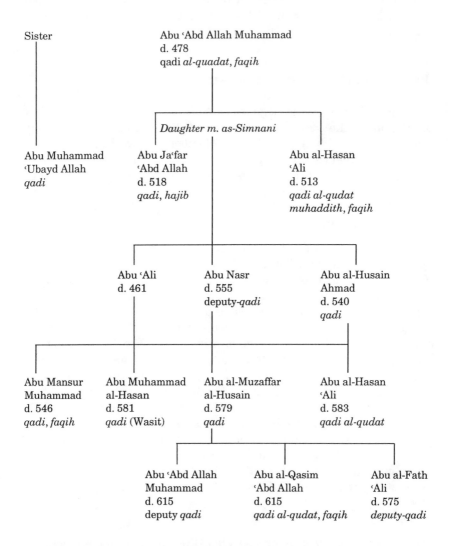

vezierate and the *niqaba*. Abu al-Qasim b. Abu Talib, known as *al-qadi al-akmal*, assumed the chief judgeship, while his paternal cousin, ʿAli b. Tirad, held both the *niqaba* and the vizierate.[13]

Two members of the family, Abu Talib Nur al-Huda and his brother Abu al-Fawaris Tirad, appear to have achieved prominence in the domains of legal scholarship and *hadith*. Nur al-Huda studied *fiqh* with Abu ʿAbd Allah ad-Damaghani and assumed the chair of *fiqh* in the great Hanafi madrasa of *mashhad* Abu Hanifa, a position which he later passed on to his son, chief *qadi* Abu al-Qasim. He held the *niqaba* for only a few months before passing it on to his brother Abu al-Fawaris.[14] The latter is described as a renowned *muhaddith*, who was devoted to the transmission of *hadith* even while preoccupied with his administrative position. He had a study circle for the dictation of *hadith* in Jamiʿ al-Mansur, the stronghold of the Hanbalis in Baghdad, as well as in locations outside the city, primarily Mecca and Medina.[15] The line of *naqib*s continued with Abu al-Fawaris, and disappeared from the historical record with the death of Qutham b. Talha az-Zainabi in A.H. 607.

Families of Shafiʿi Legal Scholars

Unlike the Hanbali and Hanafi schools, the Shafiʿi school was dominated by immigrant and transient ʿulamaʾ with worldwide experience (compare figures 2.4, 2.5, and 2.7). Only two Shafiʿi families, spanning more than three generations of scholars, emerged in the city during the period under consideration. Their first members studied with the two most influential masters of the *madhahab* during the first half of the eleventh century, Abu Hamid al-Isfaraʾini and his disciple Abu Taiyib at-Tabari, both immigrants from Iranian cities who represented the new traditions of Shafiʿi scholarship which arrived in Baghdad during the late tenth and early eleventh centuries.

1. Banu Sabbagh

According to their professional *nisba*, the Banu Sabbagh came from a family of dyers, which may have combined religious scholarship with secular profession. We may also assume that they were a wealthy family, as they resided in Bab al-Maratib. The first member to appear in the sources as a professional legal scholar is Muhammad b. as-Sabbagh (d. 448/1056), a disciple in *fiqh* of Abu Hamid al-Isfaraʾini, the *raʾis* of the Shafiʿi school in the late tenth and early eleventh centuries. Upon completing his education, he began to transmit *hadith*s and issue legal opinions in his *halqa* of *iftaʾ*, held in Jamiʿ al-Madina. He is described as a trustworthy *muhaddith* on whose authority a great number of traditions were written down.[16]

Figure A.6
The Zainabis

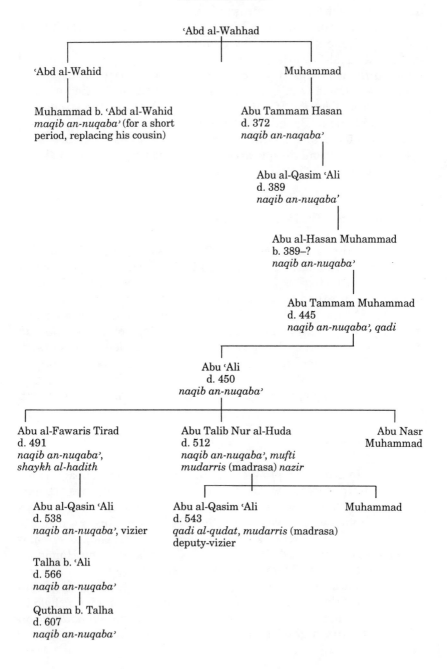

'Abd al-Wahhad

'Abd al-Wahid

Muhammad b. 'Abd al-Wahid
maqib an-nuqaba' (for a short
period, replacing his cousin)

Muhammad

Abu Tammam Hasan
d. 372
naqib an-naqaba'

Abu al-Qasim 'Ali
d. 389
naqib an-nuqaba'

Abu al-Hasan Muhammad
b. 389–?
naqib an-nuqaba'

Abu Tammam Muhammad
d. 445
naqib an-nuqaba', qadi

Abu 'Ali
d. 450
naqib an-nuqaba'

Abu al-Fawaris Tirad
d. 491
*naqib an-nuqaba',
shaykh al-hadith*

Abu Talib Nur al-Huda
d. 512
*naqib an-nuqaba', mufti
mudarris* (madrasa) *nazir*

Abu Nasr
Muhammad

Abu al-Qasin 'Ali
d. 538
naqib an-nuqaba', vizier

Abu al-Qasim 'Ali
d. 543
qadi al-qudat, mudarris (madrasa)
deputy-vizier

Muhammad

Talha b. 'Ali
d. 566
naqib an-nuqaba'

Qutham b. Talha
d. 607
naqib an-nuqaba'

His son Abu Nasr 'Abd al-Saiyid, known above all for his celebrated work *ash-Shamil,* became *ra'is al-shafi'iyya* and is classed by as-Subki both as one of the most prominent legal scholars of his time as well as a trustworthy *muhaddith.* Among those who transmitted *hadiths* from him was al-Khatib al-Baghdadi. Abu Nasr assumed the professorship in the Nizamiyya Madrasa twice, but was dismissed by Nizam al-Mulk.[17] He married his daughter to his nephew Abu Mansur Ahmad, a *muhaddith* and *faqih,* who, like Abu Nasr, studied *fiqh* with Abu at-Taiyib at-Tabari.[18]

2. The Shashis

This Shafi'i family was founded by immigrants from Mayya-fariqin in the Jazira. Both Abu Bakr Muhammad and his eldest

Figure A.7
Banu Sabbagh

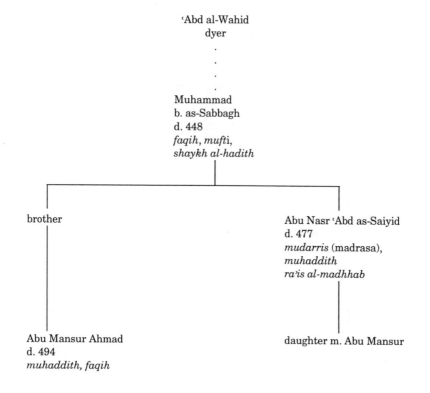

'Abd al-Wahid
dyer
.
.
.
Muhammad
b. as-Sabbagh
d. 448
faqih, mufti,
shaykh al-hadith

brother

Abu Nasr 'Abd as-Saiyid
d. 477
mudarris (madrasa),
muhaddith
ra'is al-madhhab

Abu Mansur Ahmad
d. 494
muhaddith, faqih

daughter m. Abu Mansur

brother Abu Hafs 'Umar began their studies in their hometown, but later moved to Baghdad to continue their education.[19] Abu Bakr studied law both with as-Sabbagh and ash-Shirazi and was considered to be ash-Shirazi's closest disciple (*sahib*). Upon the death of his two masters, he became the *ra'is* of the Shafi'i school in Baghdad. At first he taught Shafi'i law in a madrasa located in Qarah Zafar in the eastern side of the city, which was later named after him. Then, in A.H. 482, when Taj al-Mulk founded the Tajiyya Madrasa, he assigned to Abu Bakr the professorship in his madrasa. Upon the death of al-Kiya al-Harrasi, in A.H. 504, Abu Bakr assumed the position of *mudarris* in the prestigious Nizamiyya Madrasa and thaught there for the rest of his life.[20]

Abu Bakr had two sons, Abu Muzaffar and Abu Muhammad. Both were introduced to the doctrine of the *madhhab* by their father and heard Prophetic traditions. Abu Muzaffar died young, before he could transmit *hadiths*. Abu Bakr's younger son succeeded him in his chair in madrasa at-Tajiyya.[21]

Figure A.8
The Shashis

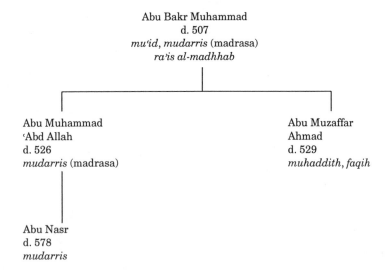

Abu Bakr Muhammad
d. 507
mu'id, mudarris (madrasa)
ra'is al-madhhab

Abu Muhammad
'Abd Allah
d. 526
mudarris (madrasa)

Abu Muzaffar
Ahmad
d. 529
muhaddith, faqih

Abu Nasr
d. 578
mudarris

Families of *muhaddithun*

Although the majority of *muhaddithun* residing in eleventh-century Baghdad were native-born (compare figures 2.4 and 2.7), there was only one local family of *hadith* experts during this period whose members are known to have held study circles for the dictation of *hadith* or who taught a large number of students. It appears that by the twelfth century, *hadith* transmission had come to be dominated either by individual scholars possessing credentials in law or by members of families that combined the fields of law and *hadith* studies. Our sources also suggest that families of Baghdadi *hadith* transmitters that survived, gradually moved into legal scholarship, professorships, and judgeships.

1. The Bishrans

This small native family of *hadith* transmitters extends back into the tenth century, but its most prominent figures taught in Baghdad during the following century. Abu al-Husain is described by Ibn al-Jawzi as one of the renowned traditionalists of his time. He is said to have taught a great number of people, probably in one or more of the great mosques of Baghdad. Among those who transmitted *hadith* from him was the Hanbali Ibn al-Banna', who studied *hadith* with his younger brother Abu al-Qasim as well.[22] By the time of his nephew Abu Bakr's rise, the family had long been well-known in Baghdadi circles. He was the teacher in *hadith* of the famous Hanbali scholar Ibn 'Aqil, and in addition to teaching the prophetic traditions, was in charge of funeral ceremonies in the great mosque of the "round city."[23]

Families of shaykhs as-sufiyya

The first scholars to bear the title of *shaykh as-sufiyya* or *shaykh ash-shuyukh*, signifying that a person is the chief of the Sufis in a certain locality, were the Sufi-Hanbali masters 'Ali b. Ibrahim al-Husri (d. 371/981) and his disciple Abu al-Hasan az-Zauzani (d. 451/1059). However, it was with the Sufi-Ash'ari Abu Sa'd b. Dust an-Nishapuri that the title was given official recognition and its holder became the director of the *awqaf* endowed for the foundation of Sufi *ribats*.[24] The creation of the office may be seen as a part of the broader process of the institutionalization of Sufism, which began in

Figure A.9
The Bishrans

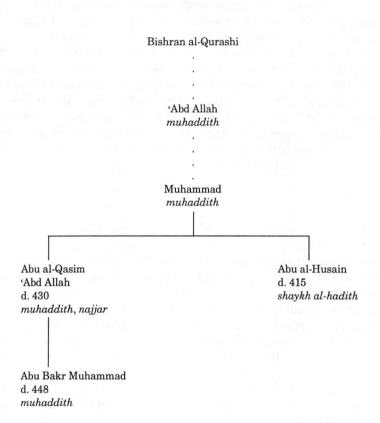

Bishran al-Qurashi

'Abd Allah
muhaddith

Muhammad
muhaddith

Abu al-Qasim
'Abd Allah
d. 430
muhaddith, najjar

Abu al-Husain
d. 415
shaykh al-hadith

Abu Bakr Muhammad
d. 448
muhaddith

the eleventh century and formed the basis for the appearance of the Sufi fraternities in subsequent centuries.

1. Banu Dust an-Nishapuri

Abu Sa'd originally came from Nishapur in the province of Khurasan, which, became a major source of Sufi recruitment in Baghdad during the period under review. He first resided in the *ribat* of 'Attab, established in the late tenth century. Eventually, he founded his own *ribat*, known as *Ribat* Abu Sa'd or *Ribat shaykh ash-shuyukh*, which was to become a major center of Sufi learning and devotion.[25] Upon his death, the supervision of his *ribat*, along with the title *shaykh as-shuyukh*, passed to his descendants (his son

Abu al-Barakat Isma'il and grandsons 'Abd ar-Rahim and 'Abd al-Latif). His grandson 'Abd al-Latif passed the title on to his own son-in-law, Ibn Sukayna. With this Sufi master's death in A.H. 607 there is no further mention of the family in the historical record.

Figure A.10
Banu Dust an-Nishapuri

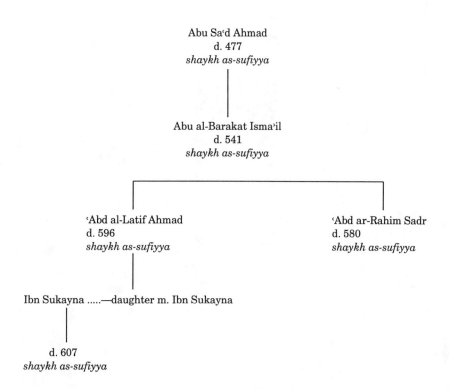

Abu Sa'd Ahmad
d. 477
shaykh as-sufiyya

Abu al-Barakat Isma'il
d. 541
shaykh as-sufiyya

'Abd al-Latif Ahmad
d. 596
shaykh as-sufiyya

'Abd ar-Rahim Sadr
d. 580
shaykh as-sufiyya

Ibn Sukayna .....—daughter m. Ibn Sukayna

d. 607
shaykh as-sufiyya

APPENDIX B

PROFESSORS
IN THE MADRASAS OF
BAGHDAD (459/1066–549/1154)

I. Shafi'i madrasas

Dates in office
or death date   Name and geographical origin

1. 459–476   Abu Ishaq Ibrahim ash-Shirazi. immigrant
2. 476–477   Abu Nasr 'Abd as-Saiyid b. as-Sabbagh (dyer). native-born
3. 477–478   Abu Sa'd 'Abd al-Rahman al-Mutawalli. immigrant
4. 479–482   Abu al-Qasim al-'Alawi ad-Dabbusi. immigrant
5. 483–484   Abu 'Abd Allah al-Husain at-Tabari. immigrant
6. 483–484   Abu Muhammad 'Abd al-Wahhab al-Farisi. immigrant
7. 484–488   Abu Hamid Muhammad al-Ghazzali. substituting for his brother. transient
8. 488–?   Abu al-Futuh Ahmad al-Ghazzali. transient
9. 493–504   Abu al-Hasan 'Ali at-Tabari, known as al-Kiya al-Harrasi. immigrant
10. 504–507   Abu Bakr Muhammad ash-Shashi. immigrant
11. Died 510   Abu Muhammad al-Andalusi as-Saraqusti. transient
12. Died 518   Abu al-Fath b. al-Hamani. native-born
13. Died 518   Abu al-Fath Ahmad b. Barhan. native-born

14. 507–513; 517	Abu al-Fath As'ad al-Mihani. transient
15. ?–517	Abu al-Fath al-Baqarki. native-born (died in Ghazna)
16. Died 520	Abu Sa'd al-Bazzar (seedsman), known as Ibn Hulwani. native-born
17. Died 525	Al-Hasan b. Salman al-Naharwani. immigrant
18. Died 528	Abu Muhammad 'Abd Allah ash-Shashi. native-born
19. Died 531	Abu Bakr al-Khujandi al-Isfahani. immigrant
20. Died 531	Abu Muhammad 'Abd ar-Rahman at-Tabari. native-born (died in Khawarizm)
21. Died 539	Abu Mansur Sa'id b. ar-Razzaz (rice-dealer). native-born
22. 545–547	Abu Najib 'Abd al-Qahir, as-Suhrawardi. immigrant
23. 535–552	Abu al-Hasan b. al-Khall. native-born
24. Died 552	Abu Bakr Muhammad al-Khujandi. transient

II. Hanafi madrasas

Dates in office or death date	Name and geographical origin
1. 459–461	Abu Tahir Ilyas ad-Dailami. native-born
2. 461–512	Nur al-Huda az-Zainabi. native-born
3. Died 515	Abu al-Qasim ad-Darir ash-Shilhi. immigrant
4. Died 537	Abu Mansur Ibrahim al-Ansari. immigrant
5. Died 543	Abu al-Qasim 'Ali az-Zainabi. native-born
6. ? –556	Abu al-Husain al-Yazdi. native-born

III. Hanbali madrasas

Dates in office or death date	Name and geographical origin
1. Died 513	Abu Sa'd al-Mubarak al-Mukharrimi. native-born

APPENDIX C

ᑎᖇ

QADIS AND KHATIBS OF
BAGHDAD (409/1018 – 549/1154)

I. Qadis

Dates in office or death date	Name and comments
1. 405–417	Abu al-Hasan Ahmad b. Abu ash-Shawarib. chief judge Native-born, Hanafi. The last member of the Shawarib family of *qadis* and chief *qadis*
2. Died 422	Abu Muhammad ʿAbd Allah al-Baghdadi al-Maliki. native-born (died in Cairo)
3. Died 425	Abu al-ʿAbbas al-Abiwardi. immigrant, Shafiʿi
4. Died 425	Abu ʿAbd Allah al-Husain as-Saimari. native-born, Hanafi
5. Died 446	Abu ʿAbd Allah Muhammad al-Isfahani. immigrant, Shafiʿi
6. 420–447	Abu ʿAbd Allah al-Husain, known as chief judge Ibn Makula. immigrant, Shafiʿi
7. 436–450	Abu at-Taiyib Tahir at-Tabari. immigrant, Shafiʿi
8. Died 458	Abu Yaʿla Muhammad b. al-Farraʾ. native-born, Hanbali
9. 436-461	Abu Tahir ʿIlyas ad-Dailami. native-born, Hanafi
10. Died 463	Abu al-Ghanaiʾm Muhammad b. ad-Dujjaji. native-born, Hanbali
11. 409–465	Abu al-Husain Ahmad al-Muhtadi, known as Ibn Ghariq. native-born, Hanbali
12. Died 466	Abu al-Hasan as-Simnani. native-born, Hanafi

173

13. 447–478   Abu ʿAbd Allah Muhammad ad-Damaghani. chief judge, immigrant, Hanafi
14. Died 470   Abu ʿAbd Allah al-Baidawi. native-born, Shafiʿi
15. Died 478   Abu al-Hasan as-Sibi, known as Hibat Allah. native-born, Hanbali
16. 478–487   Abu Bakr ash-Shami al-Hamawi. chief judge, immigrant, Shafiʿi
17. 470–?   Abu Muhammad ʿUbayd Allah ad-Damaghani. native-born, Hanafi
18. 465–479   Abu al-Hasan, Hibat Allah al-Muhtadi. native-born, Hanbali
19. Died 485   Abu Muhammd al-ʿAmani. native-born, Hanbali. Died in Basra.
20. Died 486   Abu al-Maʿali al-Baghdadi. native-born, Hanafi. Died in Anbar.
21. Died 486   Abu ʿAli Yaʿyub al-Barzabini. immigrant, Hanbali
22. 488–490   Abu Jaʿfar ʿAbd Allah ad-Damaghani. native-born, Hanafi
23. Died 494   Abu al-Maʿali ʿAzizi al-Jili. native-born, Shafiʿi
24. Died 507   Abu Mansur al-Anbari. immigrant, Hanbali
25. Unknown   Abu ʿAli Mubarak al-Baghdadi. native-born, Hanbali
26. ?–511   Abu Saʿd al-Mukharrimi. native-born, Hanbali
27. Died 512   Abu al-Barakat Talha al-ʿAquli. immigrant, Hanbali
28. Died 515   Abu al-Qasim ash-Shalaji. immigrant, Hanbali
29. 487–513   Abu al-Hasan ʿAli ad-Damaghani. chief judge, native-born, Hanafi
30. Unknown   Abu as-Saʿadat Muhammad b. Hasan. native-born, Hanafi
31. Died 523   Abu al-Fawaris Mansur al-Mosuli. immigrant, Hanafi
32. Died 535   Abu Bakr Muhammad b. ʿAbd al-Baqi, known as Qadi Maristan. native-born, Hanbali
33. Died 533   Abu ʿAli Hasan b. Saʿid. immigrant, Hanafi
34. Died 540   Abu al-Husain Ahmad ad-Damaghani. native-born, Hanafi
35. Died 541   Abu Muhammad al-Hasan b. Ahmad. immigrant, Hanafi-Muʿtazili
36. 513–543   Abu al-Qasim ʿAli az-Zainabi. chief judge, native-born, Hanafi

II. Khatibs

Dates in office
or death date   Name and comments

1. Died 428	Abu al-Fadl at-Tamimi al-Hashimi. native-born, *muhaddith*
2. 386–447	Abu Bakr at-Tammam al-Hashimi. native-born, *muhaddith*
3. Died 442	Abu al-Hasan Muhammad al-Hashimi. native-born, Hanbali
4. Died 444	Abu al-Fadl Muhammad al-Hashimi. native-born, *muhaddith*
5. Died 463	Abu Bakr Ahmad al-Khatib, known as al-Khatib al-Baghdadi. immigrant, Hanbali, later Shafi'i
6. Died 464	Abu al-Hasan Muhammad al-Hashimi. native-born, *muhaddith*
7. 409–465	Abu al-Husain Ahmad al-Muhtadi, known as Ibn Ghariq. native-born, Hanbali
8. Died 476	Abu al-Khattab al-Baghdadi. native-born, Shafi'i, later Hanbali
9. 465–479	Abu al-Hasan Hibat Allah (son of Ibn al-Ghariq). native-born, Hanbali
10. Died 507	Abu Mansur al-Anbari. immigrant, Hanbali
11. Died 539	Abu al-Hasan al-Khatib al-Baghdadi. native-born, *muhaddith*

NOTES

Introduction

1. Several historians of medieval Muslim societies have undertaken the study of the period A.D. 950–1150 and the "transformation" of Islamic civilization at the close of the twelfth century. For their interpretations, see *Islamic Civilization 950–1150*, ed. D. S. Richards (Oxford, 1973). For a perception of the period as one of transition, see also Marshall G. S. Hodgson, *The Venture of Islam: Conscience and History in a World Civilization*, vol. 2: *The Expansion of Islam in the Middle Periods* (Chicago, 1974), esp. 3, 8–9. See also Richard Bulliet, *Islam: The View from the Edge* (New York, 1994) for a social historian who abandons the historical view of looking at Islamic history "from the center," focusing instead on changes in the social structure of the vast majority of Muslims who lived at "the edge," primarily eastern Iran. Note esp. 8–12, 101.

2. See George Makdisi, "Law and Traditionalism in the Institutions of Learning of Medieval Islam," in *Theology and Law in Islam*, ed. G. E. von Grunebaum (Wiesbaden, 1971), 75–88; *EI*, 2nd edition, s.v. "Madrasa," by Johannes Pederson and George Makdisi. See also Gary Leiser, "The Restoration of Sunnism in Egypt: Madrasa and Mudarrisun, 495–647/1101–1249" (Ph.D. diss., University of Pennsylvania, 1976), 410; idem, "The Madrasa and the Islamization of the Middle East: The Case of Egypt," *JARCE* 22 (1985), 29–47. A. L. Tibawi was the first to point out that madrasas were not just colleges of law, but taught other subjects, except for philosophy, in "Origins and Character of *al-Madrasa*," *BSOAS* 25 (1962), 225–38.

3. George Makdisi was the first to argue that the Sunni revival was independent of Ash'arism and the Great Seljuks in "The Sunni Revival," in *Islamic Civilization*, ed. Richards, 155–68. See also Bulliet's remak in *The View from the Edge*, 148, that "the spread of the madrasa from the late

eleventh century on cannot be explained by a putative Sunni revival rooted in the religious policies of the rulers in the center."

4. See Makdisi, "Law and Traditionalism," 83.

5. On the early *khanqahs*, see J. Spenser Trimingham, *The Sufi Orders in Islam* (Oxford University Press, 1971), 8; *EI*, 2nd edition, s.v. "*Khanakah*," by J. Chabbi based primarily on R. Frye, *The Histories of Nishapur* (Harvard, 1965).

6. The persecution of Ibn ʿAqil is discussed in detail by Makdisi, *Ibn ʿAqil et la résurgence de l'islam traditionaliste au xie siècle* (Damas, 1963).

7. See Wael B. Hallaq, "Was the Gate of Ijtihad Closed?," *IJMES* 16 (1984), 3–14, for a study which has challenged the traditional interpretation of the development of Islamic jurisprudence, offered by Joseph Schacht, *An Introduction to Islamic Law* (Oxford, 1964) and N. J. Coulson, *A History of Islamic Law* (Edinburgh, 1964).

8. For a study which describes this process in a very persuasive manner, see W. Madelung, "Authority in Twelver-Shiʿism in the Absence of the Imam," in G. Makdisi, *La Notion d'Autorité au Moyen Age—Islam, Byzance, Occident* (Paris, 1982), 163–73.

9. Franz Rosenthal, *The Technique and Approach of Muslim Scholarship*, in *Analecta Orientalia* 24 (Rome, 1947) is undoubtedly the most comprehensive exposition on the nature of Muslim scholarship and its trends of evolution in the Middle Ages. For a general exposition of the importance of knowledge in Islamic tradition, see especially idem, *Knowledge Triumphant* (Leiden, 1970), 19–32, 277–98 (monographs in the praise of knowledge); Wan Mohd Nor Wan Daud, *The Concept of Knowledge in Islam, and its Implication for Education in a Developing Country* (London, 1989), 32–36.

10. On the freer and wider cultural dialogue of the late tenth and early eleventh centuries, see especially Roy P. Mottahedeh, *Loyalty and Leadership in an Early Islamic Society* (Princeton, 1980), esp. 29–31; and see Hodgson, *The Venture of Islam*, 2:152–200, for the variety of intellectual life in the "Earlier Middle Period."

11. See R. Stephen Humphreys' remark in his overview of scholarly literature about the ʿulamaʾ that "they are neither a socio–economic class, nor a clearly defined status group, nor a hereditary caste, nor a legal estate, nor a profession." Humphreys, *Islamic History: A Framework for Inquiry* (London, 1991), 187. For the modern era, see Michael Gilsenan, *Recognizing Islam: Religion and Society in the Modern Middle East* (London, 1982), chap. 2: "Men of Learning and Authority," 27–55.

12. See Ira M. Lapidus, *A History of Islamic Societies*, 4th ed. (New York, 1988), 176–77, for the informality of social practices and groups of this

period. The most comprehensive study of the social bonds that created the social structure in the Buyid and Seljuk periods is that by Mottahedeh, *Loyalty and Leadership*.

13. Makdisi's work was published in a number articles and in *The Rise of Colleges: Institutions of Learning in Islam and the West* (Edinburgh, 1981). For his many articles, see in the bibliography. Literature on madrasas in different places and periods includes: Jonathan Berkey, *The Transmission of Knowledge in Medieval Cairo* (Princeton, 1992); Bulliet, *The Patricians of Nishapur: A Study of Medieval Islamic Social History* (Cambridge, Mass., 1972), esp. 159, 249–50; Michael Chamberlain, *Knowledge and Social Practice in Medieval Damascus 1190–1350* (Cambridge, 1995), 69–90; Leiser, "The Restoration of Sunnism"; idem, "The Madrasa and the Islamization of the Middle East"; J. Pederson, "Some Aspects of the History of the Madrasa," *IC* 4 (1929), 527–37; H. Shumaysi, *Madaris Dimashq fi'l-ʿasr al-ayyubi* (Beirut, 1983); A. Talas, *La Madrasa Nizamiyya et son histoire* (Paris, 1939).

14. On the spread of madrasas in Iraq and Syria, note especially: Dominique Sourdel, "Réflexions sur la diffusion de la madrasa en orient du xie au xiiie siècle, *REI* 44 (1976), 165–84; Janine Sourdel-Thomine, "Locaux d'enseignements et madrasas dans l'islam médiéval," *REI* 44 (1976), 185–97.

15. Tibawi, "Origin and Character of *al-Madrasah*." Note esp. 230–31.

16. Note especially Ira M. Lapidus, *Muslim Cities in the Later Middle Ages* (Cambridge, Mass., 1967), 111. See also Roy P. Mottahedeh, *The Mantle of the Prophet* (New York, 1985), 98.

17. Berkey, *The Transmission of Knowledge*, esp. 21–27, 43, 216–18.

18. Chamberlain, *Knowledge and Social Practice*, 90.

19. Montgomery Watt, *Islamic Political Thought* (Edinburgh, 1968), 75–76, was the first to point out that education in the Nizamiyya Madrasas was designed to create an "orthodox bureaucracy." See also Bulliet's remark in *The Patricians*, 73–75, that the Nizamiyya Madrasa became a vital instrument in Nizam al-Mulk's policy of controlling what he labels the "patriciate" of Nishapur; and Gary Leiser's observation in "Note on the Madrasa in Medieval Islamic Society," *MW* 56: 1 (January, 1986), 18, that one of the reasons for the founding of colleges was "the desire of the ruling authorities to dominate, to a considerable degree, the religious elite."

20. On the significant role of the madrasas in the process of the consolidation of the legal schools and their evolution into popular factions, see especially Lapidus in *A History*, 165–66. For the importance of madrasas in the social organization of the ʿulamaʾ, see also Joan E. Gilbert, "Institutionalization of Muslim Scholarship and Professionalization of the ʿUlamaʾ in Medieval Damascus," *SI* 52 (1980), 105–34. Makdisi, in the introductory remarks to *The Rise of Colleges*, makes a clear distinction

between schools of law and colleges of law. However, he too presents a parallel and interrelated development of the two types of institutions. See esp. ibid., 1–3.

21. See especially P. M. Holt, *The Age of the Crusades: The Near East from the Eleventh Century to 1517* (New York, 1986), 80. For a different view, see Trimingham, *The Sufi Orders of Islam*, 10. It was, according to Trimingham, around persons (the Sufi *shaykhs*), rather than around places, that the institutionalization of the schools of mysticism took place. Probably the best discussion of the evolution of the Sufi *tariqa* during the late tenth and eleventh centuries is to be found in Annemarie Schimmel, *Mystical Dimensions of Islam* (North Carolina, 1975), 82–91. However, the study of the early phase in the development of the *tariqa* as an organization (as opposed to "a way") must be taken on further. See Nehemia Levtzion, "Eighteenth Century Sufi Brotherhoods: Structural, Organizational and Ritual Changes," in *Islam: Essays on Scripture, Thought and Society*, eds. P. G. Riddell and T. Street (Leiden, 1997), 147–66, for a study which has challenged the commonly accepted periodization of the institutionalization of Sufism. Levtzion argues that, up to the seventeenth century, most Sufi fraternities were diffusive affiliations, without a central organization, and without strong links between their members.

22. The most systematic body of research on the *madhhab* as a social and professional institution is represented by Henri Laoust on the Hanbali school, first in his work on Ibn Taymiyya, and then in a series of articles. For the period under consideration in this study, see "Le Hanbalisme sous le Califat de Baghdad, 241/855–656/1258," *REI* 27 (1959), 67–128.

23. Here I have been influenced by Berkey, *The Transmission of Knowledge*. By beginning his study with an examination of the patterns of instruction and the modes of scholarly communication, Berkey enables us to understand the variety and complexity of the world of higher education in Mamluk Cairo that have otherwise remained concealed.

24. See Humphreys, *Islamic History*, 187; Mottahedeh, book review of Bulliet, *The Patricians*, in *JAOS* 95 (1975), 491.

25. Lapidus, *Muslim Cities*. Lapidus deals with the ʿulamaʾ principally in chapters 4 and 5. Bulliet, *The Patricians*; Mottahedeh, *Loyalty and Leadership*, 135–50.

26. See Berkey, *The Transmission of Knowledge*, 183–218, for a discussion of the social and cultural consequences of Islam's regard for knowledge, showing how religious education was never exclusively for the learned elite, but rather open to all. See also the remarks of Mottahedeh in *Loyalty and Leadership*, 140–44.

27. W. L. Warren, "Biography and the Medieval Historian," in *Medieval Historical Writing in the Christian and Islamic Worlds*, ed. D. S. Morgan (London, 1982), 8.

28. On the development and features of biographical dictionaries and their place in Islamic historiography, see H. A. R. Gibb, "Islamic Biographical Literature," in *Historians of the Middle East*, eds. B. Lewis and P. M. Holt (London, 1962), 54–58; F. Rosenthal, *A History of Muslim Historiography* (Leiden, 1952), 82–84; I. Hafsi, "Recherches sur le genre 'Tabaqat' dans la littérature arabe," *Arabica* 23 (1976), 228–65; 24 (1977) 1–41, 150–86. And see Humphreys, *Islamic History*, 188–89 for the change in the criteria of inclusion.

29. Gibb was the first to point to the problematic characteristics of this genre in "Islamic Literature," in *Historians of the Middle East*, eds. Lewis and Holt, 56–57. His conclusions promoted a number of studies. See especially T. Khalidi, "Islamic Biographical Dictionaries: A Preliminary Assessment," *MW* 63 (1973), 53–65, for a challenge of Gibb's observation of the complete lack of the "sense of personality" in biographical notices.

30. For a detailed overview of previous research on the 'ulama', see Humphreys, *Islamic History*, 178–93.

31. Lapidus, *Muslim Cities*, chapters 4 and 5.

32. For two recent studies offering us new venues for the exploitation of biographical literature as a principal source for the study of Islamic culture and societies, see Chamberlain, *Knowledge and Social Practice*; Nimrod Hurwitz, "Ibn al-Hanbal and the Formation of Orthodoxy" (Ph.D. diss., Princeton University, 1994); idem, "Biographies and mild asceticism: A study of Islamic moral imagination," *SI* 85 (1997), 41–65.

33. The need to broaden and intensify the scope of contextualization (asking who wrote what and for whom, who listened and why, as well as the type of education the compilers and their teachers received) was first raised by Lucien Febvre in a lecture delivered on Feb. 7, 1903, in la Société d'histoire moderne under the title "Idées de quelques travaux historique à faire sur la littérature française." For an overview of Febvre's and other studies on history and literature produced by the Annales school, see Christian Jouhaud, *Annales: Histoire, Sciences Sociales* 49: 2 (1994), *Présentation*. Note esp. 273–74.

34. Pierre Bourdieu and J. C. Passeron, *La Reproduction Sociale*, trans. by R. Nice as *Reproduction in Education, Society and Culture* (London and Beverly Hills, 1977).

35. Morton White was the first philosopher to draw our attention to the narrative and its structure in history. See White, *Foundations of Historical Knowledge* (New York, Evanston, and London, 1965), 219–70. See also his previous essay: "The Logic of Historical Narration, " in *Philosophy and History: A Symposium*, ed. Sidney Hook (New York, 1963), 3–31. Since then, a number of works have been devoted to the methods of composing and interpreting historical narratives. For a comprehensive survey and analysis

of works on this topic, see Elazar Weinryb, "If We Write Novel So, How Shall We Write History?" *Clio* 17 (1988), 265–81. And see the suggestions of Humphreys, *Islamic History*, 189–93, for interpreting the material in biographical dictionaries.

36. Mentioned below are only the major sources consulted by the present study. For an extensive survey of all primary sources pertaining to eleventh-century Baghdad, see Makdisi, *Ibn 'Aqil*, 1–68.

37. For al-Khatib's *Ta'rikh baghdad* and its continuations, see ibid., 31–46. The continuations by two authors were employed in this study. These authors are Ibn as-Sa'i (d. 674/1275), the librarian of the Mustansiriyya Madrasa in Baghdad who wrote *al-Jami' al-mukhtasir*; and al-Bundari who wrote *Ta'rikh baghdad* (in manuscript).

38. For Ibn al-Jawzi and his work, see also Joseph de Somogyi, "The Kitab al-Muntazam of Ibn al-Jawzi," *JRAS*, 1932, 49–76.

39. For a detailed discussion of Ibn al-Banna' and his treatise, see the introduction to the English translation: Makdisi, *Autograph Diary of an Eleventh-Century Historian of Baghdad*, reprinted from *BSOAS* 18 (1956), 19 (1957).

40. For Sibt b. al-Jawzi and his work, see also Richard Jewett, "The Mir'at az-zaman," *AJSL* 22 (1905–6), 176.

41. On Ibn Khallikan and his work, see the introduction in the English translation: M. de Slane, *Ibn Khallikan's Biographical Dictionary*, 4 vols. (Paris, 1843–1871).

42. adh-Dhahabi's most important work is the monumental *Ta'rikh al-islam*. It is both a general narrative of the history of Islam from Muhammad to A.H. 700 and a biographical dictionary. The portion which covers the years A.H. 400–600 is unfortunately lost.

Chapter 1: The City

1. al-Ya'qubi, *Kitab al-buldan*, M. J. de Goeje ed., 2nd edition (Leiden, 1891–92), 233.

2. Ibid., 234–42.

3. A remark made by the essayist al-Jahiz and cited by the famous historian of Baghdad, al-Khatib al-Baghdadi in *Ta'rikh baghdad* (Cairo ed. 1349/1931), 1:70.

4. al-Muqaddasi, *Ahsan al-taqasim fi ma'rifat al-aqalim*, de Goeje ed., 2nd edition (Leiden, 1906), 35–36.

5. al-Khatib al-Baghdadi, Ta'rikh baghdad, 1: 22–23.

6. Sibt b. al-Jawzi, Mir'at az-zaman fi ta'rikh al-a'yan, British Museum, MS, 2 (years, A.H. 282–460), fol. 235b.

7. Sibt b. al-Jawzi, Mir'at az-zaman (Ankara, 1968: years, A.H. 448–480), 6, 23.

8. Ibn al-Jawzi, al-Muntazam fi ta'rikh al-muluk wa'l-umam (Hyderabad A.H. 1358), 8: 179.

9. Ibn al-Athir, al-Kamil fi't-ta'rikh (Beirut, 1966), 10: 90–91.

10. Cited in Ibn al-Jawzi, Manaqib baghdad (Baghdad A.H. 1342), 25.

11. R. Levy, A Baghdad Chronicle (Philadelphia, 1077), 185–203, has stressed this notion. For a different view, see H. Laoust, "Les Agitations Religieuses à Baghdad aux IVe et Ve siècle de l'Hégire," in Islamic Civilization, ed. Richards, 169–85. We shall return to Laoust's arguments.

12. Ibn al-Jawzi, al-Muntazam, 8: 215–16; Sibt b. al-Jawzi, Mir'at az-zaman (Ankara, 1968), 74. On Dar al-khilafa and Dar al-mamlaka, see G. Le Strange, Baghdad during the Abbasid Caliphate (London, 1972), 178, 233, 243. See also Jacob Lassner, The Topography of Baghdad in the Early Middle Ages (Detroit, 1970), 172–73 (based on descriptions of the city by al-Khatib al-Baghdadi), and Makdisi, "The Topography of 11th Century Baghdad," Arabica 6 (1959), 178–97, for changes in the topography of Baghdad in early Seljuk times.

13. Ibn al-Jawzi, al-Muntazam, 8:215.

14. See Hodgson, The Venture of Islam, 2:36. See also B. C. Bosworth, "The Political and Dynastic History of the Iranian World (A.D. 1000–1217)," The Cambridge History of Iran 5: 97–98.

15. Ibn al-Jawzi, al-Muntazam, 9:87.

16. Ibid., 9:35.

17. Ibid., 9:60.

18. Berkey stresses this point with regard to the role of female members of the Mamluk royal house of Cairo in the later Middle Ages as founders of educational institutions: Berkey, The Transmission of Knowledge, 162–65.

19. On the active part women of the ruling Seljuk house played in public acts of religious charity, see A. K. S. Lambton, Continuity and Change in Medieval Persia: Aspects of Administrative, Economic, and Social History, 11th–14th Century (Albany, NY, 1988), 257–58.

20. Ibid., 269–70.

21. Ibn al-Jawzi describes the great audience attending the first say of studies in the madrasa, and the esteem and honor showed to him by both the dignitaries and the common people: *al-Muntazam*, 10:252–53.

22. For the mosque as the prime forum of Hanbali teachings in medieval Egypt, see G. Leiser, "Hanbalism in Egypt before the Mamluks," *SI* 54 (1981), 155–81.

23. The fragment of the *Nizamiyya*'s deed of endowment in preserved in Ibn al-Jawzi, *al-Muntazam*, 9:66. And see Makdisi, "Muslim Institutions of Learning," 37.

24. Ibn al-Jawzi, *al-Muntazam*, 9:35–36.

25. Ibn Kathir, *al-Bidaya*, 13:129.

26. Ibn Jubayr, *Rihla*, trans. by R. J. C. Broadhurst as *The Travels of Ibn Jubayr* (London, 1952), 220–27.

27. Ibid., 220.

28. Hodgson, *The Venture of Islam*, 2:48.

29. Cited in Ibn al-Athir, *al-Kamil*, 10:54; Ibn al-Jawzi, *al-Muntazam*, 8:245.

Chapter 2: Formation

1. A distinction made by S. D. Goitein in his study on population movements and countermovements in the Middle East in the period A.D. 950–1150: Goitein, "Changes in the Middle East (950–1150) as illustrated by the Documents of The Cairo Geniza," in *Islamic Civilization*, ed. Richards, 25. For migratory patterns, see also Donald Light Jr., and Suzan Keller, *Sociology* (New York, 1982), 479.

2. There is a large selection of literature on this topic for Christian Europe. See especially Norbert Ohler, *The Medieval Traveller*, trans. Caroline Hiller (Woodbridge, 1989). See also Jacques Le Goff, *Medieval Civilization 400–1500* (Oxford, New York, 1989), 131–38; Christopher Brooke, *Europe in the Central Middle Ages*, 2nd edition (London, 1987), 153–74.

3. On the freedom of travel and commerce enjoyed by members of Jewish communities in the Mediterranean scene during the high Middle Ages, see Goitien, *A Mediterranean Society: The Jewish Communities in the Arab World as Portrayed in the Documents of the Cairo Geniza* (Berkeley, Los Angeles, 1967), 2:59–70.

4. See Bosworth, "Political and Dynastic History," *The Cambridge History of Iran*, 5:86. See also A. Bausani, "Religion in the Seljuk Period," in

ibid. 5:283–89; Frye, *Islamic Iran and Central Asia: Seventh-Twelfth Centuries* (London, 1979), 137.

5. Bosworth, "Political and Dynastic History," 86–87.

6. Sam I. Gellens, "The Search for Knowledge in Medieval Muslim Societies: A Comparative Approach," in *Muslim Travellers: Pilgrimage, migration, and religious imagination*, eds. Dale F. Eickelman and James Piscatori (London, 1990), 59.

7. Makdisi makes this point in *The Rise of Colleges*, 144–45.

8. Ibn al-Jawzi, *al-Muntazam*, 8:287.

9. Ibid., 8:28. See also the biographical notice in Ibn Jazari, *Kitab ghayat an–nihaya fi tabaqat al-qura'* (Cairo, 1933–37), 1:521–22.

10. al-Khatib al-Baghdadi, *Ta'rikh baghdad*, 11: 31; Ibn al-Jawzi, *al-Muntazam*, 8:61; Ibn al-Kathir, *al-Bidaya*, 12:32–33; Ibn al-ʿImad, *Shadharat adh-dhahab fi khabar man dhahab* (Cairo, 1350/1931) 3:223–25; Ibn Shakir al-Kutubi, *Fawat al-wafayat* (Cairo, 1951), 2:44.

11. For the history of the Zahiri school in Baghdad, see Makdisi, *Ibn ʿAqil*, 278–79.

12. Ibn al-Jawzi, *al-Muntazam*, 10:19, Ibn Kathir, *al-Bidaya*, 12:201–2; Ibn al-ʿImad, *Shadharat adh–dhahab*, 4: 70.

13. See Makdisi's remarks on the two "camps" of Sufis in eleventh-century Baghdad in *Ibn ʿAqil*, 376–83. See also Bulliet's observation that most Sufis in 10th-11th century Nishapur were Shafiʿis, compared with only one Hanafi: Bulliet, *The Patricians*, 41–43.

14. On Abu al-Hasan ʿAli az-Zauzani, see especially Ibn al-Jawzi, *al-Muntazam* 8:214; Ibn al-ʿImad, *Shadharat adh-dhahab*, 3:288–89. This Hanbali-Sufi began his course of religious learning with the study of the prophetic traditions, and gained fame as a trustworthy *hadith*–transmitter. Az-Zauzani died in Baghdad and was buried in his *ribat*.

15. See Ibn al-Jawzi, *al-Muntazam*, 9:11; Ibn Kathir, *al-Bidaya*, 12:126; Ibn al-ʿImad, *Shadharat adh-dhahab*, 4:128.

16. For the proliferation of the *ribats* in Baghdad and their consolidation as centers of religious learning (*dur al-ʿilm*), see Hussein Amin, *Ta'rikh al-iraq fi'l-ʿasr as-saljuki* (Baghdad, 1965), 239–41. See also Mustafa Jawad, "ar-Rubut al-baghdadiyya," *Sumer* 10 (1954), 218–49; Jaqueline Chabbi, "La fonction du ribat à Baghdad du vᵉ siècle au debut du viiᵉ siècle," *REI* 42 (1974), 101–21.

17. For Ibn Hamid, see the biographical notice in al-Khatib al-Baghdadi, *Ta'rikh baghdad*, 7:303; Ibn Abi Yaʿla, *Tabaqat al-hanabila*

(Cairo, 1371/1952), 2:171–77; Ibn al-Jawzi, *al-Muntazam*, 6:263–64; Ibn Kathir, *al-Bidaya*, 11:349; Ibn al-ʿImad, *Shadharat adh-dhahab*, 3:166–67; as-Suyuti, *Tabaqat al-huffaz* (Cairo, 1973), 2:171–72. For a full bibliography, see *Gal*, 1:194.

18. See al-Khatib al-Baghdadi, *Taʾrikh baghdad*, 2:256; Ibn Abi Yaʿla, *Tabaqat al-hanabila*, 2:193–230; Ibn al-Jawzi, *al-Muntazam*, 8:243–44; Ibn al-Kathir, *al-Bidaya*, 12:94–95; Ibn al-ʿImad, *Shadharat adh-dhahab*, 3:306–7; and see also *Gal*, Suppl., I:686. For the Yaʿla family, see Appendix A, below.

19. Ibn Abi Yaʿla, *Tabaqat al-hanabila*, 2:245; and the continuation by Ibn Rajab, *Dhail ʿala tabaqat al-hanabila* (Damascus, 1370/1951), 1:45–47. See also the biographical notice in Ibn al-ʿImad, *Shadharat adh–dhahab*, 3:352.

20. Ibn Rajab, *Dhail*, 1:86.

21. On al-Barzabini, see Ibn Abi Yaʿla, *Tabaqat al-hanabila*, 2, 245–47; Ibn Rajab, *Dhail* 1: 92–95; Ibn al-Jawzi, *al-Muntazam*, 9:80.

22. On Kalwadhani, see Ibn Abi Yaʿla, *Tabaqat al-hanabila*, 2; 258; Ibn Rajab, *Dhail*, 1:143–54; Ibn al-Jawzi, *al-Muntazam*, 9:190–93; Ibn Kathir, *al-Bidaya*, 12:180; *Gal*, I: 389, and Suppl. I: 687.

23. On al-Quduri, see Ibn al-Jawzi, *al-Muntazam*, 12:40; Ibn al-ʿImad, *Shadharat adh-dhahab*, 3:233; Ibn al-Hasanat al-Laknawi, *al-Fawaʾid al-bahiyya fi tarajim al-hanafiyya* (Cairo, a.h. 1324), 30–31; *Gal*, I: 183. For as-Saimari, see Ibn al-Jawzi, *al-Muntazam*, 8:119; Ibn Kathir, *al-Bidaya*, 12:52; Ibn al-ʿImad, *Shadharat adh-dhahab*, 3:256; al-Laknawi, *al-Fawaʾid*, 67, *Gal*, Suppl, I: 636.

24. See al-Khatib al-Baghdadi, *Taʾrikh baghdad*, 3:109; al-Bundari, *Taʾrikh baghdad*, MS. arabe, Paris, 6152, fol. 46a; Ibn al-Jawzi, *al-Muntazam*, 9: 22–24; Ibn al-Kathir, *al-Bidaya*, 12:129; Ibn al-ʿImad, *Shadharat adh-dhahab*, 3:362. On the marriage of ad-Damaghani's daughter to Abu al-Hasan as-Simnawi, see the latter's biographical notice in Ibn Abu al-Wafaʾ, *al-Jawahir al-mudiʾah fi tabaqat al-hanafiyya* (Hyderabad, 1332/1914) 1:95–96.

25. Ibn Khallikan, *Wafayat al-aʿyan wa-anbaʾ abnaʾ az-zaman* (Beirut, 1970), 1:73.

26. On al-Isfaraʾini, see especially as-Subki, *Tabaqat ash-shafiʿiyya al-kubra* (Cairo, 1966–67), 4:61–73. See also Ibn al-Jawzi, *al-Muntazam*, 7:277; Ibn al-Kathir, *al-Bidaya*, 12:2–3; Ibn al-ʿImad, *Shadharat adh-dhahab*, 3:178.

27. See al-Khatib al-Baghdadi, *Taʾrikh baghdad*, 4:372; Ibn al-Jawzi, *al-Muntazam*, 8:17; Ibn Kathir, *al-Bidaya*, 12:18; Ibn al-ʿImad, *Shadharat adh-dhahab*, 3:202; *Gal*, I:181.

28. See as-Subki, *Tabaqat ash-shafi'iyya*, 4:377; ash-Shirazi, *Tabaqat al-fuqaha'* (Baghdad, 1356/1937), 111; Hussaini, *Tabaqat ash-shafi'iyya*, 147–48; Ibn al-'Imad, *Shadharat adh-dhahab*, 3:275–76; Ibn Khallikan, *Wafayat*, 2:397–98; *Gal*, Suppl. I: 730.

29. See as-Subki, *Tabaqat ash-shafi'iyya*, 4:27.

30. as-Subki, *Tabaqat ash-shafi'iyya*, 3:176–79; ash-Shirazi, *Tabaqat al-fuqaha'*, 106–7; Ibn Kathir, *al-Bidaya*, 12:79–80; Ibn al-Jawzi, *al-Muntazam*, 8:198.

31. Ibn Khallikan, *Wafayat*, 6:512.

32. On ash-Shirazi, see Ibn al-Jawzi, *al-Muntazam*, 9:7–8; Ibn Kathir, *al-Bidaya*, 12:124; as-Subki, *Tabaqat ash-shafi'iyya*, 1:215–56; al-Asnawi, *Tabaqat ash-shafi'iyya* (Baghdad, 1390/1970), 2:98–99; Ibn Khallikan, *Wafayat*, 1:29–31; Ibn al-'Imad, *Shadharat adh-dhahab*, 3:349; and *Gal*, Suppl. I: 669. For as-Sabbagh, see Ibn al-Jawzi, *al-Muntazam*, 9:12; as-Subki, *Tabaqat ash–shafi'iyya*, 4:122–35; al-Asnawi, *Tabaqat ash-shafi'iyya*, 2:130–32; Ibn Khallikan, *Wafayat*, 3:217–19; *Gal*, Suppl. I:671.

33. See Ibn al-Jawzi, *al-Muntazam*, 9:179; Ibn al-'Imad, *Shadharat adh–dhahab*, 4:16–17; Ibn Kathir, *al-Bidaya*, 12:177–78; *Gal*, Suppl. I:674.

34. as-Subki, *Tabaqat ash-shafi'iyya*, 4: 281; al-Asnawi, *Tabaqat ash-shafi'iyya*, 2:560–62; Ibn al-Jawzi, *al-Muntazam*, 9:167; Ibn Kathir, *al-Bidaya*, 12:172–73; Ibn Khallikan, *Wafayat*, 3:286–90; Ibn al-'Imad, *Shadharat adh–dhahab*, 4:8–10; *Gal*, Supp., I:674.

35. Ibn al-'Imad, *Shadharat adh-dhahab*, 4:8.

36. Of the many biographical notices on al-Ghazzali, the most comprehensive is that which appears in as-Subki, the *Tabaqat ash–shafi'iyya*, 4: 81–82.

37. Trimingham, *The Sufi Orders*, 73; Schimmel, *Mystical Dimensions*, 36, 89, 159, 247–48, 364, 374. See also *EI*, 2nd edition, s.v. "'Abd al-Kadir al-Djilani," by W. Braune.

38. For dynasties of 'ulama' in 11th- and 12th-century Baghdad, see chapters 5 and 6, below. See also the genealogical charts in Appendix A.

39. For the influence of changes in the political and economic conditions of Iraq—Baghdad in particular—on the trends of migration of religious scholars, see Eliyahu Ashtor, "Un movement migratoire au haut moyen âge: migrations de l'Iraq vers les pays méditerranées," *AESC* 27 (1972), 185–215. See also Jasmin, Khidr al-Duri, "Society and Economy under the Seljuks, 1055–1160" (Ph.D. dissertation, University of Pennsylvania, 1970), 98–106, for the foundation of madrasas and *ribats* on lasting endowments as a major stimulus for the immigration of 'ulama' and Sufis to Baghdad.

40. On the proliferation of religious establishment in Syria during the second half of the twelfth and thirteenth centuries, and its effect on the immigration of 'ulama' to Damascus, see Gilbert, "Institutionalization of Muslim Scholarship and Professionalization of the 'Ulama'," 112–16. According to the author's findings, nearly one–half of the resident 'ulama' of this period in Damascus were immigrants. For the immigration of 'ulama' from the eastern part of the Muslim world to Ayyubid Egypt, see Leiser, "The Restoration of Sunnism," 417.

Chapter 3: Learning

1. See Tibawi's remark in "Origins" 230–31, that the sources rarely mentioned study in madrasas in the biographies of their subjects. Berkey, *The Transmission of Knowledge*, 18, makes the same observation with regard to biographical dictionaries pertaining to Mamluk Cairo.

2. There were twelve transient 'ulama' known in Baghdad during the first half of the twelfth century, as compared with thirty-five in the second half of the eleventh century.

3. as-Subki, *Tabaqat ash-shafi'iyya*, 4:216.

4. Ibid.

5. The best-known *hadiths* on the subject are cited in Ibn Majah, Sunan, I, no. 224, and at-Tarmidhi, *Sunan*, 39:2 (cited above).

6. Ibn Khallikan, *Wafayat*, 3:453.

7. As early as the tenth century, the Sufi al-Khuldi (d. 348/959) traced the genealogy of his mystic teaching to Hasan al-Basri (d. 110/728) and thence, through the Companion Anas b. Malik, to the Prophet himself. Later chains of transmission go back to 'Ali, in most cases through Hasan al-Basri, but sometimes through the early figures venerated by the Shi'a among the descendants of Muhammad through 'Ali and Fatima, the *sayyids*. For the construction of the early Sufi *silsilas* and the special position ascribed to 'Ali, see especially Kamil M. ash-Shaybi, *as-Sila bayna at-tasawwuf wa't-tashayyu'* (Baghdad, 1964), 2:131–37.

8. See Grunebaum, *Muhammadan Festivals* (London, 1981), 72–73. Ibn Jubayr (late twelfth century) refers to the *mawalid* as an established custom. *The Travels of Ibn Jubayr*, 114–15.

9. See *EI*, 2nd edition, s.v. "al-Harawi al-Mawsili" by J. Sourdel-Thomine. See also *The Isharat*, ed. Sourdel (Damascus, 1957), trans. as *Guide des lieux pèlerinage*.

10. Ibn Khalikan, *Wafayat*, 6:192. The story about Abu al-Hasan al-Andalusi appears in the biography of Yahya at-Tabrizi, his teacher of Arabic literature and grammar (see below).

11. al-Asnawi, *Tabaqat ash-shafiʿiyya*, 2:58–59; as-Subki, *Tabaqat ash-shafiʿiyya*, 6:32; adh-Dhahabi, *Kitab tadhkirat al-huffaz*, 4:1298.

12. Ibn Khallikan, *Wafayat*, 4:294–5.

13. Ibid., 6:191–92. On Abu Zakariyya at-Tabrizi, see also Ibn al-Jawzi, *al-Muntazam*, 9:161; Ibn al-ʿImad, *Shadharat adh-dhahab*, 4:5; adh-Dhahabi, *al-ʿIbar fi khabar man ghabar* (Kuwait, 1961–66).

14. Nizam al-Mulk, *Siyasat Nameh* (*The Book of Government*), trans. Hubert Darke (revised trans. London, 1978), 95.

15. For transient ʿulama' in twelfth and thirteenth centuries Damascus, see Gilbert "The ʿUlama' of Medieval Damascus," 26–28.

16. al-Asnawi, *Tabaqat ash-shafiʿiyya*, 2:101–2: as-Subki, *Tabaqat ash-shafiʿiyya*, 6:185.

17. See figure 6.1 in chapter 6, below.

18. al-Asnawi, *Tabaqat ash-shafiʿiyya*, 1:242; Ibn al-Jawzi, *al-Muntazam*, 9:147, Ibn Kathir, *al-Bidaya*, 12:166.

19. Ibn Khalikan, *Wafayat*, 1:37–38.

20. See remarks by Ross Dunn on the cosmopolitan scholar as the representative of the values of scripturalist Islam (the idea of the *umma*, as an integrated political and religious community) in his article "Internal migrations and the literate Muslims in the later Middle Period," in *Golden Roads: Migration, Pilgrimage and Travel in Medieval and Modern Islam*, ed. Ian Richard Netton (Richmond: Surrey, 1993), 79. See also C. F. Beckingham, "The Rihla: Fact or Fiction?" 86–94, in the same volume, for a study which stresses the fictitious character of travel narratives written in classical Islam.

21. Ibn Khalikan, *Wafayat*, 3:306.

22. Ibid., 2:97.

23. On the ambivalence of the *rihla* and its manifestations in different times and places, see Gellens, "The Search for Knowledge," in *Muslim Travellers*, eds. Eickelman and Piscatori, 56–58; and Abderrahmane El Mouden, "The ambivalence of *rihla*: community integration and self-definition in Moroccan travel accounts, 1300–1800," in ibid., 71ff.

24. as-Subki, *Tabaqat ash-shafiʿiyya*, 4:256–62; al-Asnawi, *Tabaqat ash-shafiʿiyya*, 1:59–60.

25. as-Subki, *Tabaqat ash-shafi'iyya*, 4:377; Abu Bakr al-Hussaini, *Tabaqat ash–shafi'iyya* (Beirut, 1971), 147.

26. Ya'qubi, *Kitab al-buldan*, 248.

27. For the terms *darb* and *bab* and their meanings, see Makdisi, "The Topography," 180–82. Makdisi contends that a place name should not always be understood solely on the basis of its original narrow meaning, but may also be the designation for an entire quarter.

28. On the growth of the *fada'il* literature and its various branches, see *EI*, 2nd edition, s.v. "fada'il," by R. Sellheim. See also G. E. Grunebaum, *Muhammadan Studies*, 2:128ff for books consisting largely of sayings ascribed to the Prophet, in which political and regional merits are primarily pursued. For the spread of *fada'il* traditions, particularly *fada'il Bait al-Maqdis*, see Amikam Elad, *Medieval Jerusalem and Islamic Worship: Holy Places, Ceremonies, Pilgrimage* (Leiden, 1995), 6–22.

29. Compare with the considerable number of local histories compiled by 'ulama' of Iranian cities, and which focus upon the great 'ulama' families: Bulliet, *The Patricians*, part 2.

30. Probably the best discussion of the *isnad* mentality and its effect on the method of gathering knowledge is that by Ignaz Goldziher, *Muslim Studies*, trans. C. R. Barber and S. M. Stern (London, 1971), 1, esp. 170–74. For oral transmission of rabbinic recorded literature in the period from the sixth to the tenth centuries, as indicated by variations in parallel texts, see Y. Brody, "Safrut ha-Geonim veha-Tekst ha-Talmudi," in *Mehqarei Talmud 1* (5750), eds. Y. Sussman and D. Rosenthal (Jerusalem, 1990), 237–304 [in Hebrew]. Note esp. 241–243; P. Schaefer, "Once Again the Status Quaestiones of Research into Rabbinic Literature," *Journal of Jewish Studies* 40 (1989), 89–94. And compare to the written environment and the belief that authority is invested in the book in early and middle Byzantine: Georgina Buckler, "Byzantine Education," in *Byzantium: An Introduction to the East Roman Civilization*, eds. N. H. Baynes and H. G. Wilson (Oxford, 1948), 200–20; L. D. Reynold and N. G. Wilson, *Scribes and Scholars: A Guide to the Transmission of Greek and Latin Literature*, 2nd edition (Oxford, 1974), 45–58.

31. Ibn Khallikan, *Wafayat*, 2:156.

32. See Rosenthal, *The Technique and Approach*, 6–7, for the importance ascribed to written word as the basis of all branches of knowledge during what he termed the "manuscript age" (from the late ninth century throughout the medieval period).

33. See the remark by Johannes Pederson on composition and transmission in *The Arabic Book*, trans. G. French (Princeton, 1984), 22–23. See also Berkey, *The Transmission of* Knwledge, 24–28. On the survival of

oral rituals and practices into the twentieth century, see Dale Eickelman, "The Art of Memory: Islamic Education and its Social Reproduction," *Comparative Studies in Society and History* 20 (1978), 105.

34. For the comparison between the *ijaza* and the university degree, see Makdisi, *The Rise of Colleges*, 270–72. Despite this difference, Makdisi argues that, in common with the earliest form of the academic degree, the granting of *ijaza*, certifying that the recipient was competent to issue legal opinions and to teach (*ijazat li'l-ifta'* and *ijazat li't-tadris*), involved an oral examination as a sort of thesis defense. I have found no indication of any kind of examination in the biographies of legal scholars of Baghdad during this period. On the development of the academic degree, see Charles H. Haskins, *The Renaissance of the Twelfth Century*, 8th edition (Cambridge, Mass., 1982), 370–71.

35. Makdisi, *Autograph Diary of an-Eleventh-Century Historian of Baghdad*, Reprinted from the *BSOAS* 18 (1956) and 19 (1957), pt. IV, no. 138, 289 (the Arabic text); 301 (Makdisi's translation).

36. as-Suyuti, *Tabaqat al-huffaz*, 467.

37. On the mosques of Baghdad, see Le Strange, Baghdad, 243, 252–53, 269, 278.

38. For the various *halqas* held in the city's mosques as early as the 'Abbasid era, see Makdisi, *The Rise of Colleges*, 12–24. See also Munir-ud-Rahman Ahmed, *Muslim Education and the Scholars' Social Status up to the Fifth Century Muslim Era in Light of Ta'rikh Baghdad* (Zurich, 1986), 56–60, 85–90.

39. See Makdisi, "Muslim Institutions of Learning in 11th Century Baghdad," *BSOAS* 24 (1961), 4–6.

40. as-Subki, *Tabaqat ash-shafi'iyya*, 5:296–98; al-Asnawi, *Tabaqat ash-shafi'iyya*, 1:526–27.

41. as-Subki, *Tabaqat ash-shafi'iyya*, 6:133; al-Asnawi, *Tabaqat ash-shafi'iyya*, 1:440.

42. Ibn al-Jawzi, *al-Muntazam*, 9:11.

43. al-Khatib al-Baghdadi, *Ta'rikh baghdad*, 1:355.

44. Ahmed, *Muslim Education*, 136. Based on al-Khatib al-Baghdadi, *Ta'rikh baghdad*, 6:33; 9:41.

45. Ibn al-Jawzi, *al-Muntazam*, 10:130.

46. Ibid., 10:214–17.

47. Sibt b. al-Jawzi, *Mir'at az–zaman* Part. 8, 1 (Hyderabad, 1951), 14.

48. Ibid., 5. For the effect of al-ʿAbbadi's preaching on the people of Baghdad, see chapter 6, below.

49. Ibn Khallikan, *Wafayat*, 3:139; al-Asnawi, *Tabaqat ash-shafiʿiyya*, 1:53.

50. See Sourdel, "Reflexions," 184. On the combination of orthodox and Sufi educational institutions, see also Johannes Pederson, "Some Aspects of the History of the Madrasa," *IC* 3 (1929), 529–37.

51. The literature about al-Ghazzali is almost inexhaustible. For his education and career, see especially Duncan Black Macdonald, "The Life of al-Ghazzali," *JAOS* 20 (1899); W. Mongomery Watt, *Muslim Intellectual: A Study of al-Ghazali* (Edinburgh, 1963). See also Avner Giladi, "The Educational Thought of al-Ghazzali," dissertation (The Hebrew University of Jerusalem, 1983), 14–16 [in Hebrew].

52. al-Asnawi, *Tabaqat ash-shafiʿiyya*, 2:64–65; al-Yafiʿi, *Mirʾat al-janan wa-ʿibarat al-yaqzan* (Beirut, 1970), 3:372.

Chapter 4: Forms of Social Affiliation

1. For previous research on the character of Islamic education, see in the introduction of this study: Institutionalization and Social Change.

2. See Humphrey's review of scholarship on the ʿulamaʾ in *Islamic History*, chap. 8, esp. 195–96. See also Berkey's remark in *The Transmission of Knowledge*, 22, on the impact the foundation of madrasas had on the character of the educated elite and on the forging of social relations within that group.

3. Donald Light and Suzanne J. R. Keller, *Sociology*, 3rd edition (New York, 1982), 96.

4. Ibn Rajab, *Dhail*, 1:228–29; Ibn al-ʿImad, *Shadharat adh-dhahab*, 4:98.

5. On the post of the naʾib-mudarris, see Makdisi, *The Rise of Colleges*, 188–89.

6. Ibn Abi Yaʿla, *Tabaqat al-hanabila*, 2:195.

7. See Isaiah Gafni, *Yahadut Bavel u-mosdoteha bi tekufat ha-talmud*, 2nd edition (Jerusalem, 1986), 83–87 [in Hebrew].

8. See Makdisi, *The Rise of Colleges*, 255–64. On the early development of the medieval European university, see also Hastings Rashdall, *The Universities of Europe in the Middle Ages*, 2nd edition (London, 1936), 1:4–15.

9. Ibn al-Jawzi, *al-Muntazam*, 9:53; Ibn al-Athir, *al-Kamil*, 10:123. The two professors taught on alternate days for a year, and were both dismissed in 484/1091 to make way for the appointment of al-Ghazzali. For the biographical note on Abu 'Abd Allah at-Tabari, see as-Subki, *Tabaqat ash-shafi'iyya*, 4:349; al-Asnawi, *Tabaqat ash-shafi'iyya*, 1:567-69; and Ibn al-'Imad, *Shadharat adh-dhahab*, 3:489. On Abu Muhammad al-Fami, see as-Subki, *Tabaqat ash-shafi'iyya*, 4:193; and al-Asnawi, *Tabaqat ash-shafi'iyya*, 2:273-74.

10. Sibt b. al-Jawzi, *Mir'at az-zaman* (Ankara, 1968), 135. About the disorders of the first day of studies in the Nizamiyya, see also Ibn al-Jawzi, *al-Muntazam*, 8:246-47.

11. Ibn Khallikan, *Wafayat*, 3:133 (in the biography of al-Mutawalli). It follows from this anecdote that the teacher (*mudarris*) in the *madrasa* used to teach seated on a *kursi* (a sort of chair).

12. Ibid.

13. Ibid., 2:397-98.

14. Ibn Kathir, *al-Bidaya*, 12:203; Husaini, *Tabaqat ash-shafi'iyya*, 202.

15. Ibn Khallikan, *Wafayat*, 3:139; al-Asnawi, *Tabaqat ash-shafi'iyya*, 1:121.

16. al-Asnawi, *Tabaqat ash-shafi'iyya*,1:121.

17. The most important work on the *suhba* in the context of Islamic education is that of George Makdisi. See his article "Suhba et riyasa dans l'enseignement médiévale," *Recherches d'islamologie. Recueil d'articles offert à George C. Anawati et Louis Gardet par leur collegues et amis* (Louvain, 1977), 207-21, and the corresponding sections of *The Rise of Colleges*, esp. 128-29. On the significant of *suhba* in other social contexts, see Goitein, *Mediterranean Society*, 2:275-77.

18. The tradition is cited in Muhammad Ibn Ya'qub al-Kulayni, *Usul al-Kafi* (Teheran, A.H. 1381), 1:64.

19. On the transmission of the *imam*'s superior knowledge, and the sources from which he derives his knowledge, see Etan Kohlberg, "Imam and Community in the Pre-Ghayba Period," in *Authority and Political Culture in Shi'ism*, ed. Said Arjomand (Albany, 1988), 25-30.

20. The tradition is found in the collections of sound *hadiths* of al-Bukhari, *Sahih* (Leiden, 1862-68), 3 (*Kitab al-'ilm*): 10; at-Tirmidhi, *Sahih* (Cairo, A.H. 1292), 39 (*Kitab al-'ilm*): 19.

21. On the method of publishing, see Pederson, *The Arabic Book*, esp. 23-24. See also Berkey, *The Transmission of Knowledge*, 24-27, for a detailed description of the methods of instruction and publication. For the social uses of this transmitting system, see chapter 5, below.

22. Ibn Rajab, *Dhail*, 1:118–22; Ibn Kathir, *al-Bidaya*, 12:166.

23. Ibn al-Jawzi, *al-Muntazam*, 7:277.

24. as-Suyuti, *Tabaqat al-huffaz*, 435.

25. Ibn Khallikan, *Wafayat*, 1:93.

26. Husaini, *Tabaqat ash-shafiʿiyya*, 148.

27. Ibn Rajab, *Dhail*, 1:109–10. The *mustamli* was primarily associated with the transmission of the prophetic traditions. In large circles in which *hadith* was transmitted, he repeated in a loud voice what the teacher himself had dictated and explained his words to the listeners. On the role of the *mustamli*, see A. S. Tritton, *Materials on Muslim Education in the Middle Ages* (London, 1957), 35–37. See also Makdisi, *The Rise of Colleges*, 213–14. And compare with the *tanna*, the "living book", in the Jewish schools and academies, whose function it was to recite authoritative texts which others then analyzed. Goitein, *Mediterranean Society*, 2:199–200.

28. Ibn Khallikan, *Wafayat*, 2:478.

29. Since the function of the *muʿid* was peculiar to the field of law itself, it had already existed in the mosques, and did not appear only with the advent of the madrasa, as was once thought. See Makdisi, *The Rise of Colleges*, 193. On the duties and responsibilities of the *muʿid*, see also chapter 5, below.

30. Ibn Rajab, *Dhail*, 1:20–21. On the term *taʿliqa*, see Makdisi, *The Rise of Colleges*, 114–15.

31. Ibn Abi al-Wafaʾ, *al-Jawahir*, 1:119; Al-Laknawi, *al-Fawaʾid*, 40.

32. Ibn Khallikan, *Wafayat*, 1:626.

33. Ibn Abi Yaʿla, *Tabaqat al-hanabila*, 2, 239.

34. Ibid., 182–86. See also Ibn al-Jawzi, *al-Muntazam*, 8:93; Ibn Kathir, *al-Bidaya*, 12, 41; Ibn al-ʿimad, *Shadharat adh-dhahab*, 3:238–41.

35. This is in line with Berkey's main argument in *The Transmission of Knowledge* that the great variety of educational institutions (many called madrasas) in Mamluk Cairo supported educational efforts without ever becoming essential to them. For a different view, which virtually ignores the role of the madrasas in the study and transmission of Islamic law and the Islamic religious sciences, see Chamberlain, *Knowledge and Social Practice*, 69–90. Madrasas, in Chamberlain's view, should not be seen as educational institutions, but as key elements in the competition between ʿulamaʾ over *mansabs* (endowed positions).

36. For this interpretation, see in the introduction of this study (Institutionalization and Social Change).

37. As opposed to the *khutba*, the formal address of the Friday prayer, the *wa'z* was not considered a formal part of the religious requirements, and was not restricted as to place and time. On the nature of the *wa'z*, see Makdisi, *The Rise of Colleges*, 217–18. See also Laoust, "Les Agitations," 178–89, for its missionary function in the Shafi'i madrasas in eleventh-century Baghdad.

38. Sibt b. al-Jawzi, *Mir'at az-zaman* (Ankara, 1968), 187.

39. Ibid., 187–88. See also Ibn al-Jawzi, *al-Muntazam*, 8:305–6.

40. This in line with the views of Richard Bulliet, whose study of the 'ulama' of tenth- and eleventh-century Nishapur has offered us new avenues for interpreting the meaning of affiliation to the legal schools and the source of conflicts among them. See his concluding remarks in *Islam: The View from the Edge*, 110–11.

41. The first systematic legal compilation of the Hanbali school was written in Damascus in the beginning of the thirteenth century by Ibn Qudama Muwafaq ad-Din (d. A.H. 1223).

42. Ibn al-Jawzi, *al-Muntazam*, 10:216.

43. Makdisi, *Autograph Diary*, pt. II, no. 35, p. 246 (the Arabic text), p. 258 (Makdisi's translation); pt. III, no. 96, p. 25 (the Arabic text), p. 44 (Makdisi's translation).

44. For the *madhhab* as a solidarity group—a framework for religious, social, political, and economic life—beyond its scholarly unit, see chapter 6, below.

45. Literally: one of those who became a companion from among the community of followers of our *imam* was so and so.

46. Ibn Abi Ya'la, *Tabaqat al-hanabila*, 2:393.

47. See the remarks of Michael Winter on the place of books in Sufi education in *Society and Religion in Early Ottoman Egypt: Studies in the Writings of 'Abd al-Wahhab al-Sha'arani* (New Brunswick and London, 1982), 192–95.

48. Ibn Abi Ya'la, *Tabaqat al-hanabila*, 407. The phenomenon of "inherited *baraka*" is well-known in the world of Islam. See W. N. Brinner, "Prophet and Saint: Two Exemplars in Islam," in *Saints and Virtues*, ed. J. S. Hawley (Berkeley, 1987), 8.

49. On this (and by far more frequently encountered) type of ascetic, see Makdisi, "The Sunni Revival," in *Islamic Civilization*, ed. Richards, 166.

50. Ibn Abi Ya'la, *Tabaqat al-hanabila*, 363.

51. Ibid., 362.

52. See N. Hurwitz, "Ibn al-Hanbal and the Formation of Orthodoxy," for a study which points to the social ramifications of the belief system he labels as "mild asceticism."

53. Ibn Abi Ya'la, *Tabaqat al-hanabila*, 401.

54. Ibid. The biography of Abu Isma'il al-Harawi al-Ansari is included in the *tabaqa* of the disciples of Qadi Abu Ya'la, even though the latter is not mentioned in the list of his teachers. Nor is the date of his death specified. It may be suggested that the biographer included this biography due to the fame and importance of al-Ansari within the Hanbali school of this period, or that it was added by a later generation of copyists.

55. For legal scholars bearing the appellations associated with Sufism, see figures 2.4–2.7 in chapter 2, above.

56. ash-Shirazi, *Tabaqat al-fuqaha'*, 147; al-Khatib al-Baghdadi, *Ta'rikh baghdad*, 1:345.

57. ash-Shirazi, *Tabaqat al-fuqaha'*, 147.

58. al-Asnawi, *Tabaqat ash-shafi'iyya*, 2:499–50.

59. See Sophia Saadeh, "The Development of the Position of the Chief Judge during the Buyid and Seljuk Periods" (Ph.D diss., Harvard University, 1977), 222–26.

60. as-Subki, *Tabaqat ash-shafi'iyya*, 6: 30–31.

61. Ibn Kathir, *al-Bidaya*, 13:69.

62. For example, the Shafi'i Ibn as-Sabbagh issued a legal opinion in A.H. 461 in which he set himself against Ibn Sukkara, one of the leading Hanbalis who had burned tambourines and broken lutes, requiring him to be accountable and therefore punished. See Ibn al-Banna' *Autograph Diary*, pt. 3, no. 110–11, p. 282 (the Arabic text), p. 284 (Makdisi's translation).

63. See for example Ibn al-Jawzi, *al-Muntazam*, 9:58 (in his account of the important events of the year A.H. 484).

64. Ibn al-Jawzi, *al-Muntazam*, 8:272; Ibn al-Athir, *al-Kamil*, 10:99; Ibn Kathir, *al-Bidaya*, 12:105.

Chapter 5: Mechanisms of Inclusion and Exclusion

1. For the problem of defining the 'ulama' "class", see the introduction of this study (the 'Ulama' and the Problem of Self-Presentation), especially the remarks of Mottahedeh in *Loyalty and Leadership*, 138–44.

2. Ibn al-'Imad, *Shadharat adh-dhahab*, 4:8. For al-Kiya al-Harrasi, see also in chapter 2, above (From Journeys to Schools).

3. On al-'Askalani and his compilations, notably the *Lisan an–nizam*, see the article by Franz Rosenthal in *EI*, 2nd edition.

4. Several studies have concluded that the 'ulama' who lived before the twelfth century were primarily part-time scholars of religion who engaged in other occupations, mostly trade. See especially Hayyim J. Cohen, "The Economic Background and the Secular Occupations of Muslim Jurisprudents and Traditionists in the Classical Period of Islam (until the middle of the eleventh century)," *JESHO* 13 (January, 1970), 16–61.

5. Ibn Khallikan, *Wafayat*, 3:203.

6. The most important work on the *kuttab* under the early 'Abbasids is that by Dominique Sourdel, *Le vizirat abbaside de 749 à 936 (132 à 324 de l'Hégire)*, 2 vols. (Damascus, 1959–60).

7. The earliest of these didactic treatises known to us is the *Risala ila 'l-kuttab*, written in the eighth century by 'Abd al-Hamid, chief secretary of the last Umayyad caliph.

8. Cited in G. E. Grunebaum, *Medieval Islam*, 2nd edition (Chicago, 1953), 2:253–54.

9. Ibn Khallikan, *Wafayat*, 3:342–43.

10. Ibn al-Jawzi, *al-Muntazam*, 8:280.

11. Ibn Kathir, *al-Bidaya*, 12:226.

12. Ibn al-Jawzi, *al-Muntazam*, 10:131–32.

13. Medieval Arabic literature provides little information about Islamic education in the Middle Ages, particularly the elementary level of education. For modern literature, see especially Ahmad Shalabi, *History of Muslim Education* (Beirut, 1954), 5–6; A. F. al-Ahawani, *at-Tarbiyya fi'l-Islam* (Cairo, 1955), 42; Bayard Dodge, *Muslim Education in Medieval Times* (Washington, 1962), 5–7.

14. Berkey demonstrates this point nicely with regard to the transmission of knowledge in Mamluk Cairo, arguing that "education in this society cannot be considered in isolation; rather, it must be seen as one element in the broader continuum of Islamic piety and worship": Berkey, *The Transmission of Knowledge*, 50. See also his remarks on the wide social horizons of *hadith* studies in ibid., 210–18.

15. Ibn Jama'a, *Tadhkirat as-sami' wa'l-mutakallim fi adab al-'alim wa'l-muta'allim* (Hyderabad, A.H. 1353), 123. For a full citation, see Berkey, *The Transmission of Knowledge*, 26.

16. See especially Gilbert, "The 'Ulama' of Medieval Damascus," 69–76. See also Mottahedeh's suggestion that, although many people who considered

themselves learned in the Seljuk period were outside the madrasa system, the madrasas "gave an air of professionalism" to the scholars who taught or studied in them: Mottahedeh, *Loyalty and Leadership*, 140.

17. as-Subki, *Mu'id an-ni'am wa-mubid an-niqam* (London, 1908), 152–53. Cited in Makdisi, *The Rise of Colleges*, 189–90.

18. al-Asnawi, *Tabaqat ash-shafi'iyya*, 2:273–74; as-Subki, *Tabaqat ash-shafi'iyya*, 5:229–30.

19. Ibn as-Sa'i, *al-Jami' al-mukhtasar* (Baghdad, 1353/1939), 9:11; al-Asnawi, *Tabaqat ash-shafi'iyya*, 2:279–81.

20. On the *mu'id* and *mufid*, see Makdisi, *The Rise of Colleges*, 193–96.

21. as-Subki, *Mu'id an-ni'am*, 154–55.

22. The surviving deeds of endowments from the Mamluk period suggest that no institution ever supported an endowed position called *ifada*. The *mufid*, therefore, seem to have functioned as a private assistant to a professor. See Berkey, *The Transmission of Knowledge*, 41.

23. Ibn al-Jawzi, *al-Muntazam*, 10:261.

24. Ibid., 10:11 (chronicle); 10:135–36 (biographical note).

25. The following basic works each contains a bibliography: Schacht, *An Introduction to Islamic Law*, especially chap. 25; Coulson, *History of Islamic Law*; E. Tyan, *Histoire de l'organization judiciare en pays d'islam*, 2nd edition (Leiden, 1960). For a fuller bibliography, see *EI*, 2nd edition, s.v. "Kadi," by E. Tyan.

26. See Schacht, *Introduction to Islamic Law*, 49ff; Lambton, *Continuity and Change*, 71–77.

27. Ibn al-Jawzi, *al-Muntazam*, 9:15.

28. For a general discussion of the prerogatives of the *qadi* under the Seljuks, see Lambton, *Continuity and Change*, 72. For further discussion of the status and actual powers of the *qadi* under the Seljuks, see chapter 6, below.

29. See Appendix C below: *Qadis* and *khatibs* of eleventh-century Baghdad.

30. On the functions of the *mufti*, see Schacht, *An Introduction to Islamic Law*, 73–75.

31. See Makdisi, *The Rise of Colleges*, 199–200.

32. as-Subki, *Tabaqat ash-shafi'iyya*, 5:133; al-Asnawi, *Tabaqat ash-shafi'iyya*, 1:272.

33. Ibn as-Sa'i, *al-Jami' al-mukhtasar*, 9: 280–81.

34. See especially the remarks of Montgomery Watt in *Islamic Political Thought*, 74. See also Carla Klausner's conclusion that the Great Seljuks founded madrasas in order to create an "orthodox bureaucracy" imbued with echoes of administrative practice, which might serve them as an effective counterweight to the power and ambitions of the military chiefs: Klausner, *The Seljuk Vezirate*, 5–7.

35. See Klausenr, *The Seljuk Vezirate*, 62–66.

36. See Chamberlain's important remark that, in high medieval Arabic, there is no word for "curriculum," "lists of books," or "program of study": Chamberlain, *Knowledge and Social Practice*, 87.

37. On the weakening of the civil administration during the Seljuk period, see especially Klausner, *The Seljuk Vezirate*, 79–81.

38. al-Bundari, *Kitab zubdat an-nusrat wa nukhbat al-'usra*, abridged from 'Imad ad-Din al-Isbahani, *Nusrat al-fatra wa 'usrat al-fitra*, and edited by M. T.h. Houtsma in *Recueil de Textes relatifs à l'Histoire des Seljoucides* (Leiden, 1889), vol. 2 (*Histoire des Seljoucides de l'Iraq*), 57.

39. as-Subki, *Tabaqat ash-shafi'iyya*, 6:178; al-Asnawi, *Tabaqat ash-shafi'iyya*, 2:344–45; Ibn Khallikan, *Wafayat*, 5:147–50.

40. Ibn Khallikan, *Wafayat*, 5:149.

41. as-Subki, *Tabaqat ash-shafi'iyya*, 6:149.

42. See the stories about *shaykhs* who refused to accept anything from "this world," in chapter 6, below.

43. For examples, see chapter 2, above (Travel and the Worldwide Scholarly Connections).

44. Jean-Claude Garcin makes the same observation with regard to the process of upward mobility among the people of the Upper Egyptian countryside created by education in the madrasas of Qus: Garcin, *Un centre musulman de la Haute-Egypte médiévale: Qus* (Cairo, 1976), 356. See also Bulliet, *Islam: The View from the Edge*, 106, for a distinction between major and minor 'ulama' in eleventh-century Mishapur.

45. The first clear-cut rules regarding the organization of the 'ulama' would seem to be those found in the so-called *Kanuname* of the Ottoman sultan Mehmet II (1451–1481). The principal provisions pertaining to the structure of the scholarly profession determined that a *mulazim*—that is, a candidate for office—should first teach in a graded series of madrasas, one after the other, and only when he had reached a certain grade would he become eligible for the great offices of the religious establishment, headed by the *mufti* of Istanbul. See Richard C. Repp, *The Mufti of Istanbul: A Study*

in the Development of the Ottoman Learned Hierarchy (London, 1986), 31–41. The term *mulazim*—literally: one who is assiduous, constant in attendance—came to be used for a candidate for office at any stage of his career; for the *mudarris*, or *qadi* awaiting his next post, as well as for a beginner.

46. See ibid., 51, for reflections in biographical literature of this change in the perception of success among the 'ulama'.

47. Ibn as-Sa'i, *al-jami' al-mukhtasar*, 9:188–89; al-Asnawi, *Tabaqat ash-shafi'iyya*, 2:285.

48. as-Subki, *Tabaqat ash-shafi'iyya*, 5:133; al-Asnawi, *Tabaqat ash-shafi'iyya*, 1:271; Ibn al-'imad, *Shadharat adh-dhahab*, 4:311; adh-Dhahabi, *al-'Ibar*, 4:280.

49. as-Subki, *Tabaqat ash-shafi'iyya*, 4:210; al-Asnawi, *Tabaqat ash-shafi'iyya*, 1:104–5.

50. Ibn Khallikan, *Wafayat*, 5:134–35.

51. Ibn al-Jawzi, *al-Muntazam*, 10:4–7; Ibn Rajab, *Dhail*, 1:255–89.

52. For a discussion of the legal literature surrounding the law of the *waqf* as it pertained to the madrasas, see Makdisi, *The Rise of Colleges*, 35ff. The *fatwas* of medieval jurisconsults on which much of his discussion is based were, as Makdisi himself notes, nonbinding legal opinions.

53. See Leiser, "Madrasa and Mudarrisun," 44.

54. See Berkey, *The Transmission of Knowledge*, 103.

55. See especially Lapidus, *A History*, 174; Bulliet, *The Patricians*, 73–74.

56. as-Subki, *Tabaqat ash-shafi'iyya*, 6:134.

57. Ibid.

58. Ibn Abi Wafa', *al-Jawahir*, 1:163; ad-Dari, *Tabaqat as-saniyya*, 2:217–18.

59. Ibn al-Jawzi, *al-Muntazam*, 9:179; Ibn al-'Imad, *Shadharat adh-dhahab*, 4:16–17.

60. Ibn Kathir, *al-Bidaya*, 12:219; Ibn al-'Imad, *Shadharat adh-dhahab*, 4:122.

61. al-Asnawi, *Tabaqat ash-shafi'iyya*, 2:87–88.

62. Ibn al-Jawzi, *al-Muntazam*, 10:226 (chronicle). For the Banu Shashi, see the genealogical chart in Appendix A, below.

63. Ibn as-Sa'i, *al-Jami' al-mukhtasar*, 9:11; al-Asnawi, *Tabaqat ash-shafi'iyya*, 2:280–81.

64. Of the total number of forty-seven 'ulama' holding teaching positions in the city's mosques and for whom family background is indicated, twenty-one are explicitly said to have been born into 'ulama' families. Of them, sixteen were native-born. In addition to teaching positions, some of the native-born 'ulama' families succeeded in securing for themselves the office of the *qadi*, as well as the *khatib*ship in the great mosques of Baghdad. For the number of native-born 'ulama' holding scholarly positions in general, see figure 6.1 in chapter 6, below.

65. On the definition of the term *hasab*, see Mottahedeh, *Loyalty and Leadership*, 100. The author argues that *hasab*—the honor acquired through virtuous deeds—was not, as has been thought, merely the personal achievements of its possessor, but rather acquired through the deeds performed by his ancestors.

66. For the *mudarrisun* of this period, see Khuda Bukhsh, *Die Academien der Araber und ihre Lehrer*, translated by F. Wustenfeld as "The Arab Academies and their Professors" in *Contributions to the History of Islamic Civilization* (Pakistan, 1975), 2:147–48.

67. See the genealogical charts in Appendix A: Scholarly Families of Baghdad.

68. For dynasties of 'ulama' in Nishapur, see Bulliet, *The Patricians*, part. 2. See also Gilbert, "The 'Ulama' of Medieval Damascus," 145–88, for the scholarly families of Damascus.

69. For the number of immigrant 'ulama' holding top-level positions in our period in Baghdad, see figure 6.1 in chapter 6, below.

70. as-Suyuti, *Tabaqat al-huffaz*, 454–55. For Abu Zakariyya, see also Ibn al-'Imad, *Shadharat adh-dhahab*, 4:32.

71. Compare to Chamberlain, *Knowledge and Social Practice*, 2, that "in the high medieval Middle East, it was the household . . . that held power, and that exercised it in most of its social, political, cultural, and economic aspects." The elite household, according to Chamberlain, was the sole important framework in the public sphere of high Medieval Damascus.

Chapter 6: Place and Role in the Public Sphere

1. See the remarks of Humphreys, *Islamic History*, 188ff.

2. This is in line with the views of Lapidus, who offered us a very important interpretation of the role and status of the 'ulama' in high medieval Muslim cities, first in his study of urban life in Mamluk Cairo and Syria, *Muslim Cities in the Later Middle Ages*, chaps. 4 and 5, and later in

his article "Muslim Cities and Islamic Societies," in *Middle Eastern Cities: A Symposium on Ancient, Medieval, and Modern Middle Eastern Urbanism,* ed. Lapidus (Berkely and Los Angeles, 1969), 47–79. For a summary of his conclusions, see idem, *A History,* 162–80. For a different interpretation, see Bulliet, *The Patricians,* 24–26. Bulliet describes the 'ulama' of Nishapur as a civilian elite with "class" interests separate from those of other social categories, such as merchants and landowners. Made up of a small number of local families, this elite succeeded in guaranteeing its continuity by heredity. The difference in the interpretation of the role and status of the 'ulama' must be related, at least to some extent, to the different political conditions in these cities. In contrast to high medieval Mamluk cities studied by Lapidus, medieval Nishapur was placed under relatively indirect political control. Consequently, a "patriciate" evolved (between the mid-tenth and mid-twelfth centuries) that enjoyed a greater degree of freedom and autonomy.

3. See, for example, the story about the Ash'ari al-Qushairi in chapter 4 (The *Madhhab*).

4. Modern scholarship on the administration of justice under the Great Seljuks is vast. The most comprehensive studies are those by Lambton, "Internal Structure," esp. 213, 270, 277ff; *Continuity and Change,* esp. 70.

5. See also the lists of *mudarrisun, qadis,* and *khatibs* in Appendices B and C.

6. For a detailed discussion of the history of the judiciary under the Buyids and Seljuks, see Saadeh, "The Development of the Position of the Chief Judge," 183ff.

7. Watt, *Islamic Political Thought,* was the first to argue that by supporting Ash'arism, the Great Seljuks played a significant role in the process of Sunni revivalism. See esp. 75–76. This view has been disputed by Makdisi, "The Sunni Revival," in *Islamic Civilization,* ed. Richards, 155–68, who argues that the renewed activity of Sunni Islam was independent of the Seljuks and Ash'arism.

8. Al-Kunduri's official ban forced hundreds of Ash'aris out of their posts and put many of them on the road to exile. For a detailed account of this episode, see Bulliet, "The Political-Religious History of Nishapur," in *Islamic Civilization,* ed. Richards, 80–85.

9. For a different view, see Laoust, "Les Agitations," 175–85.

10. Ibn al-Jawzi, *al-Muntazam,* 9:208.

11. Ibid., 9:24

12. Ibid., 9:109.

13. Ibid., 9:136.

14. For the Zainabis, see the genealogical chart in Appendix A.

15. Lambton, *Continuity and Change*, 224–48; and see also Klausner, *The Seljuk Vezirate*, 70.

16. For the recruitment and education of the vizier and other high-ranking officials in the Seljuk bureaucracy, see Klausner, *The Seljuk Vezierate*, 50–68.

17. Sibt b. al-Jawzi, *Mir'at az-zaman* (Ankara, 1968), 80–88. See also Ibn al-Jawzi, *al-Muntazam*, 8:218–24; Ibn al-Athir, *al-Kamil*, 10:20–22.

18. Sibt b. al-Jawzi, *Mir'at az-zaman* (Ankara, 1968), 87–88.

19. Abu Ja'far ad-Damaghani was appointed by his brother Abu al-Hasan, *qadi al-qudat*, over Rusafa and Bab at-Taq in A.H. 488, but left his post two years later. He then assumed the *hijaba*, a post he was afterwards asked to resign. Ibn al-Jawzi, *al-Muntazam*, 9:150, 156; Ibn Abi Wafa', *al-Jawahir*, 1:758.

20. al-Kindi, *Kitab al-wulah wa-kitab al-qudah* (London, 1912), 311.

21. Cited in al-Kindi, *Kitab al-wulah*, 471.

22. Ibn Abi Ya'la, *Tabaqat al-hanabila*, 380–81.

23. Ibn al-Jawzi, *al-Muntazam*, 9:96; Ibn Kathir, *al-Bidaya*, 12:151; al-Bundari, *Ta'rikh baghdad*, fol. 71a.

24. Ibn Rajab, *Dhail*, vol. 1, 129.

25. N. A. Faris, *The Book of Knowledge*, translation of *Kitab al-'ilm* of al-Ghazzali's *Ihya 'ulum ad-din* (Lahore, 1962), 179.

26. Ibid., 182.

27. Ibid., 108–9.

28. Ibn Khallikan, *Wafayat*, 5:137.

29. Ibn al-Jawzi, *al-Muntazam*, 9:283.

30. Sibt b. al-Jawzi, *Mir'at az-zaman* (Hyderabad, 1551), part. 8, vol.1, p. 17.

31. Ibn al-Jawzi, *al-Muntazam*, 8:16.

32. Ibid., 10:215.

33. Ibid., 10:217.

34. Ibid., 7:277.

35. Mottahedeh makes this point in *Loyalty and Leadership*, esp. 149–50, 162.

36. Sibt b. al-Jawzi, *Mirʾat az-zaman* (Hyderabad, 1551), part. 8, vol. 1, p. 83 (in the biography of his Hanbali disciple Ibn ʿAqil).

37. For historians who have tried to show that the schools of law were indeed meaningful social organizations in tenth-fifteenth century Muslim cities, see Lapidus, "Muslim Cities," 47–79; Bulliet, "The Political-Religious History of Nishapur," in *Islamic Civilization*, ed. Richards, 71–91; Makdisi, "Hanbalite Islam," in *Studies on Islam*, ed. M. Swartz (New York, 1981), 216–74. See also a different view—Mottahedeh, *Loyalty and Leadership*, 163; idem, Book Review of Bulliet, *The Patricians*, 491–92.

38. For the internal structure of the schools, see Lapidus, "Muslim Cities," 112.

39. Such was the case when (in A.H. 475) the Ashʿari theologian, al-Bakri, who had previously accused the Hanbalis of heresy, claimed the right to preach Ashʿarism in the mosque. See Ibn al-Jawzi, *al-Muntazam*, 9:3–4; Sibt b. al-Jawzi, *Mirʾat az-zaman* (Ankara, 1968), 217–18; Ibn al-Athir, *al-Kamil*, 10:124–25.

40. See the example of the Shafiʿi *mudarris*, Abu Bakr al-Khujandi, in as-Subki, *Tabaqat ash-shafiʿiyya*, 6:134.

41. See the description of the conditions of the Shafiʿis in Baghdad in Abu Ishaq ash-Shirazi's letter to Nizam al-Mulk in Sibt b. al-Jawzi, *Mirʾat az-zaman* (Ankara, 1968), 187–88.

42. Ibn al-Jawzi, *al-Muntazam*, 9: 484.

43. See Appendix A, below.

44. Ibn al-Bannaʾ, *Autograph Diary*, pt. III, no. 80, p. 21 (the Arabic text); p. 38 (Makdisi's translation).

45. Ibid., pt. III, no. 114, p. 282 (the Arabic text), p. 293 (Makdisi's translation).

46. Ibn al-Athir, *al-Kamil*, 10:90–91. See also Ibn al-Jawzi, *al-Muntazam*, 8:272–73.

47. Ibn Rajab, *Dhail*, 1:20–33.

48. Ibn al-Bannaʾ, *Autograph Diary*, pt. III, no. 100, p. 26 (the Arabic text), p. 45 (Makdisi's translation).

49. Ibid., pt. III, no. 63, p. 16 (the Arabic text), p. 33 (Makdisi's translation).

50. Ibid., pt. III, no. 68, p. 18 (the Arabic text), p. 35 (Makdisi's translation).

51. Sibt b. al-Jawzi, *Mir'at az-zaman* (Ankara, 1968), 36–37.

52. Ibn al-Banna', *Autograph Diary*, pt. III, no. 83, pp. 21–22 (the Arabic text), p. 40 (Makdisi's translation).

53. See Sabri, *Mouvements Populaires à Baghdad*, 121–26. For the *'ayyarun*, see also Claude Cahen, "Mouvements populaires et autonomise urbain dans l'Asia musulmane du Moyen Age," *Arabica* 5 (1958), 225–50; 6:25–26, 230–60. Tirage à part Leiden, 1959. Cahen sees the *'ayyarun* as the "déclasses" element of society, for the Turks refused to incorporate them into the army or the police force.

54. Ibn al-Jawzi, *al-Muntazam*, 8:326–27.

55. Ibn Abi Ya'la, *Tabaqat al-hanabila*, 402–3.

56. Sibt b. al-Jawzi, *Mir'at az-zaman*, part. 8, vol. 1 (Hyderabad, 1951), pp. 5–6.

57. Ibid., 6.

58. Ibn Abu Ya'la, *Tabaqat al-hanabila*, 407.

59. See E. Gellner, Saints of the Atlas (Chicago, 1936)—an anthropological work carried out in Berber Sufi hostels (*zawiyyas*). Also see Talmon-Heller, "The Shaykh and the Community," 108–9 for the holy man in a rural society of twelfth-century Jabal Nablus.

60. Goldziher made this point in his famous article on the veneration of the holy men in Islamic tradition in *Muslim Studies*, 2:338. See also D. B. Macdonald, "Karama," *SEI*, 216–17.

Conclusion

1. See P. Selznick, *Leadership in Administration* (New York, Evanson, and London, 1957), 16–22. For the process of institutionalization, see also Leonard Broom and Philip Selznick, *Essentials of Sociology* (New York, 1975), chap. 5; B. L. Berger and T. Luckmann, *The Social Construction of Reality* (London, 1969), chap. 2.

Appendix A: Scholarly Families of Eleventh-Century Baghdad

1. For al-Qadi Abu Ya'la, see the biographical references in chapter 2 (From Journeys to Schools).

2. For Abu Ya'la's eldest son, Abu al-Qasim, see Ibn Rajab, *Dhail*, 1:16–17. For his youngest son, Abu Khazim, see ibid., 1:220–21. Unlike his brother, Abu Qasim, who resided in Bab al-Maratib, the quarter of the wealthy, Abu Khazim resided in the more humble Hanbali quarter of al-Azaj and led an ascetic life.

3. Ibn Abi Ya'la, *Tabaqat al-hanabila*, 2:139; Ibn al-Jawzi, *al-Muntazam*, 7:110.

4. For 'Abd al-Wahid, see *Tabaqat al-hanabila*, 2:179; Ibn al-Jawzi, *al-Muntazam*, 7:295; Al-Khatib al-Baghdadi, *Ta'rikh baghdad*, 11:4. For his brother, 'Abd al-Wahhab, see *Tabaqat al-hanabila*, 2:183; *al-Muntazam*, 8:81.

5. For Abu Muhammad at-Tamimi, see especially *Tabaqat al-hanabila*, 2:250–51; *al-Muntazam* 9:89–90; and Ibn al-'Imad, *Shadharat adh-dhahab*, 3:385.

6. Ibn Rajab, *Dhail*, 1:107.

7. Ibid., 1:106–7.

8. For Abu 'Ali al-Hashimi, see especially the long biographical notice in Ibn Abi Ya'la, *Tabaqat al-hanabila*, 2:182–86.

9. See Ibn al-Jawzi, *al-Muntazam*, 8:299.

10. See especially Ibn Rajab, *Dhail*, 1:20–33.

11. For Ibn al-Ghariq, see especially Ibn al-Jawzi, *al-Muntazam*, 8:283. For his cousin, Abu al-Hasan, see ibid., 8:147. For his son, Abu al-Hasan Hibat Allah, see ibid., 9:34.

12. For a survey of all members of the family, see Saadeh, "The Development of the Position of the Chief Judge," 231–45.

13. See chapter 5.

14. Ibn Abi Wafa', *al-Jawahir*, 2:19–22; Ibn al-Jawzi, *al-Muntazam* 9:201; Ibn al-'Imad, *Shadharat adh-dhahab*, 4:34. Upon the death of Nur al-Huda, in A.H. 512, the position of the *mudarris* passed to his son Abu al-Qasim. For a list of the *naqib*s of 11th-century Baghdad, see Massignon, "Cadis et naqibs," 11–12.

15. Ibn Abi Wafa', *al-Jawahir*, 1:266; Ibn al-Jawzi, *al-Muntazam*, vol. 9, p. 108; Ibn al-'Imad, *Shadharat adh-shahab*, 3:396–97.

16. See especially as-Subki, *Tabaqat ash-shafi'iyya*, 4:188; al-Asnawi, *Tabaqat ash-shafi'iyya*, 2:131.

17. See the bibliographical references in chapter 2 (From Journeys to Schools).

18. as-Subki, *Tabaqat ash-shafiʿiyya*, vol. 4, p. 85; al-Asnawi, *Tabaqat ash-shafiʿiyya*, vol. 2, p. 132, Ibn al-Jawzi, *al-Muntazam*, 9:125; Ibn Kathir, *al-Bidaya*, 12:16.

19. For Abu Hafz, see as-Subki, *Tabaqat ash-shafiʿiyya*, 4:285.

20. See especially ibid., 6:70.

21. For Abu Muzaffar, see al-Asnawi, *Tabaqat ash-shafiʿiyya*, 2:87–88. For Abu Muhammad, see ibid.; Ibn al-Jawzi, *al-Muntazam*, 10:52. as-Subki does not include Abu Bakr's two sons in his *tabaqat*.

22. Ibn al-Jawzi, *al-Muntazam*, 8:18–19; al-Khatib al-Baghdadi, *Taʾrikh baghdad*, 12:98–99. For Abu al-Qasim, see *Taʾrikh baghdad*, 10:432–33.

23. Ibn al-Jawzi, *al-Muntazam*, 3:176; Ibn al-ʿImad, *Shadharat adh-dhahab*, 3: 278.

24. For the creation of the *mashyakhat ash–shuyukh as-sufiyya*, see Massingnon, "Cadis et naqibs," 112.

25. For Abu Saʿd and his house, see Ibid. See also the biographical references in chapter 2 (The Baghdadi ʿUlamaʾ and Worldwide Scholarly Networks).

BIBLIOGRAPHY

Primary Sources

Al-ʿAbbadi, Abu ʿAsim Muhammad. *Kitab tabaqat al-fuqaha> ash-shafiʿiyya.* Leiden, 1964.

Al-Asnawi, Abu Muhammad ʿAbd ar-Rahim. *Tabaqat ash-shafiʿiyya.* 2 vols. Baghdad, 1390/1970.

Al-Bundari, Fakhr ad-Din al-Fath. *Taʾrikh baghdad.* Paris, MS. Arabe, 6152.

―――. *Kitab zubdat an-nusrat wa-nukhbat al-ʿusra,* abridged from ʿImad ad-Din al-Isbahani, *Nusrat al-fatra wa-ʿusrat al-fitra.* Edited by M. T.h. Houtsma in *Recueil de Textes relatifs à l'histoire des Seljoucides.* Leiden, 1889, vol. 2 (Histoire des Seljoucides de l' Iraq).

Ad-Dari, Taqi ad-Din b. ʿAbd al-Qadir at-Tamimi. *at-Tabaqat as-saniyya fi tarajim al-hanafiyya.* Riyad, 1983.

Adh-Dhahabi, Shams ad-Din Abu ʿAbd Allah Muhammad. *al-ʿIbar fi khabar man ghabar.* Edited by Salah ad-Din Munajjid and Fuʾad Sayyid. Kuwait, 1961–66.

―――. *Kitab tadhkirat al-huffaz.* Hyderabad, 1315/1897.

Al-Ghazzali, Abu Hamid. *Kitab al-ʿilm.* Translated by N. A. Faris as *The Book of Knowledge.* Lahore, 1962.

Al-Husaini, Abu Bakr b. Hidayat Allah. *Tabaqat ash-shafiʿiyya.* Beirut, 1971.

Al-Khatib al-Baghdadi. *Taʾrikh baghdad.* 14 vols. Cairo, 1349/1931.

Al-Kindi, *Kitab al-wulah wa-kitab al-qudah.* London, 1912.

Al-Laknawi, Ibn al-Hasanat, *al-Fawaʾid al-bahiyya fi tarajim al-hanafiyya,* Cairo, 1324/1906.

209

Al-Muqaddasi, Shams ad-Din Abu ʿAbd Allah Muhammad. *Ahsan at-taqasim fi maʿrifat al-aqalim*, edited by M. J. Goeje. Leiden, 1906.

Ash-Shirazi, Abu Ishaq Ibrahim. *Tabaqat al-fuqahaʾ*. Baghdad, 1356/1937.

As-Subki, Taj ad-Din ʿAbd al-Wahhab. *Tabaqat ash-shafiʿiyya al-kubra*. 6 vols. Cairo, 1966–67.

———. *Muʿid an-niʿam wa-mubid an-niqam*. Edited by David Myhrman. London, 1908.

As-Suyuti, Jalal ad-Din ʿAbd al-Rahman. *Tabaqat al-huffaz*. Edited by ʿAli Omar. Cairo, 1973.

———. *Taʾrikh al-Khulafaʾ*. Cairo, 1964.

Al-Yafiʿi, ʿAfif ad-Din Abu Muhammad ʿAbd Allah b. Asʿad. *Mirʾat al-janan wa-ʿibrat al-yaqzan*. 4 vols. Beirut, 1970.

Al-Yaʿqubi, Ahmad b. ʿAli Yaʿqub. *Kitab al-buldan*. Edited by M. J. De Goeje. Leiden, 1892.

Ibn Abi Wafaʾ, ʿAbd al-Qadir al-Qurashi. *al-Jawahir al-mudiʾah fi tabaqat al-hanafiyya*. 2 vols. Hyderabad, 1332/1914.

Ibn Abi Yaʿla, Abu al-Husain Muhammad. *Tabaqat al-hanabila*. 2 vols. Cairo, 1371/1952.

Ibn al-Athir, Abu al-Hasan. *al-Kamil fiʾt-taʾrikh*. 12 vols. Beirut, 1965–67.

Ibn al-Bannaʾ, Abu ʿAli al-Hasan b. Ahmad. *Taʾrikh*. Translated and edited by Makdisi George as *Autograph Diary of an 11th-Century Historian of Baghdad*. In *BSOAS* 18 (1956); 19 (1957).

Ibn al-ʿImad, ʿAbd al-Hayy. *Shadharat adh-dhahab fi khabar man dhahab*. 8 vols. Cairo, 1931–32.

Ibn al-Jazari. *Kitab ghayat an-nihaya fi tabaqat al-qurraʾ*. Cairo, 1933–37.

Ibn al-Jawzi, Abu al-Faraj Muhammad. *al-Muntazam fi taʾrikh al-muluk waʾl-umam*. 6 vols. [=vols. V-X, yrs. 257–574/870–1197]. Hyderabad, 1358/1940.

———. *Manaqib baghdad*. Baghdad, 1342/1923.

Ibn Jubayr. *Rihla*. Translated by R. J. C. Broadhurst as *The Travels of Ibn Jubayr*. London, 1952.

Ibn Kathir, ʿImad ad-Din Abu al-Fidaʾ Ismaʿil. *al-Bidaya waʾl-nihaya*. 14 vols. Beirut, 1966.

Ibn Khaldun, ʿAbd al-Rahman b. Muhammad. *The Muqaddimah*. Translated by Franz Rosenthal. 2nd edition. New York, 1967.

Ibn Khallikan, *Wafayat al-aʿyan wa-anbaʾ abnaʾ az-zaman*. 7 vols. Beirut, 1970.

———. *Ibn Khallikan's Biographical Dictionary*. Translated by MacGuckin de Slane. 4 vols. Paris, 1843–71.

Ibn as-Saʿi, Taj ad-Din Abu Talib. *al-Jamiʿ al-mukhtasar*. Baghdad, 1934 (vol. 9).

Ibn Rajab, Zain ad-Din Abu al-Faraj ʿAbd al-Rahman. *Dhail ʿala tabaqat al-hanabila*. Cairo, 1372/1952–53.

Ibn Shakir al-Kutubi, Salah ad-Din Abu ʿAbd Allah Muhammad. *Fawat al-wafayat*. 2 vols. Cairo, 1951.

Ibn Qadi Shuhba. *Tabaqat ash-shafiʿiyya*. Beirut, 1987.

Nizam al-Mulk. *Siyasat-Nameh*. Translated by Hubert Darke as *The Book of Government*. 2nd edition. London, 1978.

Sibt b. al-Jawzi, Yusuf b. Qizughli. *Mirʾat az-zaman fi taʾrikh al-aʿyan*.

a) Manuscript—British Museum, Or. 4619. Years: 282/895–460/1067

(b) Partial edition by Ali Servin. Ankara, 1968. [events connected with the Seljukids, 448/1056–479/1086]

(c) Printed edition of part 8, vol. 1 of J. R. Jewett text. Hyderabad, 1951–52. [events connected with the Seljukids, 495/1101–589/1193].

Secondary Works

Arberry, A. J. *Sufism: An Account of the Mystics of Islam*. London, 1950.

Ahmed, Kamal ad-Din Hilmi. *al-Salajika fiʾt-taʾrikh wal-hadara*. Kuwait, 1975.

Ahmed, Munir ad-Din. *Muslim Education and the Scholars' Social Status up to the 5th Century Muslim Era (11th Century Christian Era) in Light of Taʾrikh Baghdad*. Zurich, 1968.

Al-Ahawani, A. F. *at-Tarbiyya fiʾl-islam*. Cairo, 1955.

Amin, Husein. *Taʾrikh al-ʿIraq fiʾl-ʿasr as-saljuki*. Baghdad, 1965.

Ashtor, Eliyahu. *A Social and Economic History of the Near East in the Middle Ages*. London, 1967.

———. "Un mouvement migratoire au haut moyen age: migrations de l'Iraq vers les pays méditerranées." *AESC* 27 (1972), 185–215.

Bausani, A. "Religion in the Seljuk Period." *The Cambridge History of Iran*, 5:283–303.

Berkey, Jonathan. *The Transmission of Knowledge in Medieval Cairo: A Social History of Islamic Education*. Princeton, 1992.

Bosworth, C. E. "The Political and Dynastic History of the Iranian World (A.D. 1000–1217)." *The Cambridge History of Iran*, 5:1–202.

Bourdieu, Pierre. *Reproduction in Education: Society and Culture*. London, 1977.

Brooke, Christopher. *Europe in the Central Middle Ages*. 2nd edition. London, 1987.

Brody, Y. "Safrut ha-Geonim veha-Tekst ha-Talmudi." *Mehqarei Talmud 1* (5750), eds. Y. Sussman and D. Rosenthal (Jerusalem, 1990), 237–304 [in Hebrew].

Buckler, Georgina. "Byzantine Education." In *Byzantium: An Introduction to the East Roman Civilization*, edited by N. H. Baynes and H. G. Wilson, 299–320. Oxford, 1948.

Bukhsh, Khuda, S. "The Arabs Academies and their Professors." In *Contributions to the History of Islamic Civilization*. Hyderabad, 1975.

———. "The Educational System of the Muslims in the Middle Ages." *IC* 1 (1927), 442–72.

Bulliet, Richard W. *The Patricians of Nishapur: A Study in Medieval Islamic Social History*. Cambridge, Mass., 1972.

———. "The Shaikh al-Islam and the Evolution of Islamic Society." *SI* 35 (1972), 53–67.

———. "The Political-Religious History of Nishapur." In *Islamic Civilization, 950–1150*. Papers on Islamic History: III, edited by D. S. Richards, 71–91. Oxford, 1973.

———. *Islam: The View from the Edge*. New York, 1994.

Cahen, Claude. "Movements populaires et autonomisme urbain dans l'Asie musulmane du Moyen Âge." *Arabica* 5 (1958), 225–50; 6 (1959), 25–56, 233–65.

Chabbi, Jacqeline. "La fonction du ribat à Baghdad du ve au debut du viie siecle." *REI* 42 (1974), 101–21.

Chamberlain, Michael. *Knowledge and Social Practice in Medieval Damascus, 1190–1350*. Cambridge, Great Britain, 1994.

Chr. Jouaud. "Présentation." *Annales: Histoire, Sciences, Sociales* 49 (Mars-Avril, 1994): *Littérature et Histoire*, 270–76.

Cohen, Hayyim J. "The Economic Background and the Secular Occupations of Muslim Jurisprudents and Traditionists in the Classical Period of Islam (until the middle of the eleventh century)." *BSOAS* 13 (1970), 16–61.

Coulson, N. J. *A History of Islamic Law*. Edinburgh, 1964.

Daud, Wan. *The Concept of Knowledge in Islam*. London, 1989.

Decobert, Ch. *Le Medinat et le Combattant*. Paris, 1991.

Dodge, Bayard. *Muslim Education in Medieval Times*. Washington, 1962.

Al-Duri, Khidr Jasmin. "Society and Economy of Iraq under the Seljuks (1055–1160) with Special Reference to Baghdad." Ph.D. diss., University of Pennsylvania, 1970.

Eickelman, Dale, F. "The Art of Memory: Islamic Education and its Social Reproduction." *Comparative Studies in Society and History* 20 (1978), 485–516.

Elad, Amikam. *Medieval Jerusalem and Islamic Worship: Holy Places, Ceremonies, Pilgrimage*. Leiden, 1995.

El-Ali, S. A. "The Foundation of Baghdad." In *The Islamic City*. Papers on Islamic History: III, edited by A. H. Hourani and S. M. Stern, 87–101. Oxford, 1970.

El-Moudden, Abderrahmane. "The ambivalence of *rihla*: Community integration and self-definition in Moroccan travel accounts." In *Muslim Travellers: Pilgrimage, Migration, and the Religious Imagination*, edited by Dale F. Eickelman and James Piscatori, 69–84. Berkeley and Los Angeles, 1990.

Gafni, Isaiah. *Yahadut Bavel u-mosdoteha bi-tekufat ha-talmud*. 2nd edition. Jerusalem, 1986 [in Hebrew].

Garcin, Jean-Claude. *Un centre musulman de la haute Egypte médiévale: Qus*. Cairo, 1976.

Gellens, Sam I. "The Search for Knowledge in Medieval Societies: A Comparative Approach." In *Muslim Travellers*, edited by Eickelman and Piscatori, 50–65.

Gellner, Ernest. *Saints of the Atlas*. Chicago, 1936.

Gibb, H. A. R. "Islamic Biographical Literature." In *Historians of the Middle East*, edited by B. Lewis and P. M. Holt, 54–58. London, 1962.

———. *Studies on the Civilization of Islam*. 2nd edition. Princeton, 1982.

Giladi, Avner. "Mahshavto Hahinuhit shel al-Ghazzali." Ph.D. diss., The Hebrew University of Jerusalem, 1983 [in Hebrew]

Gilbert, Joan E. "The 'Ulama' of Medieval Damascus and the International World of Islamic Scholarship." Ph.D. diss., University of California, 1977.

———. "Institutionalization of Muslim Scholarship and Professionalization of the 'Ulama' in Medieval Damascus." *SI* 52 (1980), 105–34.

Gilsenan, Michael. *Recognizing Islam: Religion and Society in the Modern Middle East*. London, 1982.

Goitein, S. D. "Changes in the Middle East 950–1150 as illustrated by the Documents of the Cairo Geniza." In *Islamic Civilization*, edited by Richards, 17–33.

———. *A Mediterranean Society: The Jewish Communities in the Arab World as Portrayed in the Documents of the Cairo Geniza*. Berkeley, 1967–88.

Goldziher, Ignaz. *Muslim Studies*. Translated by C. R. Barber and S. M. Stern. 2 vols. London, 1971.

Grunebaum, G. E. *Muhammadan Festivals*. London, 1981.

Hafsi, I. "Recherches sur le genre 'Tabaqat' dans la littèrature arabe." *Arabica* 23 (1976), 228–65.

Hallaq, Wael B. "Was the Gate of Ijtihad Closed?" *IJMES* 16 (1984), 3–14.

Haskins, Charles H. *The Renaissance of the Twelfth Century*. 8th edition. Cambridge, Mass., 1982.

Heer, Friedrich. *The Medieval World: Europe 1100–1350*. Translated by George Weidenfeld. New York, 1962.

Hodgson, Marshall, G. S. *The Venture of Islam*. 3 vols. Chicago, 1974.

Holt, P. M. *The Age of the Crusades: The Near East from the Eleventh Century to 1517*. London, 1986.

Hourani, A. H. "The Islamic City in Light of Recent Research." In *The Islamic City*, edited by Hourani and Stern, 9–24.

Humphreys, Richard Stephen. *Islamic History: A Framework for Inquiry*. No. 9. Minneapolis, 1988.

Hurwitz, Nimrod. "Ibn Hanbal and the Formation of Orthodoxy." Ph.D. diss., Princeton University, 1994.

———. "Biographies and mild asceticism: A study of Islamic moral imagination." *SI* 85 (1997), 41–64.

Jawad, Mustafa. "ar-Rubut al-baghdadiyya." *Sumer* 10 (1954), 218–49.

Khalidi, Tarif. "Islamic Biographical Dictionaries: A Preliminary Assessment." *MW* 63 (1973), 53–65.

Klausner, Carla. *The Seljuk Vezirate: A Study of Civil Administration.* Cambridge, Mass., 1973.

Kohlberg, Etan. "Imam and Community in the pre-Ghayba Period." In *Authority and Political Culture in Shi'ism*, edited by Said Arjomand, 25–30. Albany, NY, 1988.

Lambton, A. K. S. *Continuity and Change in Medieval Persia: Aspects of Administrative, Economic, and Social History, 11th–14th Century.* Albany, NY, 1988.

―――. "The Internal Structure of the Seljuk Empire." *The Cambridge History of Iran*, 5:203–83.

Laoust, Henri. "Le hanbalisme sous le califat de Baghdad 241/855–656/1258." *REI* 27 (1959), 67–128.

―――. "Les Agitations Religieuses à Baghdad aux IVe et Ve siècles de l'Hégire." In *Islamic Civilization*, edited by Richards, 169–87.

Lapidus, Ira M. "Muslim Cities and Islamic Societies." In *Middle Eastern Cities: A Symposium on Ancient Islamic and Contemporary Urbanism*, edited by Lapidus, 47–79. Berkeley and Los Angeles, 1969.

―――. *Muslim Cities in the Later Middle Ages.* Cambridge, Mass., 1967.

―――. *A History of Islamic Societies.* 1st edition. New York, 1988.

Lassner, Jacob. "The Caliph's Personal Domain: The City Plan of Baghdad Re-Examined." In *The Islamic City*, edited by Hourani and Stern, 103–18.

―――. *The Topography of Baghdad in the Early Middle Ages.* Detroit, 1970.

Le Goff, Jacques. *Medieval Civilization 400–1500.* Translated by Julia Barrow. Oxford and New York, 1988.

Le Strange, G. *Baghdad During the Abbasid Caliphate.* 3rd edition. London, 1972.

―――. *The Lands of the Eastern Caliphate.* 2nd edition. Cambridge, 1930.

Leiser, Gary. "Hanbalism in Egypt before the Mamluks." *SI* 54 (1981), 155–81.

―――. "The Restoration of Sunnism in Egypt: Madrasa and Mudarrisun, 495–647/1101–1249." Ph.D. diss., University of Pennsylvania, 1976.

―――. "Note on the Madrasa in Medieval Islamic Society" *MW* 56, no. 1 (January, 1986), 16–23.

Levtzion, Nehemia. "Eighteenth Century Sufi Brotherhoods: Structural, Organizational and Ritual Changes." In *Islam: Essays on Scripture, Thought and Society*, edited by Peter G. Riddell and Tony Street, 147–66. Leiden, 1997.

Levy, Reuben. *Baghdad Chronicle*. Philadelphia, 1977.

Light, Donald, and Keller, Suzanne JR. *Sociology*. 3rd edition. New York, 1982.

Madelung, W. "Authority in Twelver-Shi'ism in the Absence of the Imam." In *La Notion d' Autorité au Moyen Age—Islam, Byzance, Occident*, edited by George Makdisi, 163–73. Paris, 1982.

Makdisi, George. *Ibn 'Aqil et la Resurgence de l'Islam Traditionaliste au xie Siècle*. Damas, 1963.

————. "Muslim Institutions of learning in Eleventh-Century Baghdad," *BSOAS* 24 (1961), 1–56.

————. "Suhba et riyasa dans l'enseignement mèdièvale." In *Recherches d'islamologie. Recueil d' articles offert à George C. Anawati et Louis Gardet par leurs collègues et amis*. Louvain, 1977.

————. "The Sunni Revival." In *Islamic Civilization*, edited by Richard, 155–68.

————. "The Topography of 11th-Century Baghdad." *Arabica* 6 (1959), 178–97.

————. *The Rise of Colleges: Institutions of Learning in Islam and the West*. Edinburgh, 1981.

————. "Hanbalite Islam." In *Studies on Islam*, translated and edited by M. L. Swartz, 216–74. New York, 1981.

————. *Humanism in Classical Islam and the Christian West*. Edinburgh, 1990.

Marrou, Henri-Irenée. *Histoire de l' Education Dans l'Antiquité*. Paris, 1948.

Massignon, Louis. "Cadis et naqibs Baghdadiens." *WZKM* 31 (1948), 106–15.

Morgan, D. O., ed. *Medieval Historical Writing in the Christian and Islamic Worlds*. London, 1982.

Mottahedeh, Roy P. *Loyalty and Leadership in an Early Islamic Society*. Princeton, 1980.

————. *The Mantle of the Prophet: Religion and Politics in Iran*. New York, 1985.

————. *Book Review of R. Bulliet, The Patricians*. *JAOS* 95 (1975), 491–92.

Netton, Ian Richard, ed. *Golden Roads: Migration, Pilgrimage and Travel in Medieval and Modern Islam*. Richmond (Surrey), 1993.

Nisbet, Robert. *Key Concepts in the Social Sciences: Social Change*. Oxford, 1972.

Ohler, Norbert. *The Medieval Traveller*. Translated by Caroline Hillier. Woodbridge, 1989.

Pederson, Johannes. "Some Aspects of the History of the madrasa." *IC* 3 (1929), 527–37.

———. *The Arabic Book*. Translated by Geoffrey French. Princeton, 1984.

Petry, Carl. *The Civilian Elite of Cairo in the Later Middle Ages*. Princeton, 1981.

Rashdall, Hastings. *The Universities of Europe in the Middle Ages*. 2nd edition. London, 1936.

Repp, Richard C. *The Mufti of Istanbul: A Study in the Development of the Ottoman Learned Hierarchy*. London, 1986.

Reynold, L. D., and Wilson N. G. *Scribes and Scholars: A Guide to the Transmission of Greek and Latin Literature*. 2nd edition. Oxford, 1974.

Rosenthal, Franz. *A History of Muslim Historiography*. Leiden, 1952.

———. *Knowledge Triumphant: The Concept of Knowledge in Medieval Islam*. Leiden, 1970.

Saadeh, Sophia. "The Development of the Position of the Chief Judge During the Buyid and Seljuk Periods." Ph.D. diss., Harvard, 1977.

Sabri, Simha. *Mouvements Populaires à Baghdad à l'Epoque ʿAbbaside, IXe-XIe Siècles*. Paris, 1981.

Schacht, Joseph. *An Introduction to Islamic Law*. Oxford, 1964.

Schaefer, P. "Once Again the Status Quaestionis of Research into Rabbinic Literature." *Journal of Jewish Studies* 40 (1989), 89–94.

Schimmel, Annemarie. *Mystical Dimensions of Islam*. Chapel Hill, 1975.

Shalaby, Ahmad. *History of Muslim Education*. Beirut, 1954.

Ash-Shaybi, Kamil M. *as-Sila bayn at-tasawwuf waʾt-tashayyuʿ*. 2 vols. Baghdad, 1964.

Sourdel, Dominique. *Le visirat abbaside de 749 à 936 (132 à 324 de l'Hègire)*. 2 vols. Damas, 1959–60.

———. "Réflexions sur la diffusion de la madrasa en orient aux VIe et VIIIe Siècle." *REI* 44 (1976), 165–84.

Sourdel-Thomine, Janine. "Locaux d'enseignements et madrasas dans l'islam médiéval." *REI* 44 (1976), 185–97.

Talmon-Heller, Daniella. "The Shaykh and the Community: Popular Hanbalite Islam in 12th–13th Century Jabal Nablus and Jabal Qasyun." *SI* 79 (1994), 103–20.

Tyan, Émile. *Histoire de l'organization judiciare en pays d'islam*. 2 vols. 2nd ed. Leiden, 1966.

Tibawi, A. L. "The Origins and Character of the Madrasa." *BSOAS* 25 (1962), 225–38.

Triminghan, J. Spencer. *The Sufi Orders in Islam*. New York, 1971.

Tritton, A. S. *Materials on Muslim Education in the Middle Ages*. London, 1957.

Vajda, Georges. "De la transmission orale du savoir dans l'Islam traditionnel." *L'Arabisant* 4 (1975), 2–8.

Wan Daud, Wan Mohd Nor. *The Concept of Knowledge in Islam, and its Implications for Education in a Developing Country*. London and New York, 1989.

Watt, Montgomery. *Islamic Political Thought*. Edinburgh, 1987.

Wensinck, A. J. *A Handbook of Early Muhammadan Tradition*. Leiden, 1927.

White, Morton. *Foundations of Historical Knowledge*. New York, Evanston, and London, 1965.

———. "The Logic of Historical Narration." In *Philosophy and History: A Symposium*, edited by Sidney Hook, 3–31. New York, 1963.

INDEX OF PROPER NAMES

GENERAL INDEX

'Abbasid caliphate, 'Abbasids, 1,
6–7, 99, 113, 130, 135, 142–43.
Individual caliphs: al-Mansur, 21;
al-Muqtadi, 60, 117–18; al-
Muqtafi, 117–18, 131; al-Mustadiʾ,
26; al-Mustanjid, 117; al-
Mustazhir, 131; an-Nasir li–Din
Allah, 116
ʿabid (pious), 48, 62, 89–90, 91, 145
adab (belles-lettres), as part of the
madrasa's curriculum, 13. See
also adib
adib (the "cultured and educated
man"), 99–100, 117
ahl al-hadith ("people of hadith ,"
traditionalists), 2, 3, 4, 87
ahl al-raʾy, ashab al-raʾy,
mutakallimun ("people of
opinion," rationalists), 3, 4, 87. See
also Ashʿaris; Muʿtazilis
ʿamid (provincial governor), 24
ʿamma (the masses), 142–43
ancient (rational) sciences, 2, 127
arbab al-qalam. See kuttab
ashab (followers, closest disciples),
30, 60, 143; relationships with
their shaykhs, 81, 84–85, 88, 137
Ashʿaris, Ashʿarism, 2, 41, 127, 130,
138, 139, 88, 177n.3. (2), 4. See
also ahl al-raʾy; mutakallimun

asnaf (professional classes), 96,
99–100. See also kuttab; tujjar
aʿyan (the most eminent people in
the community), ʿulamaʾ as, 35
ʿayyarun (youth gangs or gallants),
142–43
Ayyubids, 38, 57, 65, 114, 118–19,
123
Azerbaijan, 63, 73, 91

Baghdad, as a center of learning, 22,
35, 41, 47, 55–56, 142; changes in
the conditions of, 22, 23–25, 30,
55–56; descriptions and image of,
21–23, 30, 65–66, 67–68; distinctive areas and quarters of: al-
Anbariyyin, 67; Bab al-Azaj, 27,
112; Bab al-Basra, 7, 24, 27, 70,
138; Bab al-Maratib, 80; Bab ash-
Shaʿir, 78; Bab ash-Sham, 66–67;
Bab at-Taq, 24, 25, 67; Dar al-
khilafa, 24, 25–26, 27, 133, 142;
Dar as-saltana as-saljukiyya, 24,
25, 26, 131; al-Karkh, 24, 52, 53,
120–21, 142; at-Tustariyyin, 67
Baihaq, 54, 66–67
Balkh, 38, 67
baraka (divine blessing), transmission and bestowing of, 89, 144, 145

223